JERRELL H. SHOFNER

ORLANDO

THE CITY BEAUTIFUL

ORLANDO
THE CITY BEAUTIFUL

by Jerrell H. Shofner

Dedicated to Donald A. Cheney

Publisher
Douglas S. Drown

Editor
Lynn Rollins Price

Photo Editor
Jerrell H. Shofner

Art Director and Designer
Rusty Johnson

Current Photography
David Cotton

Project Director
Bud Brewer

Historical Photography Reproduction
John Markham

Copyright 1984 by Continental Heritage Press,
1612 S. Boston Avenue, Townhouse Three,
Tulsa, Oklahoma 74119

Library of Congress Catalog Card Number: 84-072652
ISBN Number: 0-932-986-39-0

Publisher's Acknowledgement:
Continental Heritage Press extends its appreciation to
the Orange County Historical Society, the major
sponsor and a primary resource for the research and
photography of *Orlando: The City Beautiful.*

Special gratitude is extended to the society's president, Delaney Way and the curator of the Orange
County Historical Museum, Jean Yothers.

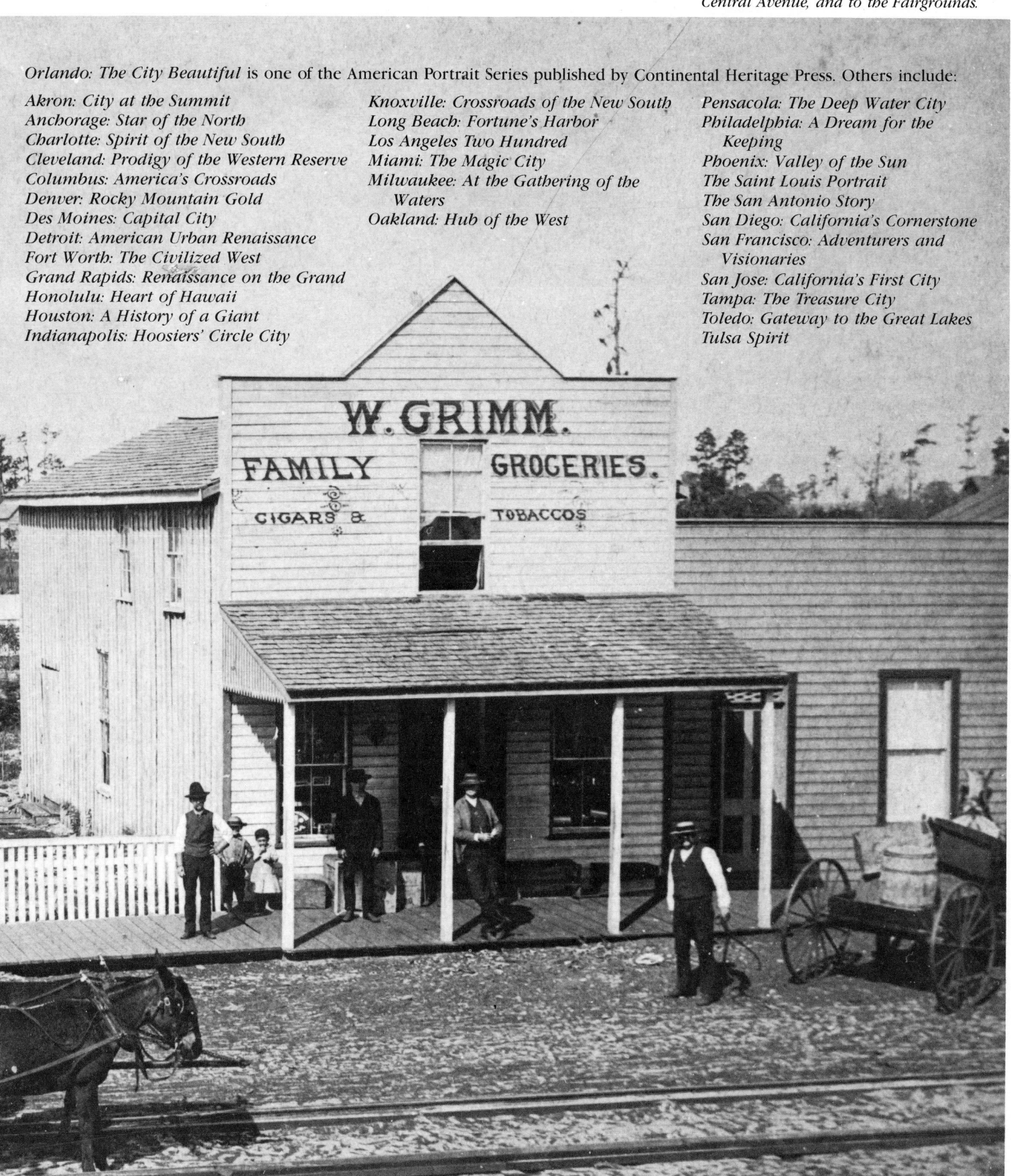

Even as the Orlando skyline looms in the distance, Lake Eola remains a placid reminder of the city's many great natural resources.

SPONSORS AND BENEFACTORS

The following firms, organizations, institutions and individuals have invested toward the quality of this historic book and thereby expressed their commitment to the future of this great city and to the support of the book's principal sponsor, the Orange County Historical Society.

AT&T Technology Systems
Aagaard-Juergensen, Inc.
*Akerman, Senterfitt & Eidson
*Anderson & Rush
*Arts, Inc.
*Barnett Bank of Central Florida, N.A.
Barnie's Coffee & Tea Co., Inc.
Bellows TV & Appliances
Boone Community School
*Brookwood Community Hospital (AMI)
Grover Bryan, Inc.
Cablevision of Central Florida
*Cardinal Industries
*Carlton, Fields, Ward, Emmanuel, Smith & Cutler, P.A.
Central Constructors

*Central Florida Lumber & Supply Co.
*Church Street Station
Colley, Trumbower & Howell
*Colonial Plaza Mall
*Philip Crosby Associates, Inc.
*Community Communications, Inc.
Wayne Densch, Inc.
Dixie Textile & Supply Co., Inc.
Doerrs Trailer Leasing Co.
*Downtown Development Board
*Eastern Airlines
*Ernst & Whinney
Feelin' Great, Inc.
Robert Feldman, SMR, Inc.
Ferncreek Properties, Inc.
*Ferran Engineering Group, Inc.
*Financial Security Corporation of America
*THE FIRST, F.A.
The First Banks of Orange County
*First Baptist Church/Orlando
*First Fidelity
*Florida Citrus Bowl/Tangerine Bowl
Florida Fruit & Vegetable Association
*Florida Gas Transmission Company

*Florida Hospital
Florida Hospital Foundation
*Florida National Bank/Orlando
*Florida Power Corporation
*Florida Ranch Lands, Inc.
Florida Sun International, Inc.
Fred's Crane Service, Inc.
*Freedom Savings and Loan Association
Genstar Southern Development
Gilbane Building Company
*Giles, Hedrick & Robinson, P.A.
*Gray, Harris & Robinson, P.A.
Greater Orlando Aviation Authority
Headquarters Companies
David W. Hedrick
Holiday Inns, Inc.
Hubbard Construction Company
Hughes, Inc.
*Humana Hospital — Lucerne
Huskey Realty
*Industrial Development Commission of Mid-Florida, Inc.
Invenex Laboratories
*Ivey's Florida

*Jaymont Realty Incorporated
KMS Mortgage & Investment Co.
*The Kirchman Corporation
*The Landmarks Group
*LeeVista Center
Let's Travel of Orlando, Inc.
*M.G. Lewis & co.
*Harry P. Leu, Inc.
*Litton Systems, Inc.
Lovelace, Roby & Company
*Lowndes, Drosdick, Doster & Kantor, P.A.
*Maguire, Voorhis & Wells, P.A.
*Martin Marietta Orlando Aerospace
McDee Services
Bruce McEwan
McGrath Management, Inc.
Mid Florida Technical Institute
Modern Welding Co., Inc.
NCNB National Bank
Nadeau Construction Co., Inc.
Orange County CTA
*Orlando Central Park, Inc.
*Greater Orlando Chamber of Commerce
*Orlando General Hospital

*Orlando Magazine
*Orlando Regional Medical Center
Orlando Utilities Commission
*Palmer Electric
Carl Patterson
*Peirsol, Boroughs, Grimm, Bennett & Griffin, P.A.
*The Dr. Phillips Companies
Plyworld Corp.
*Red Lobster Inns of America
Rich-United Corp.
*The Thomas W. Ruff and Company
*Sea World of Florida
*Sentinel Communications Company
*Sheraton-Twin Towers
*Skyline Restaurant
*Southeast Bank
Southeast Business Corporation
*Southern Bell Telephone and Telegraph Company
Starline Manufacturing Corporation
*Sun Bank, N.A.
Sverdrup & Parcel & Associates
*Swann & Haddock, P.A.

TDC Corporation of Florida
*Thomas Lumber Company, Inc.
Tip Top Roofing Co., Inc.
Trammell Crow Company
United States Cold Storage Inc.
United Telephone Co. of Florida
*The United Way
Visiting Nurse Association
WBJW/WCOT Radio
*WCPX-TV, Channel 6
*WESH-TV
*WFTV
Williams C. Webb Company
*Winderweedle, Haines, Ward & Woodman, P.A.
*The Winter Park Land Company
*Winter Park Memorial Hospital

*Denotes corporate sponsor. The histories of these organizations and individuals appear in a special section beginning on page 172.

Orlando's 1st Regimental Band, under the direction of drum major James Spellman. The building at the rear of the drill field is the Orlando Gas Plant.

Downtown Orlando's rebirth is evident everywhere. Above, a hot dog vendor does a brisk business in the warm afternoon. Right, window washers keep The First Bankers Building glistening.

CONTENTS

Employees and customers of the South Lake Apopka Citrus Growers Association gathered in front of its packing house in the late 1930s.

Orlando's lakes are among its most popular attractions. Left, an egret at sunset on Lake Underhill. Above, a popular swimming hole on Lake Maitland.

LOCATION IS EVERYTHING

*T*here are few places where the influence of geography on human affairs is better illustrated than the Florida peninsula. Having risen from the sea as an appendage to the North American continent some 20 to 40 million years ago, it protruded daggerlike into Spain's western hemispheric empire in the sixteenth and seventeenth centuries. Although of doubtful intrinsic value to Europeans of that time, Florida was a region which Spain did not necessarily want but could not permit an antagonist to possess. Its geographic location thus propelled Florida into an otherwise disproportionate role in the international rivalries of early modern Europe.

As the Spanish Empire declined and the United States began to grow in the early nineteenth century, Florida's location again became significant. When the Spanish were no longer able to control the area, the exuberant and expansive United States determined to acquire peninsular Florida from Spain in order to quiet its southern border — and extend its frontier.

Americans settled throughout the peninsula, but seemed particularly drawn to the Orlando area. They were farmers and ranchers, lumbermen and citrus growers, builders and dreamers — and remarkable promoters. "Our county is filled with the most delightful, deep, health-giving, clear water lakes," wrote one nineteenth-century developer. "And upon these lakes nature has modeled the lands so as to make the most beautiful building sites on earth."

This was Orlando. Nature had blessed her with an incomparable climate and unrivaled resources. And if the Spaniards hadn't noticed, the Americans certainly had. From a pristine forest in the 1850s, Orlando's people would mold a metropolis, sometimes exploiting the bounty which had been bestowed upon them, but always striving to make their city the best that a city could be.

First Annual Me
At The Fair Gr

In October 1911, members of the Pioneer Association of Orange County gathered at the Fairgrounds for their first annual meeting.

Pioneer Association of Orange County
s, Orlando, Fla. Oct. 11th 1911.
Photo by Robinson

*Cinderella's Castle at Walt Disney
World draws thousands of tourists to the
Orlando area every year.*

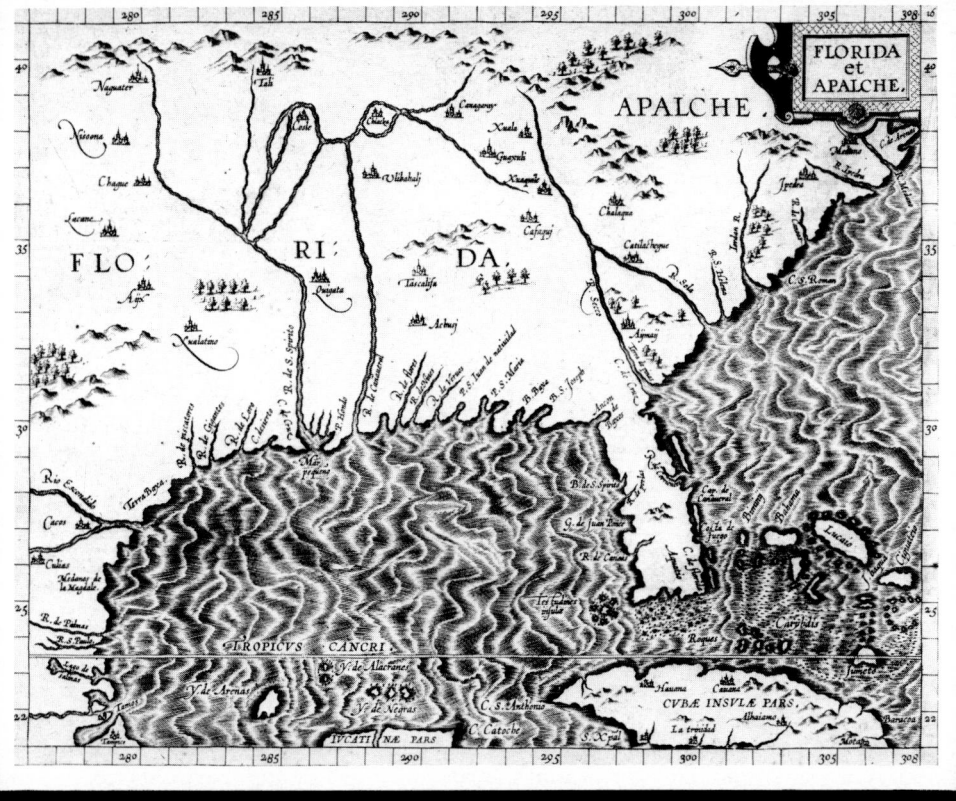

In the late sixteenth century, Spain and some of her European neighbors regarded most of North America as Florida. This 1597 map by Corneille Wytfliet reflects that view.

Artist's rendering of a native alligator
hunt, date unknown.

LAND OF LAKES

Underlying most of the Florida peninsula is a
thick layer of limestone formed by marine
deposits from the long period when it lay
beneath the sea. Since the limestone is soluble
it occasionally gives way. The resulting sinkholes account
for the numerous surface lakes which now enhance the
physical beauty of the Orlando area. Although the coastal
areas of the peninsula are low and flat, there is a long
ridge of rolling terrain extending down the peninsula
almost to Lake Okeechobee. Orlando lies on the eastern
edge of this central ridge, but the greater Orlando area
of the 1980s extended westward into the hills where
citrus groves abound and eastward into the flat coastal
area where range cattle were still grazing, even as the
subdivisions began crowding them out.

Florida's earliest inhabitants, however, were a different
type. They were saber-toothed tigers, camels, bears,
wolves, and various mastodons forced southward by the
encroaching glaciers of the Ice Age. There probably were
fewer sinkholes seventeen million years ago, and thus
fewer lakes, but the glacial melting to the north may
have helped form some of Florida's first freshwater rivers.
These huge animals foraged off the land or ate one

another. (Fossils of some prehistoric animals have been
found in Rock Springs only a few miles northwest of
Orlando.)

The prehistoric animals were long gone when man
appeared about 10,000 — and possibly as early as
40,000 — years ago. Florida's first people were hunters,
rarely staying in one place long enough to build villages.
Later cultures fished the coastal areas and inland rivers
and lakes and developed primitive agricultural methods.
These people did occupy villages, often leaving mounds
upon which records of their existence were left. Early
inhabitants of the Lake Apopka area, about 7,500 B.C.,
also apparently carried on some form of trade with other
villagers. Several dugout canoes have been uncovered in
the mucklands from which the lake has since receded.
The layering of artifacts at the Lake Apopka site suggests
that it was inhabited until about A.D. 100 and then
abandoned. Several other cultures occupied the area for
brief periods, then moved on.

When Ponce de León claimed Florida for Spain in
1513, the peninsula was occupied by still other Indian
groups. Along the southern shores of the Atlantic lived
the Ais, a small, but fierce group which hunted and
fished as far inland as the St. Johns River. The much
larger Timucuan group had drifted into northeastern and
central Florida. The Orlando area was the southernmost

*D'Ayllon's unsuccessful encounter with
the mythical Chicoreans along the
Atlantic coast, circa 1515.*

part of their territory. During the next two decades, Spanish explorers would encounter several Timucuan tribes.

Nearest the Orlando area were the Acueras, farmers who lived along the Oklawaha chain of lakes. When Hernando de Soto camped in the Ocali province in 1539, he purchased corn from the Acueras. The tribe was again mentioned in the reports of a military expedition in 1604, but disappeared from the records by about 1650, probably victims of European diseases or wars.

GOD AND GLORY, BUT NO GOLD

Spanish explorers spent the next several centuries struggling to conquer and settle Florida. The conquistadores were fortune hunters, searching for gold and precious metals such as had been found in South America. Along the way, they were expected to claim all new lands for their king, and establish permanent settlements, mostly by converting the local heathens to Christianity. In Florida, they found no gold — but tremendous obstacles.

The land, for one thing, was hardly inviting. The lakes frequently overflowed, leaving the surrounding sands waterlogged and difficult to traverse. Even during dry

spells, the wind would cause the deep sands to shift constantly. Some areas were perpetually swampy, and stagnant pools of water bred mosquitos that could bite through the thickest cloth. After Tristan de Luna's abortive effort at Pensacola in the 1550s, the Spanish crown was almost ready to abandon the seemingly invulnerable and worthless spit of sand. Still, Florida pointed directly into Spain's bullion-rich Latin American empire. Then in 1564, the Spanish were forced to defend a land they no longer really wanted. The French, who had arrived and built Fort Caroline on the St. Johns River, were threatening Spain's hold, but they were about to meet a very worthy opponent.

Pedro Menendez de Aviles, a member of a noble Asturian family, had proven his genius as a sea captain at the age of 19. He then became one of the celebrated conquistadores who explored the New World in the name of Spain. He served successfully as Captain General of the treasure fleet, twice a year transporting the bullion which the Spanish were then extracting from Latin America. By 1564, he had been rewarded for his efforts by being appointed *adelantado* of Florida. The territory's new governor had the authority to settle the new lands for his personal profit as well as for his king and church.

Menendez quickly vanquished the luckless French from Fort Caroline, chased the survivors to Matanzas

Sixteenth century con-
querors. Above, an art-
ist's version of De
Soto's landing at
Tampa in 1539.
Although Tampa is
most often listed as the
landing site, there is a
dispute as to whether
De Soto actually
landed there or at a
point further south.
Right, Jean Ribeault
placing a marker as he
claims Florida for
France in the 1560s.

Inlet, and massacred them. Free of the French, Menendez set out to explore the coastline and interior of his new domain. Convinced that he could find a cross-Florida waterway, in August 1566 he led about 100 men with three small vessels up the St. Johns. Passing Chief Calabay's town near present-day Palatka, he crossed Lake George and entered the much narrower river beyond, intent on negotiating with Chief Mayaca, whose territory extended from south of Lake George into the Orlando area and eastward toward the coast. Menendez hoped to leave several Catholic missionaries with Mayaca, to instruct the Indians in the Christian faith. Mayaca claimed to want friendship with Menendez, but apparently was not interested in accepting the faith. The expedition suddenly found itself under attack from the shore, and the river blocked by stakes. Menendez withdrew rather than risk a violent encounter in which he was clearly at a disadvantage.

Over the next ten years, Menendez negotiated more successsfully with other Indian tribes and established the first permanent Spanish settlement at St. Augustine. In the words of Jeanette Thurber Connor, "Pedro Menendez, of all his countrymen, not only conquered and explored Florida, but began in earnest to settle and organize it, and with a skill, an executive talent, which would have given Spain a much firmer hold on her colony during the following two centuries, had his successors been half as efficient as he was."

Menendez' successors continued to deal with the Florida Indians through combinations of religious instruction and force. The Mayacas remained in the area between Orlando and Lake George, accepting some religious instruction, but retaining their independence from the Spaniards. In 1699, Governor Laureano de

Torres y Ayala instigated a revolt by the Iroros, a subordinate tribe of the Mayacas which inhabited the St. Johns valley near present-day Sanford. Seizing one of the Iroros, the governor had him taken to St. Augustine, where the unfortunate Indian was enraged by his failure to get a fair hearing. After two unsuccessful years of trying to obtain justice, the Iroros fled from their village and headed for the hills to the north. The new governor, Joseph de Zuniga y Cerda, dispatched 26 infantrymen and 30 armed Indians to stop them. Three Iroros were killed, the rest brought back to their village.

The Mayacans were also generally obliged to cooperate with the Spaniards in their efforts to resist English incursions. The French were never again a threat, but British colonies had gradually pushed the Spanish borders south toward the St. Johns River by the 1730s. After British Governor James Moore of South Carolina virtually demolished the Spanish mission system in the early eighteenth century, most of the Indians of the region were annihilated or evacuated by Moore's forces. By the time Florida was transferred from Spain to England in 1763, the Mayacas and their neighbors were being succeeded by bands of Miccosukees and other Muskogean groups who would subsequently be known as Seminoles.

CHANGING OF THE GUARD

Long more successful in their relations with the southeastern Indians than their Spanish adversaries, the English attempted to settle their countrymen along the St. Johns River during their twenty-year occupation of Florida. They also pursued a more peaceful

PARAOVS TI SATOVRIO NA ROY DE LA FLORIDE.

Saturiba was the leading Timucuan chief in the 1560s, when Menendez and Ribeault were contesting each other's claim to Florida for Spain and France.

Artist's rendering of an Indian sacrificial ceremony.

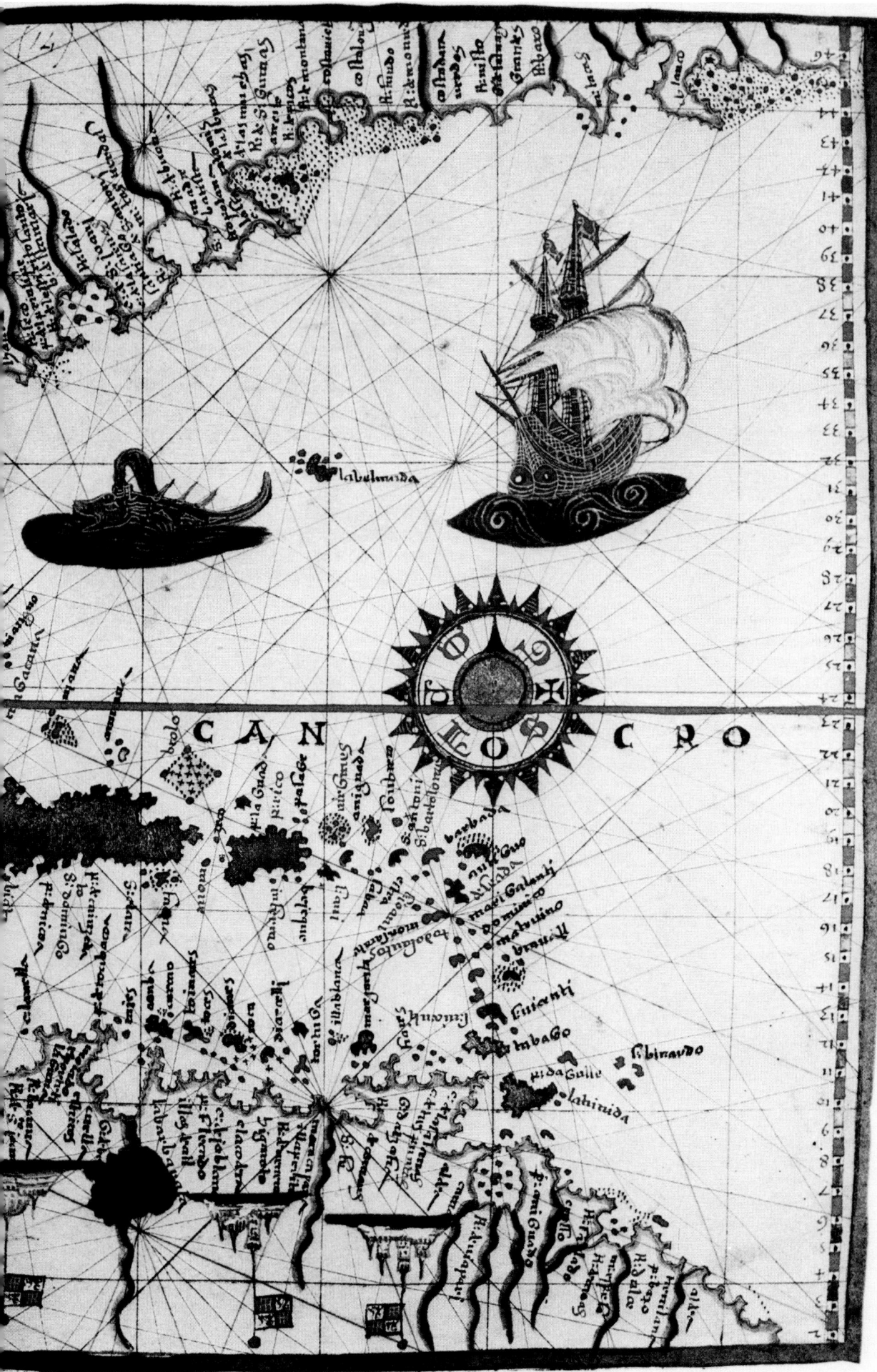

An early map of the Spanish-American empire showed a crudely shaped Florida peninsula.

Spanish St. Augustine, circa 1671, a century after its founding by Pedro Menendez.

Indian policy. Governor James Grant met with Cowkeeper and other chiefs, entertaining them with elaborate ceremonies and plying them with gifts, and generally succeeding in keeping the peace.

Although the Spanish regained control in the mid-1780s, it was with a declining empire and much diminished financial resources. They conceded a virtual monopoly of the Indian trade to the British-run Panton, Leslie Company in return for substantial financial assistance. Panton, Leslie continued a lucrative trade with the peninsular Indians from the site of Spalding's Upper Store, near present-day Astor. When Governor Vicente Mañuel de Zespedes y Velasco visited it in 1787, he found a greatly expanded enterprise involving more than 50 blacks engaged in agriculture, stock-raising, and fur-packing. Under the management of John Hambly, the store purchased furs from the natives and shipped them in barrels down the St. Johns for exportation to England.

While the British and Spanish were contending for Florida territory, the Indians were caught in the middle. During the transitional years, more and more Creek bands had filtered into the area. Although most were of Muscogean stock, the Creeks were a loose association of independent groups, frequently unable to understand one another's dialects. Recognizing no authority beyond their own village chiefs, they traded with a British company, lived on land claimed by Spain, and had little concern for either private property or international boundaries. With Napolean's brother claiming the throne of Spain and King Ferdinand VII in exile, the Spanish governors had little support in their efforts to maintain order in Florida.

To further complicate matters, the recently independent United States was growing in strength, its people pushing outward all along the southern and western frontiers. As planters opened up new cotton lands in Georgia, their slaves sometimes escaped and joined the Florida Indians. The Indians themselves often raided the plantations, stealing slaves or causing them to run away. Angry frontier planters retaliated with raids in Spanish Florida to retrieve their lost property. By 1810, the United States was pressing the Spanish to stabilize the border situation, and ultimately, unashamedly invading Spanish territory with U.S. troops.

A major turning point was reached in 1812-13 when the United States simultaneously went to war with England and the Creek Indians. After Indians massacred several hundred settlers at Fort Mims in southwestern Alabama, General Andrew Jackson caught a large band of Red Stick Creeks at Horseshoe Bend and destroyed the effective fighting force of that large confederation. The results were particularly significant for Florida's future. Jackson forced the defeated Red Sticks to cede about twenty million acres of land to the United States, accelerating the move of still more settlers into the South. He also drove the surviving Red Sticks into

Florida. There they would join the Miccosukee tribes, significantly augmenting the Seminoles who would ultimately — and most certainly inadvertently — bring the first white settlers into the Orlando area.

The pugnacious General Jackson continued his war against the Indians, chasing them into the peninsula. He captured Spanish Pensacola before dashing to New Orleans to defeat British forces at the famous Battle of New Orleans on January 8, 1815.

Frontier turmoil continued, however. By 1816, Jackson was again battling the rebellious Indians. His forces destroyed a Miccosukee encampment in northern Florida, then took over a Spanish fort in St. Marks. Jackson pursued one elusive Indian band nearly 100 miles into Florida and executed two British citizens whom he believed were giving aid to his Indian adversaries. This unfriendly action brought about an English protest and a crisis for President James Monroe. Monroe was advised, on the one hand, to punish Jackson for insubordination and, on the other, to endorse his actions to show Spain that it must either govern Florida or give it up to the growing United States.

Secretary of State John Quincy Adams had been involved in lengthy negotiations with a foot-dragging Spanish minister over the possible cession of Florida to the United States. He reasoned that if Monroe supported Jackson, Don Diego de Onis was more likely to agree to a treaty. Monroe agreed, and in 1819, the Adams-Onis Treaty was completed. Finally ratified in 1821, the treaty gave Florida to the United States and set in motion a series of events which brought white settlers to the Orlando area.

A WATER ROUTE ACROSS FLORIDA

Pedro Menendez' sixteenth-century search for a waterway across Florida was but the first of many such efforts during the past 400 years. During territorial days, Floridians tried to construct a cross-Florida canal to shorten the distance between their plantations and the eastern seaboard markets. The idea was revived in the 1880s, when a private firm was chartered to build a ship canal across the peninsula. That venture failed, as did another in 1900.

The federal government funded another attempt during the Depression, and some work on a canal was done in the Ocala area, but federal money was withdrawn in 1937 and that project also failed. The next effort came with World War II, when German submarines played havoc with American oil tankers plying the dangerous Bahama Channel. Envisioned this time as a barge canal, a project was launched to connect the St. Johns River with the Gulf along a route following the Oklawaha River. After decades of work on both ends of the canal, conservationists convinced President Nixon that the barge canal threatened Florida's fragile ecology. The project was halted in the early 1970s. It is unlikely, however, that the last has been heard of the cross-Florida waterway — a dream that dates back to the very beginnings of Florida history.

CHAPTER TWO

THE SECOND SEMINOLE WAR AND THE SETTLEMENT OF CENTRAL FLORIDA

The Econlockhatchee River offered pristine beauty and an abundant supply of fish.

The Second Seminole War. Above, the Indians declaring war, as interpreted by a German tourist in the United States. Below, the German visitor's rendition of an Indian war ceremony.

CONFLICT SEEMED INEVITABLE

The Seminole Indians were a seminomadic people, engaging in primitive agriculture, fishing, and cattle-grazing. Their villages were made of buildings that could be easily constructed and readily abandoned. Although their relative mobility had helped them survive the many moves forced upon them by white settlers, they had often suffered the loss of both cattle and crops. Finally, pressed into Florida in the 1800s, the Seminoles were beginning to run out of room — and tolerance.

As the new territorial government was just taking shape in Florida in 1822, word spread quickly that the lands between the Apalachicola and the Suwanee rivers — soon to be known as Middle Florida — were ideally suited to growing short staple cotton, by then the South's most popular crop. By the time Tallahassee was designated the territorial capital in 1824, a small land rush was already underway in the region. Many of the hapless Seminoles were living in scattered villages across this same territory. Once again, they were about to be pressured to leave the lands upon which they had chosen to live.

The United States government policy toward the Indians was still ambivalent in the early 1820s. Middle Florida's new settlers, however, almost immediately began demanding the Indians' removal from the desirable lands along the southern frontier. Some even suggested they be moved to someplace west of the Mississippi River, an area which explorers and cartographers had recently described as "the Great American Desert."

The government first tried to move the Seminoles to an unsettled part of peninsular Florida. Many Seminoles were reluctant even to consider moving again, and there were bitter disagreements among the various chiefs. A meeting with the whites was finally arranged in the fall of 1823 at Moultrie Creek. By agreeing to allow several of the older chiefs to remain on lands along the Apalachicola River, Governor William P. Duval, James Gadsden, and Bernardo Sequi induced the chiefs to sign the Treaty of Fort Moultrie, by which they agreed that the remainder of the Seminoles — numbering between 4,000 and 5,000 — would move to a reservation of about four million acres in the south-central part of the peninsula. The northern border of their new reservation was not far from present-day Orlando, but the treaty provided that if the land proved insufficient to sustain the Seminoles, the line would be moved northward. There was also a provision that the treaty was to cover a period of twenty years.

After much delay, the still reluctant Seminoles began moving to the new territory in 1824. They were soon to learn the value of their new treaty.

Controversies arose almost immediately. The land was of poor quality and game was scarce, but requests to expand the reservation's boundaries were ignored. White settlers who claimed to be looking for runaway slaves sometimes kidnapped blacks who had long ago joined the Seminole tribe. The government often was late in paying the annuities it had promised the Seminoles. Territorial judges assigned to settle grievances between the Indians and whites almost always sided with the settlers. Finally, the enraged Indians began launching raids against the white communities. By the time Andrew Jackson was elected to the presidency in 1828, the demand for removal of the Indians to a western territory had become loud and insistent.

The Seminoles still believed that the Fort Moultrie treaty would be sustained, and that they could stay in Florida for the rest of the twenty years promised to them. But by the early 1830s, many were near starvation. In 1832, the chiefs again reluctantly agreed to discuss removal. At a meeting with Commissioner James Gadsden at Payne's Landing, some of the chiefs agreed to send six of their members to investigate the so-called Indian Territory. If it proved acceptable, they would move there within three years. A year later, the expedition signed a document at Fort Gibson in Indian Territory, agreeing to the move. Upon their return to Florida, however, the six chiefs learned that several of the younger chiefs had declared they would not be bound by the new agreement.

Wiley Thompson, a powerful, strong-willed man who had served with General Jackson, had the misfortune to have recently become the commissioner charged with completing the removal of the Seminoles from the territory. Frustrated and provoked by the turn of events, Thompson summarily declared Micanopy, Jumper, Alligator, Black Dirt, and Arpeika (Sam Jones) deposed as chiefs. When authorities in Washington objected to his arbitrary action, Thompson agreed to another meeting with the Indian chiefs. At that meeting, Powell (better known as Osceola), a half-breed who was not a chief, appeared for the first time as an opponent of removal. During the next several months the United States prepared for removal while most of the Indians gradually decided to resist it.

There were no settlers in the Orlando area at the time, but there were several in the Tomoka area who were busily growing sugar cane and other crops. There were also several crews of timber workers cutting live oak for the United States Navy along the St. Johns River not far above Lake Monroe. All were vulnerable to the rapidly deteriorating Indian situation.

Osceola was a great Seminole warrior who was arrested at a meeting that took place under a truce flag.

A WAR WITH NO WINNERS

The Second Seminole War began suddenly and violently on December 28, 1835. As Wiley Thompson and a companion walked outside Fort King late in the afternoon, Osceola and a small band ambushed and killed them both. Earlier that day a larger group led by Jumper, Alligator, Micanopy, and Coacoochee (Wildcat) attacked and annihilated a column of troops led by Major Francis L. Dade on the way from Tampa Bay to Fort King. Other Indian bands attacked, burned, and destroyed the sugar plantations along the Tomoka River. Nearly all the inhabitants of Mosquito County fled. In 1838, there were only three qualified voters in the entire county, and the 1840 census takers could not find a single resident.

When the Seminole War began, there were at least two Indian villages in the Orlando area. King Philip was the chief of a band living at Yalaka near Lake Tohopekaliga. His son Coacoochee lived with a group of about 200 Indians at Lake Apopka. Both Coacoochee and Philip became important war leaders. Coacoochee would never return to his Lake Apopka home, but by the time he left for Indian Territory in the early 1840s, he had distinguished himself as one of the ablest and most respected Seminole chiefs.

The war seemed to be moving in the United States' favor early in 1837. General Thomas S. Jesup opened an offensive in a sweep along the Oklawaha River, and part of his force surprised Chief Osuchee near Lake Apopka in January 1837. Osuchee and four other Indians were killed; several others were captured. After another costly battle a few days later, several chiefs agreed to suspend hostilities and confer with Jesup. But neither Philip nor Coacoochee were among them. On February 8, with several hundred warriors, they attacked Captain Mellon's detachment at Lake Monroe. In a fierce fight, Mellon was killed. (A fort at the site of that battle was later named for him.)

Some of the Indians then claimed they were ready to move to Indian Territory, but Jesup was becoming suspicious. In a move which earned him calumny from many historians, Jesup arrested Osceola, Wildcat, and other chiefs at a meeting that took place under a truce flag. The chiefs were taken to Fort Marion; their women and children were herded to Tampa Bay. From there,

Osceola was moved to Fort Moultrie where he soon died. Wildcat starved himself until he was thin enough to escape through a small window at the top of his cell.

Coacoochee subsequently led his band in the largest battle of the war at Okeechobee, where Zachary Taylor and about 1,000 soldiers inflicted considerable damage on the Indians. Although the war continued for several more years, this was the last pitched battle.

In 1839, another attempt was made to peacefully remove the remaining Seminoles. The plans were interrupted in July when Colonel William S. Harney's detachment was ambushed on the Caloosahatchie River. Forced to flee without his trousers, Harney lost eighteen of his 30 men and subsequently became a vengeful Indian fighter. (In the 1870s he also became one of the first of many professional soldiers to make Orlando his retirement home.)

By 1841, warfare had decimated the Indian population, and its economic condition was desperate. Band after band of Indians gave up and went to Tampa for expatriation. Colonel William J. Worth took over the American forces at about that time, and when Wildcat was captured, Worth induced him to help bring in the

ONE OF THE BEST AND BRIGHTEST

Coacoochee, whose name means "wildcat," was a lifelong inhabitant of the Orlando area before the Second Seminole War. He emerged during the war as one of the ablest of the Seminole warriors and became the leader of the war faction of the tribe after Osceola's death. He also made a favorable impression on all the whites with whom he came in contact during his tragic life — including newspaper editors who published the eloquent letters he wrote, pleading for fair treatment from a government which had promised much and delivered little.

Captured under a truce flag in 1837, he was briefly imprisoned at St. Augustine. Curious residents of the city were taken aback when Coacoochee unabashedly offered to trade wives with George Anderson, a leading merchant of the town, who had brought his wife to view the "savages."

After his heroic escape from Fort Marion, Coacoochee eluded the U.S. armed forces for four more years before finally surrendering to Colonel William J. Worth, an officer who expressed in glowing terms his estimate of Coacoochee as a guerilla leader and an adversary.

Agreeing to emigrate to Indian Territory, Coacoochee and his band found conditions there much different from what had been expected. Determined to improve the lot of his people, in 1850 he led a band across Texas into Mexico, where the Mexican government granted him a reservation. There he survived several battles with the ferocious Comanches, only to perish in a typhoid epidemic in 1857. The surviving expatriates finally returned to a reservation in Indian Territory in the 1860s.

remaining Indians. Then, upon Worth's recommendation, the government agreed to let the remaining warriors — only about 112 — remain with their families in deep southern Florida.

With only a handful of Indians remaining by 1842, central Florida was little more than an empty expanse of pine forest and lakes that often overflowed their banks. The area showed little of the promise that had drawn new settlers to Tallahassee. To attract homesteaders, the government enacted the Armed Occupation Act. Those brave enough to settle the area would be granted land upon which they could live as citizen-soldiers, forming a barrier between the Indians and the more populated portions of the Florida territory. These citizen-soldiers often homesteaded near the temporary forts that had been built during the war. Fort Gatlin attracted one such settlement which eventually emerged as Orlando. Aaron Jernigan, with his brother Isaac, arrived from Georgia in 1843 and settled his family on the northwest shore of Lake Holden, not far from Fort Gatlin. He opened a trading post, which soon became the site of the area's first post office. The name Jernigan was adopted for the fledgling village.

While that was happening, Mosquito County communities soon began vying for designation as the county seat. Since population was a major criterion, serious contenders struggled to attract new settlers. Cornelius Taylor, a controversial town builder who owned several acres of valuable live-oak lands near Lake Monroe, brought about twenty people to the lake's north shore and founded Enterprise in 1842. Practically a metropolis for central Florida at the time, Enterprise was named the county seat. Three years later, after Florida was granted statehood, the first legislature changed the county's name from Mosquito to Orange, and named Mellonville the county seat.

Daniel Stewart had founded Mellonville near the site of Fort Mellon in 1842. Using the Armed Occupation Act, Stewart brought in about 160 settlers from Georgia. Although many of these first arrivals soon returned to their old homes, the handful of settlers who remained built a permanent community.

FORCIBLY IF THEY MUST

Floridians, especially the frontiersmen in central Florida, had not been pleased with the government's decisions to leave some of the Seminoles in the Everglades. Although Arpeika and Billy Bowlegs, the chiefs of the remaining bands, were anxious to avoid further confrontations with the white settlers, they were not always able to control errant tribal members. Occasional cattle thefts kept the frontier wary and tense. In 1845, Governor William Moseley wrote President James K. Polk, demanding that the Seminoles be removed from the state "peacefully if they can, forcibly if they must."

Four years later, Congress responded by enacting a law forbidding the Seminoles from leaving the reservation. But at the same time, it was looking for a way to remove the Indians from Florida altogether. When a small number of Seminole renegades attacked some white villages, settlers all over central Florida began leaving their homes for safer environs. About 1,400 regulars of the Florida militia were called out to guard the few

settlers who stayed on. When the renegades were finally caught, most of the remaining Seminoles agreed to leave Florida for Indian Territory. Still, General David E. Twiggs decided to keep his militia in the region and build a chain of forts from Tampa Bay to Indian River. Troops were stationed at these posts intermittently for the next

KING PHILIP.

King Philip was a Seminole war chief from the Kissimmee area.

Judge J.G. Speer, a prominent early
settler, took a leading role in securing
the county seat for Orlando.

William Wright Patrick, one of Orlando's
first merchants, served as county
sheriff in the 1850s.

several years, sometimes figuring largely in the early history of Orlando.

Despite the frequent Indian alarms, the Orlando area seems to have been increasingly attractive to settlers during the 1840s and 1850s. Several hundred settlers came to Orange County during that period, including several pioneers of Orlando and its neighboring communities.

Robert Ivey and John R. Worthington settled near Jernigan in the late 1840s. J.J. Patrick moved to the Conway area in 1852, followed shortly by his brother

William. William Patrick and W.G. White both opened stores at Orlando. James P. Hughey moved to Lake Lucerne in 1855, and William B. Hull settled at Lake Fairview (later called Lake Lancaster). D.K. Hall and William A. Lovell had sawmills at Orlando in the 1850s. James G. Speer, one of Orlando's most prominent early settlers, arrived at Lake Jenny Jewel in 1854, later moving to Mellonville and then Oakland. Andrew Barber took up land near Lake Conway and David Mizell settled near the lake which was later named for him.

L.H. Clay was farming near Clay Springs by 1850, and shortly afterward Robert Barnhart built a sawmill on the upper Wekiwa River. William Delk built another sawmill on his Rock Springs plantation in the early 1850s. Matthew Stewart and his numerous relatives took up land near present-day Apopka. They and their neighbors organized a Masonic Lodge, and when the lodge building was erected, members from miles around came to meetings which became major social events. The area was known as "The Lodge" for many years before the name Apopka was adopted.

The 1855 legislature divided Orange County to better accommodate the area's growing population. Volusia County was carved out of the territory north of Lake Monroe between the St. Johns River and the coast. Not surprisingly, this touched off another contest for the county seat. The possible sites were Fort Reed (Mellonville), Fort Gatlin (Jernigan), and The Lodge. According to various sources, Judge Speer invited soldiers from a nearby post to a picnic at Fort Gatlin on election day. He then asked them to cast their votes for that site. Fort Gatlin won the election. No one knows why Speer might have favored the Fort Gatlin location, since he appeared on the 1860 census as a resident of Mellonville. Nonetheless, the town of Orlando came into existence on the site of the old Jernigan post office near Fort Gatlin and thus became the county seat for a territory encompassing present-day Orange, Osceola, and Seminole counties as well as portions of present-day Lake County.

A MOON LODGE

Orange Lodge No. 36, F. & A.M., the oldest Masonic lodge in central Florida, has been meeting in the same building longer than any other lodge in the state.

Early-day members met on the dates of a full moon so that those who had to ride — or even walk — for miles at night could better find their way. Thus it was designated a "moon lodge." The lodge was the focal point of one of the oldest settlements in the Orlando area. Chartered in January 1856, the lodge has met continuously since that time and in the same building since 1869.

In its early days, the building was used as a church by several religious denominations, and was the community's first school. Part of the building also housed Apopka's first store. The community which evolved on the site was known simply as "The Lodge" until it was renamed Apopka in the 1870s. The lodge building remains a central part of the Apopka community and a historic site in central Florida.

CHAPTER THREE

SECESSION, CIVIL WAR, AND RECONSTRUCTION

Postwar Orlando, circa 1879. This view is of Orange Avenue, north from Central and Orange.

FLORIDA JOINS THE CONFEDERACY

Many of central Florida's residents in 1860 were from southern states where slave labor was important to cotton-plantation agriculture. Some were growing cotton, and several owned a few slaves. Like most southerners, they generally subscribed to the concept of state's rights. But they were somewhat isolated from the increasingly heated debate over slavery and state's rights, and they were too busy with their own affairs to become excited over it. By 1860, however, they were obliged to take a position. Shortly after Abraham Lincoln's election, a secession convention was held in Tallahassee. Orange County residents, although divided over the secession issue, elected William Woodruff, a staunch Unionist, to represent them at Tallahassee. During the convention debates, Woodruff consistently voted with the minority who opposed secession. When the delegates finally voted 62-7 for leaving the Union, Woodruff was one of the seven who still opposed it.

Once Florida joined the Confederacy, many Orange County residents supported their state, and a large number actually marched off to war. The county's sparse population and isolated location spared it from direct military conflict, but the Orlando area, nevertheless, felt the inconvenience, hardships, and privations of the war. With supply lines cut off by coastal and river blockades, resourceful residents found new ways of providing for themselves. Store owner James P. Hughey made bimonthly trips to Gainesville, where goods were still coming in through the Florida Railroad. Though many items soon became unavailable and the railroad was interdicted late in the war, Hughey was able to provide at least some of the necessities of life to his neighbors.

Others survived by drawing much needed salt from the coastal waters and selling it to the Confederacy for $50 a bushel. Military wives learned to cultivate their own fields. When the post office was discontinued early in the war, Mrs. W.B. Hull, who ran a rooming house while her husband was in the army, established an unofficial postal facility.

Despite the hardships and shortages, Orlando was one of the few Confederate communities that actually grew during the war. William H. Holden left northern Florida and purchased 1,200 acres on what became Lake Holden, where he eventually developed a 100-acre citrus grove. Several settlers came from war-torn Georgia, including William and Charles Hansel and Nathan and Hiram Beasley. Orlando's first physician, Dr. Whittle, arrived in 1865.

These signs of growth were still far short of a boom. In

DATELINE PINECASTLE

From Kentucky in 1869 came one of Orlando's most prolific and influential promoters. Will Wallace Harney was seeking a place where his wife might find better health when he built "Pine Castle" on Lake Conway. Although his wife soon died and he subsequently lived a reclusive life, he continued to write glowing — if occasionally overzealous — articles about the riches and glory to be found in central Florida. Published by the Cincinnati Commercial *and other newspapers as well as by national magazines, his writings are sometimes credited for transforming nineteenth-century Orlando. Harney also contributed many accurate accounts of daily life in Orlando. The following description of building a new home is from Paul W. Wehr's* Dateline Pinecastle, *a study of Harney's writings:*

"After the trees are felled and cut into practical logs he has a 'log-rollin,' the simple practice of a neighbor exchanging labor with neighbor, with a gratuitous dinner as make-weight.

"Preparations for such a day bring about great housewifery excitement. There must be a goodly size of fat bacon to cook 'the long sass,' greens, cabbage and the like . . . .[She] scours the country for eggs; and the day before the feast the old gun is got down, cleaned, oiled, and there is a still-hunt, that means business, for venison. But all is solid refreshment. Bacon, venison, cowpeas, a very nutritious bean, sweet potatoes, pumpkins, and plenty of coffee, too weak to stand up in a cup without a saucer. The men provide picks and levers of oak or persimmon, and the test of

Will Wallace Harney is seated in the doorway of Pinecastle, the home he built during the 1870s.

physical strength is to 'carry your end of the log.' By nightfall it is all ready . . . ."

The next step was the "house-raisin," in which the wife took an even greater interest. She gathered eggs, butter, and sugar to feed the workers, while the men went in search of more food for the feast:

"John must hunt a bee-tree for wild honey; Jim must fish in the lake; bananas and guavas must be provided; poultry cackles in terror, and the hunter is notified that the venison must be supplemented with wild turkey, duck, or, if he be ambitious and bold, the fisherman must get a soft-shelled turtle for soup . . . ."

EVERYTHING THAT BITES OR STINGS

*T*he mosquito was the scourge of central Florida from the very beginning, and Will Wallace Harney was quick to notice:

"Everything that buzzes or flies, everything that bites or stings is familiar in Florida. The red bug, of the loathsome chinch genus, I think, buries itself under the cuticle, and makes a purulent sore. Mosquitos and sand flies, of course . . . . It [the mosquito] flies in clouds, darkening the air and fouling the dishes . . . .They have forceps that will plug through a two-double army blanket. Until the woods and grasses are cleared off, for two or three months of the year they are bad . . . ."

Harney later boasted that there had "not been a mosquito netting up at Pinecastle for three years, but if you sit down in a hollow they can pick you through four doubled blankets."

866, Orlando was still a small settlement, concentrated ound the log courthouse at the corner of Central and ain (now Magnolia) streets. There were two stores, one loon, the Lovell House, and John Worthington's store d hotel, which catered almost exclusively to the wyers and judges who attended the periodic sessions of ourt. Dr. Whittle was soon joined by another physician, P. Preston, who opened his office in his newly onstructed home on Lake Jenny Jewel.

WHERE THE NEGRO IS NOT AND NEVER WILL BE"

*T*he turbulent Reconstruction period caused more bitterness, more disruption of southern society, and ultimately more migration to central Florida, an the war itself. When Andrew Johnson, a southern nionist, assumed the presidency after Lincoln's sassination, he inherited a growing controversy over ow to "reconstruct" the Union. Lincoln had favored a mple and speedy readmisssion of the southern states ithout alteration of their social structures. Some ongressmen, known as Radical Republicans, argued for a orough reorganization of the South. They believed the rmer Confederates should be denied political rights, d that those rights — along with Confederate lands — ould be given to the former slaves.

Johnson proceeded with a plan similar to Lincoln's. e Radical Republicans launched a campaign to thwart s efforts and place Congress in charge of national econstruction. This struggle between the president and ongress lasted two years, during which southerners ere left under military occupation, wondering about eir ultimate fate. When the Radical Republicans finally feated the president, impeached him, and implemented eir own Reconstruction plan, southerners were smayed. The congressional plan called for Negro ffrage to be supervised by military commanders. outherners talked of immigration to Brazil, Mexico, lifornia, and other places "where the Negro is not and ver will be." Although a few did leave for those places, number of prominent families from northern Florida

MORE ON MOSQUITOS AND A BIT ON BEDBUGS

Built by Jacob Summerlin in 1875, the Summerlin Hotel was expanded in 1892, and served as a hostelry until it was razed in 1941.

*B*uilt by Jacob Summerlin in 1875 at the extravagant cost of $15,000, the Summerlin Hotel quickly became a center of activity in Orlando. The proprietor and his staff went to great lengths to see that their guests were comfortable, according to this article by Louise Frisbie, printed in the Polk County Democrat in 1981.

"On the desk of the hotel, during its first days of operation, there was placed a sign reading that '10 cents hard cash' would be paid to any roomer who could produce a mosquito actually caught in the hotel. Not a cent was ever paid to any person, for none were ever caught. Strangely enough, the woods surrounding Orlando were filled with the pests . . . .

"Rates at the new hotel were $2 daily. This included the dubious privilege of bathing in a wash bowl, and the delights of eating at a family table loaded with food. Vegetables were raised at the back of the hotel . . . . Summerlin kept a number of cows on hand to furnish milk for the guests, despite the fact that milk was a scarcity in those days . . . .

"The mailman was a little-seen person and communications were bad, train service not being available until late in 1880. When the mailman arrived by horseback, he was roundly welcomed, gently and considerately escorted to a room on the third floor of the hotel.

"But just as soon as the postman departed, his room was soundly deloused with a bath of kerosene. Postmen in those days, sleeping in all sort of quarters, were great carriers of bedbugs!"

Jacob Summerlin was one of Orlando's greatest benefactors, as well as one of the most prosperous cattlemen in the state. Summerlin is identified as the man in both of these photos, although the identity of the man in cowman's regalia has been disputed.

IN HONOR OF HIS HOMELAND

P eter A. Demens was born Peter A. Dementiev, the son of a prominent family of St. Petersburg, Russia. Serving as an officer in the czar's palace guard, he became embroiled in a political controversy and decided to leave his native land. Arriving in Florida in the 1870s, he acquired extensive tracts of virgin pine timberland and engaged in a successful lumber business for several years. Amazed at the economic and political freedom of his adopted land, he became an intensely patriotic American, but was also obsessed with the idea of founding a counterpart to his native St. Petersburg. When he began cutting out his timber, Demens conceived the idea of converting his lumber tram road into a railroad from Longwood to the south end of Lake Apopka. There he hoped to found his new St. Petersburg.

With more audacity than resources, Demens began constructing what eventually became the Orange Belt Railroad, but by the time the tracks reached the Lake Apopka site, Judge J.G. Speer and others had already named the spot Oakland. Using what today would be called creative financing, Demens managed to obtain a series of loans to continue building his railroad. He extended the line across Florida and down the Pinellas peninsula to a settlement he managed to get renamed St. Petersburg. By the time the road was completed, however, Demens had lost control of it to a financial group headed by E.T. Stotesbury. Still, he was apparently satisfied with his accomplishment. He left Florida and subsequently engaged in similar activities in California, carrying on a tradition of individualism and private enterprise which would scarcely have been possible had he remained in Russia.

and other southern states packed their remaining belongings and headed down the St. Johns River to Orange County.

Among them was Francis Eppes. As mayor of Tallahassee when Andrew Johnson proclaimed civil law restored in the South, Eppes arrested several United States soldiers for "fast riding" on the town's main street. An exasperated General John Foster, who still believed that martial law was supreme, demanded that Eppes return his troops to the post for discipline. Eppes refused, to which Foster responded disdainfully, "You misapprehend the importance of your position." With that, Eppes had had enough. He arrived in Orlando in early 1867. A grandson of Thomas Jefferson, he was quite favorably received and became a prominent citizen.

Eppes' relative, William Randolph, a Virginian who had been practicing law in New Orleans, arrived in Orlando a little later. Other prominent Orlandoans who migrated from the old plantation belt included David and Thomas Shine and James D. Beggs. Matthew R. Marks, a future Orlando mayor and aggressive promoter, arrived from Georgia in 1869. E.T. Sturdivant, Dr. Elijah Martin, Nathaniel Poyntz, J.B. Parramore, and Cassius A. Boone also arrived at about that time.

On the heels of the southern emigrés came northern visitors. Some made permanent homes around Orlando, and others bought land on which to build winter homes. After passage of the Homestead Act of 1866, several freedmen (former slaves) took up land in Orange County. Others were brought in as laborers, but with the exception of a disturbance at Sanford in 1870, there was little racial trouble in the area.

CATTLE RUSTLING IN THE WILD, WILD SOUTH

P ostwar central Florida was an open-range cattle frontier of the type most often associated with the American West. Cattle rustling and range wars were common. Self-reliant frontiersmen protected their rights — as they understood them — with direct and sometimes violent action. Range disputes led to frequent shootings and killings. Confrontations on the streets of Orlando between feuding cowmen became common, and efforts to bring about justice through the courts were rarely successful.

A sensational cattle-rustling case was on the circuit docket in the fall of 1868. Prominent attorneys from Jacksonville and St. Augustine were present, and rumors of impending violence circulated through Orlando. Shortly before the trial, the community awoke one night to a blazing fire at the courthouse. Volunteers in various states of dress rushed to the scene. They doused nearby buildings with water, but were unable to save the courthouse. When evidence of arson — a bottle of turpentine — was found at the scene, it was naturally assumed (though never proven) that someone had burned the courthouse to destroy evidence related to the impending trial.

The Barber-Mizell feud marked the zenith of the range-related violence. David Mizell Jr. was the Orange County sheriff, and his brother John was county judge. Members of the Barber family were grazing cattle over open range extending about 70 miles south of Orlando. According to various versions of the feud, Moses Barber Jr. either owed money for cattle he had purchased or had been fined for

A typical central Florida cowman in the 1890s.

minor crime. Sheriff Mizell took his brother Morgan and young son, Billy to collect the money from Barber. Along the way, Sheriff Mizell was ambushed and killed while crossing Bull Creek. The murderer had not been seen, but when Judge Mizell learned of his brother's death, he sent a posse to capture Barber. When Barber escaped to Georgia, the posse ran down and killed two of his sons.

Violence continued over the next several years as the cattle industry expanded, but improvements were on the way. Jacob Summerlin transferred his huge cattle empire from Bartow to Orlando in 1873, and he and other cowmen gradually brought order to the industry. The county improved its methods of registering marks and brands, and prominent cattlemen took turns serving as inspectors. There were still occasional thefts, but the wholesale rustling of herds became uncommon.

Farmers, too, were having difficulties. Some Orange County farmers were still growing cotton, but prices were unstable and usually on the decline. In 1871, a devastating hurricane destroyed most of the crops. High winds preceded a 48-hour rain which dumped at least a foot — some argued 48 inches — on central Florida. Another damaging storm in 1873 destroyed the cotton fields again and caused some damage to the young citrus groves as well.

Very few people were actually earning any real money anyway. Both the war and Reconstruction had so severely depleted state and county resources that the governments resorted to issuing scrip in payment of their obligations. The scrip fluctuated from as little as 40 cents on the dollar to as much as 90 cents. Then, in 1873, the entire nation went into a depression which lasted six years. Thus it was not until the end of the decade that Florida and Orange County were able to redeem their outstanding paper and begin using cash.

The Barber-Mizell feud. Above, Sheriff David W. Mizell, who was killed while attempting to arrest a member of the Barber family. Left, members of the Mizell family stand in front of the log cabin built by Mizell's wife Angeline.

Still, Orange County continued to grow. Several new communities were emerging. Mellonville had been engulfed by the new town of Sanford which, as head of the St. Johns River transportation and the site of Henry S. Sanford's real-estate and citrus activities, was competing with Orlando for recognition. Orlando claimed only about 85 inhabitants inside its limits, but the surrounding area encompassed many more. In 1875, the growing community erected its third courthouse, the second to be built since the original burned in 1868.

Construction of the new courthouse stimulated Orlandoans to greater civic pride, and they soon decided to incorporate their village. Wanting the boundaries to extend one mile in each direction from the courthouse, community leaders found that there were 29 qualified voters in that area, four more than needed by law. At an

James DeLaney, shown here with his family, came to Orlando about 1875 and purchased 40 acres near lakes Lucerne and Cherokee. He served as postmaster, kept a store, and built the Kuhl-DeLaney block, one of the city's first brick buildings.

election in July 1875, the voters agreed to call the new town Orlando, the name its post office had had since 1857. William J. Brack became the first mayor.

As Orlando gained prominence in central Florida, the region itself was receiving greater attention in state politics in 1876. Anxious to oust the Republicans who had controlled state offices since 1868, the Democratic party nominated George F. Drew of Madison County for governor and Noble A. Hull of Orlando for lieutenant governor. Drew and Hull defeated incumbent Republican Governor Marcellus L. Stearns and his running mate, David Montgomery, but the results came only after almost four months of uncertainty about who the nation's president would be. After a hard fought campaign that was very close in Florida, Republican Rutherford B. Hayes defeated Democrat Samuel J. Tilden by an electoral-college vote of 185 to 184. And although the state races had gone to the Democrats, Florida's electoral votes were counted for Hayes.

Many Floridians questioned the Republican version of the electoral college vote, but they didn't protest because they believed Hayes would bring an end to more than ten years of national intervention in the affairs of southern states. They were right. No president used national troops to enforce civil rights in the South again until 1957. The turbulent politics of the post-Civil War era gradually quieted, the Republican party practically disappeared as a viable political entity by the early 1890s, and Floridians concentrated more and more on making a living. The older, more settled portions of the state languished in depression for many years, but by the late 1870s Orlando and most of central Florida were on the verge of a population and economic boom.

BUMBY'S EXPRESS

When Joseph Bumby arrived from England in the 1870s he, like many of his neighbors, planted citrus trees. Since there was a delay of several years before the grove would become profitable, he set out to find other ways to make a living. Although Bumby was best known during his lifetime for the extensive hardware business he eventually operated, it was during the transitional period between his arrival and later success that he made history.

Like many others, Bumby had had a memorable experience trying to get from the St. Johns River to Orlando upon his arrival to Florida. And having been engaged in the transportation business in England, Bumby saw an opportunity to earn a living while offering a public service. When a mail route was designated over a new public road between Sanford and Orlando, Bumby obtained the mail contract and began hauling both freight and passengers.

Driving a team of horses for the morning trip from Orlando, he changed teams at Sanford at noon and made the return journey in the afternoon. The round trip required some twelve hours. This so-called "Bumby's Express" was the first regularly scheduled public transportation system in central Florida.

Nine Orlando women dressed in costumes representing local businesses in an 1890 promotional event.

The City of Jacksonville was one of the Clyde Line steamers on which people traveled to Orlando from Jacksonville and points north. Built in 1884, the vessel was on the river well into the twentieth century.

THE FIRST BOOM

Florida's first land and population boom occurred in the 1880s with central Florida as its focus. A combination of readily available water transportation down the St. Johns River, exuberant advertising, the Driston land sale, and the first railroad construction contributed to the boom, but it was founded upon climate, suitable land, and citrus.

In 1879, a Tampa newspaper lamented ruefully that Orange County land values were much greater than those in Hillsborough County, and wondered why. A Tallahassee editor declared the answer obvious since "Orange County has been advertised and puffed to the four corners of the earth and has no end of land agents and speculators who manipulate the market."

Much of that was true. Will Wallace Harney of Pinecastle, Zelotes Mason of Apopka, and others with literary leanings were writing voluminously of the

The South Florida Railroad Station, circa 1885. In the foreground is the street railway.

wonderful possibilities of central Florida land and its climate. John G. Sinclair, former governor of New Hampshire, was proclaiming the attractions of central Florida from his new Orlando real estate agency. Henry Sanford's sales of acreage to President Ulysses Grant and Rhode Island Senator Henry Anthony were "news" events. (Less was said about another sale to William Tecumseh Sherman.) And M.R. Marks, a future Orlando mayor, attracted attention with his claim that "the frost line " was north of Lake Monroe and that anyone settling south of the lake could expect year-round balmy temperatures.

Such claims attracted people from both north and south. Many who arrived in the late nineteenth century became permanent residents, but numerous others were winter visitors — snowbirds — looking for potential citrus grove lands.

Equally as important as advertising, however, was availability of transportation. The St. Johns River gave central Florida an advantage over other areas of the peninsula. Sometimes by rail and sometimes by water, seekers of land and warm climates made their way first to Jacksonville. From there they could easily find steamer transportation up the St. Johns River to Sanford.

From Sanford it was a different matter. Orlando and its neighbors south of Sanford could be reached only by foot or wagon over deeply rutted, sandy roads. Several of the early settlers complained of the arduous journey and the price-gouging of those who furnished occasional wagon service. As late as 1880, an Orlando visitor noted the casual attitude of the local livery operator. Anyone wanting transportation had to give him two-days' notice so he could round up the horses which roamed through the woods around Orlando.

The railroad, however, brought rapid changes. Chartered by two Maitland residents with Boston ties and financed by the owners of the *Boston Herald*, the South Florida Railroad was to run from Lake Monroe to Charlotte Harbor. The line was begun in January 1880. With Henry Sanford and other dignitaries present, former President Ulysses Grant turned the first shovel of earth in a festive launching of the project. Completed to Orlando that fall, the narrow-gauge line began service from that point. Joseph Bumby, who had had previous railroad experience in England, became the company's Orlando agent. For the first year, Bumby's feed and grain store served as the depot for both freight and passengers. The line was extended to Kissimmee and, after it was acquired by Henry Plant in 1883, to Tampa.

Orlando's transformation began immediately. A village of some 200 souls in 1880, by 1885 Orlando was a full-fledged town with nearly 50 businesses serving a large area. A widely distributed promotional pamphlet applauded Orlando's growth as "phenomenal as there are no oil wells, factories or mines, the population depending entirely on its orange groves, truck gardens

THE ENGLISH COLONY

The Englishmen who moved to the Orlando area in the late nineteenth century became legends almost as soon as they set foot on Florida soil. The younger ones were especially lively, if occasionally mischievous, but they were nevertheless fondly regarded. Winifred Browning, who was a young English girl of 12 when her family came to Orlando, wrote about the Englishmen in her memoirs, The Moss of a Rolling Stone.

"They were fine fellows, and, like ourselves, very musical, and so night after night was devoted to music. Many of the young Britishers 'batched it' in twos and threes. They worked their groves by day and visited different families in the evenings, when most of said families, like ours, kept open house.

"Some drank pretty heavily but those we did not see much of, and strange as it may seem, nearly all the wild ones were clergymen's sons . . . .

"One of them we considered the character of the English settlement, Conway. I can picture him now as I saw him once go galloping past us, on foot, and neighing like a horse, he trotted into the livery stable where he began to chew hay and oats from the manger, and would kick if interfered with.

"We were told later that he was used to having periodic attacks of the D.T.s when he would imagine he was a horse and go galloping into town, where he was always kept in a stall and treated like a horse until sober.

"Another of these boys opened his alarm clock with a can opener, after an evening at the English Club, mistaking it for a can of beef. It was kept at the club as an exhibit. Yet another, who was particularly amusing when he had had a trifle too much, told this story on himself the next day at Polo.

"He was on his way home the night before when suddenly his pony stopped and couldn't be persuaded to go on. What was wrong he couldn't tell, nor could he recognize the road, so he gave up, dismounted, unsaddled and hitched the pony to a post he COULD see. He camped out on the spot until morning, only to find he was outside his own gate and the poor little pony had simply stopped for him to open it."

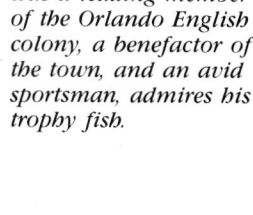

Leslie Pell-Clarke, who was a leading member of the Orlando English colony, a benefactor of the town, and an avid sportsman, admires his trophy fish.

Mr. and Mrs. Arthur G. Smyth prepared for a ride. Note the English tack and side-saddle.

Winter Park's Seminole Hotel, viewed from the south.

NO. 95. "THE SEMINOLE" FROM SOUTH, WINTER PARK, FLA.

and unrivaled climate. Orlando is built on the peel of the orange."

For many potential landowners in 1880, there was yet one more hurdle. Francis Vose, a Pennsylvania iron manufacturer, had furnished the rails to build the first Florida railroad nearly two decades before. But he had never been paid. Vose went to court to get his money, and the state was forbidden to sell any of its vast public lands unless it could raise the cash to settle its debt to Vose. Finally, in the late 1870s, Hamilton Disston, a wealthy saw manufacturer from Philadelphia, became interested in draining Florida lowlands and raising sugar on them. By 1881, he and Governor William D. Bloxham agreed on the sale of four million acres of ostensibly wet lands for 25 cents an acre in cash. The transaction liquidated the Vose debt and removed the court injunction. The state subsequently disposed of sixteen million acres of land to the benefit of dozens of railroad companies — including the South Florida Railroad.

Disston may have fared even better in the deal. He bought the swamps, but also some of central Florida's best agricultural lands. He almost immediately resold half his land to Sir Edward Reed and an English syndicate which had been negotiating with the state for several years. Reed and his associates, in turn, advertised their Florida land throughout England. The British settlers paid about one dollar an acre, and settled throughout Orlando and Winter Park, especially near Lake Conway.

The so-called "English colony" caused quite a stir. The British came by the hundreds, bringing with them their love of opera and sport, and such curious customs as their daily teatime. The locals, or "crackers," were much impressed and tried to imitate many British habits. They studied nearly every aspect of their new neighbors, eventually dividing them into three categories. There were the "retired generals," older military and civil officials who were retiring to Florida's warm climate. Next came the "second sons," younger members of wealthy families who, since they would not inherit the family fortunes, came to Florida seeking fortunes of their own in the citrus groves. The third group, the "remittance men," were also sons of wealthy British families. They had, for various reasons, fallen out of favor at home and were being paid to live elsewhere. The young English bachelors worked hard in the citrus groves all day, then played equally hard all night. It was they who became the subjects of most intent interest. Fond of drink, music, and sport, their arrival changed the social environment of Orlando immediately and permanently. (The Rogers Building which housed the English Club, focal point of many nineteenth-century social events, is one of Orlando's oldest remaining structures.)

A group of English settlers in front of the Bennett House, which was located on East Central Avenue.

THE CITY MOVES WEST

Arrival of the railroad shifted the business district from the courthouse square toward the railroad depot. In the late 1870s, A.M. Hyer had built a store at the corner of Church and Orange "out in the pine woods" where most people thought it would fail. It was acquired in 1880 by W.G. White, who anticipated the impact of the railroad. He was soon joined by John G. Sinclair and N.L. Mills, who opened a real-estate office there. Then H.H. Luckie from South Carolina built the

Orange County's second courthouse and town well as they appeared in 1884. The building subsequently became part of the Tremont Hotel.

Charleston House on the same corner. As the focal point of social activities, it also helped draw the town westward. By 1883, the new business district was joined by the Shine and Butler Store, McElroy's Blue Drug Store, C.A. Boone's Hardware, and the Peak and Mullins Drug Store. Sidney Ives opened his grocery store there, then soon formed a partnership with H.H. Dickson. (The Dickson and Ives Grocery was the nucleus of the department store which served Orlando until the 1960s.)

A string of hotels soon went up to accommodate the growing number of winter residents. And in 1883, at the initiative of Nathaniel Poyntz, the First National Bank was opened.

The Orlando Fire Department with its new equipment, shortly after the company was organized.

PROGRESS BY FIRE

In the early morning hours of January 12, 1884, the town was awakened by a fire in James Delaney's grocery store. Despite a welcome rain the previous evening, flames soon spread to Bassett's Millinery Store, Gilliams' Drug Store, and the building which housed Mahlon Gore's *Orange County Reporter*. All were consumed, and only the timely use of explosives by the recently organized volunteer fire department saved the rest of the business district.

Delaney's building and stock were insured, but the destruction of his records left him dependent upon his customers' integrity. Most of them paid up. An even greater demonstration of community spirit was the reaction to the newspaper's demise. After the fire, Gore went to Sanford and arranged to have his paper printed there. Upon his return, the harried editor was met by a group of neighbors who presented him with $1,200 to help defray his losses, and with $300 worth of new subscriptions.

Though the fire was an immediate disaster, it brought further progress to Orlando. Within months, a city hall and jail were built. The city also organized the Orlando Hook and Ladder Company, which was soon equipped with three 55-gallon chemical fire engines. Regulations were also enacted to encourage brick rather than wood construction.

One of the first brick structures was the Kuhl-Delaney block, a three-story affair built by Edward Kuhl and James Delaney, whose store had been lost in the fire. Adjacent to it was a two-story building constructed by Norman Robinson. The high point of the new construction was the San Juan de Ulloa Hotel, Orlando's first brick hostelry. Constructed at a cost of $150,000 by

Edgar Dann and Monroe Matthews, seated on two Florida cow ponies in front of the livery stable in the 1890s.

Henry S. Kedney, an immigrant from Minnesota who had lived in Maitland since 1870, the three-story San Juan was launched into Orlando history by a lavish opening ceremony. Two stories were added in 1893, when it was purchased by Harry L. Beeman, an heir to the Beeman chewing-gum fortune. With a popular dining room, a pharmacy, and other businesses on its main floor, it was frequented by many Orlandoans as well as winter visitors.

John Sinclair's Orlando real-estate booklet for 1886 listed 50 stores, seven churches, a seminary, an opera house, five large hotels, three bakeries, two newspapers, a machine shop, two carriage shops, an ice factory, four drug stores, and several restaurants — compared to 200 people and half a dozen businesses only six years earlier. In his 1886 directory, Wanton S. Webb was so impressed by the enormous changes since the 1884 fire that he could give Orlando but one description — "the phenomenal city."

Phenomenal as the town may have seemed, life in Orlando was still somewhat basic. The first telephone service had its inauspicious beginning in 1881 when a single line was installed from P.A. Foster's livery stable to his home. The system soon expanded to include eight subscribers and an exchange above the McElroy Drug Store. Mass transit came to Orlando in 1886. N.L. Mills and his son, Ernest, operated the Orlando Street Railway, occasionally pulling a mule-drawn car along wooden rails. The only requirement imposed by the city was that the speed not exceed six miles per hour.

In 1886, the city commissioned the Orlando Water Works to provide water to the community. Embroiled in controversy from its inception, the company became defunct after the 1894-95 freezes. It was reorganized by John M. Cheney as the Orlando Water and Light Company. Cheney, a strong-willed gentleman, decided

once that Orlandoans were wasting their water, and shut the system down to entice them to change their ways.

Street maintenance was yet another matter. Since no one was willing to clean the streets, that job was left to the razorback hogs living under the courthouse. However, Columbus Sweet agreed to tackle the job of removing the tree stumps from the rights-of-way, clearing 659 of them in two years. There was as yet no city pound, but Put Myers became the town cow-sitter for a while. His job was to round up the town's milk cows each morning and drive them to a range outside the city

THE MAN WHO MADE THE "CITY BEAUTIFUL"

The Branham family has been a positive force in Orlando since the arrival of Albert Gallatin Branham from Tennessee in 1885, but perhaps the most noticeable impact on the city was made by the elder Branham himself. During the administration of Mayor M.R. Marks — at a time when "Arbor Day" was being celebrated across the nation — the city decided to plant oak trees along some of the downtown streets. Under a contract with the city, Branham set out 400 oak trees — and the idea caught on. During the next several years he planted for the city, as well as for many individuals, about 5,000 live and water oaks.

Its tree-lined streets are a major reason for Orlando's designation as "The City Beautiful." Albert Gallatin Branham is probably more responsible for this epithet than any other person.

Alligator roping was a form of entertainment in Orlando in the 1880s. The man seated on the alligator was Bunk Baxter, who sometimes wrestled alligators in the street, to the delight of the Saturday crowds.

45

THE RAZORBACK HOG

A FLORIDA RAZOR-BACK.
You have heard of roosters before
But this is the champion I'm sure
He's the original Razor-back Hog
Hones himself on the side of a log
Then is ready to root some more.

A Florida razorback hog.

There was no animal more aptly suited to cleaning the streets of early-day Orlando than the razorback hog, for — according to this report by Mahlon Gore in 1895 — the animal was good for very little else.

"...divested of head, tail, intestines and hair, he is a hollow deception. His hams are remarkable for the concavity of their outlines and the wonderful disproportion of meat to your expectations, while his sides look like a miserable failure of nature, in an attempt to make a fair article of whip leather. Architecturally, the razorback is built on four legs — the two hind ones at the rear corners; the front ones just far enough in front of center to prevent the long snout from tilting the tail end into the air. The pure breed has three tails — one at the proper place and one suspended from each lower jaw.

"The Creator never made anything in vain, and no doubt there was a wise purpose in providing the razor-back with tails on his jaws; but man has never yet been able to penetrate this veiled mystery. There is an excess of tails and paucity of brains. He has no sense and his instincts are perverse and lead to destruction. With his long snout he can smell a potato patch five miles against the wind. If he cannot find a leaning tree that he can climb and jump into the patch, he will burrow under the fence. It is claimed that no owner of a potato patch can be truly pious in a razor-back section. The razor-back never gets fat — he is a hollow delusion and an empty mockery. He eats anything that comes his way . . . . Whatever adheres to his ribs from the food he consumes could be wiped off with a woolen rag. He is mostly made up of bowels and sin."*

near Lake Cherokee, where they grazed until they were driven back each evening.

Town beautification projects were more successful. Orlando celebrated its first Arbor Day in 1888 when Mayor Matthew Marks contracted with Albert G. Branham to set out 400 oak trees on public property. Citizens joined in and began setting out trees in front of their homes as well. A racecourse was added to the city's first public park, which became known as Eola Park.

As the city grew and cowmen continued their raucous weekend activities, the national temperance movement made its way to Orlando. The town was voted dry in 1883, but the cowmen still obtained liquor illegally.

For most Orlandoans, however, Saturday became known as "Cracker Day." Families gathered from miles around to trade and exchange the latest news.

Sometimes the entertainment took unusual forms. One popular activity was watching Bunk Baxter wrestle his pet alligator at the corner of Orange Avenue and Pine Street. On another weekend, the main event was the public hanging of a murderer, Henry Stokes. A huge crowd of acquaintances gathered 'round while Stokes called out good-humored farewells as he went to his eternal rest.

By 1884, the weekend activities had shifted to the newly built opera house and community hall on Court Street. There, the locals presented plays and occasional musical performances, sometimes supplemented by traveling players and minstrel shows. One of the opera house's finest hours was a benefit performance by Emma Thursby, a prominent opera singer who was vacationing on the coast.

Not all events there were "high culture." After a skating rink was added to the hall, several youths planned a major extravaganza. They persuaded "Uncle Dan" Prescott to provide them with a wild razorback hog, which the skaters planned to chase with hockey sticks. The hog, dazed by the noise and lights, simply lay down and refused to move.

GROWTH ALL AROUND

The boom years following Reconstruction were felt not only in Orlando but throughout Orange County. New communities sprouted all around the city; older ones established themselves as separate towns with distinct personalities.

Along the railroad to the north (near present-day Princeton and Orange) was the flag-stop of Wilcox, renamed Formosa in 1887. Among its several residents was C.W. Jacocks, a prominent local official and grove caretaker. Mrs. Jacocks developed an improved variety of pecan and had a sizable pecan grove there until the freezes of 1894-95. Still identifiable as a separate community as late as 1910, when Russell Park on Lake Ivanhoe was described as "a short distance north of the city," Formosa was annexed into Orlando in 1925 as the

A four-ox team draws a wagon carrying three crackers into Orlando by way of Main Street. The building to the left is the Armory.

THE CRACKER IN TOWN

Orlando in the nineties. Above, Orange County delegates to the World's Fair Convention in Chicago in 1891. The Opera House behind them was later used as a skating rink. Left, West Central Avenue, as viewed from the courthouse tower in 1894.

central business district spread to the north.

Near the site of old Fort Maitland on the shore of Lake Maitland, C.C. Beasley was homesteading land in quiet seclusion in the post-Civil War years. Some of the numerous Partin family also had groves nearby. From Minnesota, seeking a winter home, soon came Bishop H.B. Whipple, who had previously visited the area. He and B.R. Swope set out some of the earliest groves, and the latter purchased considerable acreage in what was to become the Maitland-Winter Park area. Soon joining them were John C. Eaton, Maitland's first mayor, John Bigelow, Isaac Vanderpool, and the family of S.B. Hill. George Packwood set out a grove on Lake Sybelia and his brother, Richard, became Maitland's first physician. E.R. Hall, a wealthy Chicago banker, established a winter residence in 1875 and moved there permanently about 30 years later.

Already a post office since 1872, the town was laid out in 1876 and incorporated in 1885. N.J. Bayard opened the first store, Bishop Whipple built the Church of the Good Shepherd in memory of his son, and Isaac Vanderpool opened the first citrus packing house. H.S. Kedney managed several of the groves for absentee owners.

C.C. Haskell of Boston moved to Maitland in the late 1870s and, with E.W. Henck of Longwood, was instrumental in starting the South Florida Railroad, which reached Maitland in mid-1880. Despite its charm, Maitland remained until the 1950s "back among the groves and the evergreen oaks," with a business section "scattered and small, for Maitland [was] a residential town for citrus growers and business folk of nearby towns."

Altamonte Springs was originally situated at Palm Springs near the Little Wekiwa River, then relocated to the railroad when it came through in 1880. A large hotel was frequented by winter residents, some of whom purchased land nearby. One of them was H.H. Westinghouse — of the famed family — who purchased Spring Lake Grove. R.S. Fuller operated the first store at Altamonte Springs and also served as postmaster. J.M. Lewis began promoting local real estate in 1881.

Early tourist attractions. Below, a horse-drawn railway was often used to carry hotel guests from the railroad station. Right, a fair at the first Fairgrounds on Lake Eola in the 1880s.

49

With its winter residents and orange groves, Altamonte Springs remained a pretty little town with oak-lined streets until the explosive growth of central Florida in the 1960s. Made a part of Seminole County in 1913, it has become more and more a part of the Orlando metropolitan area as recent growth has merged several communities of the area.

About thirteen miles north of Orlando, Longwood was the junction of three railroads in the 1880s. E.W. Henck's role in constructing the South Florida has been discussed. P.A. Demens, a Russian immigrant who operated a large sawmill at Longwood, transformed a logging tram road into the Orange Belt Railroad, which eventually extended from Longwood through the Apopka area and Oakland to St. Petersburg. The Florida Midland also ran from Longwood and Lake Jesup through Apopka and Ocoee to Kissimmee. A large hotel was built in the mid-1880s by N.B. Clouser, who operated it for many years, entertaining numerous winter visitors who enjoyed the excellent hunting and fishing along the nearby Wekiwa River. The hotel has survived the changes of time and now comprises the center of a restored historical district in Longwood. Clouser, his son, and an associate ran Longwood's first store. After Demens had cut much of the timber and moved on to his railroad interests, Longwood had an extensive turpentine industry for several years. D.H. Horne opened the first large turpentine still there about 1900.

A black congregation in the late 1890s. The newspaper displayed by the man at right was the Winter Park Advocate *, a newspaper published by and for blacks.*

Winter Park's origins were much different from its neighbors. Planned and laid out before it was settled, it was intended to attract "men and women of intelligence, culture, character, taste and means." Loring A. Chase and Oliver E. Chapman, both from Massachusetts, purchased 600 acres near Osceola Station on the railroad in 1882.

Frankly stating their aim to make Winter Park "a first class place for northern and southern men of wealth," they priced their lots so as "to insure purchasers of means, substantial buildings, and well-ordered grounds." Streets were laid out with adequate space for parks, schools, hotels, and a business district, and "a separate and adequate area for the negro population."

Advertising their new town throughout the eastern United States in 1881, Chase and Chapman proceeded to transform their ideas into reality. With some assistance from the railroad and such early settlers as Lewis Lawrence, W.C. Comstock, J.C. Stovin, Dr. Ira Geer, Wilson Phelps, L.L. Galt, and Royal R. Thayer — several of whom lived in the older community of Osceola, where David Mizell had settled in 1858 — they erected a railroad station at a cost of $1,100. A two-story building was constructed and the first floor was leased to John Ergood and Robert White Jr. for a store. The second floor became the town hall. H.H. Berry moved his wagon shop from Osceola, and William S. Lane did the same with his cabinet shop. Chapman and Chase gave A.E. Rogers a lot on which he built Winter Park's first hotel. Early purchasers of lots included Charles H. Morse and Franklin Fairbanks of Chicago, Frederick Lyman, Dr. J.R. Tantum, J.F. Adams, William C. Comstock, and T.C. Hill. Before the end of 1881, a road was completed to connect the new town with the Osceola settlement.

When a telegraph office was opened on New Year's Day in 1883, the first message from Lewis Lawrence to his good friend, President Chester A. Arthur, read tersely "Happy New Year. First message from office opened here today. No North No South." Chapman and Chase must have been pleased with its nonsectional theme.

By 1885, Winter Park boasted several businesses and

dwellings housing permanent or winter residents. The
[fir]m of Chapman and Chase was dissolved that year when
[Ch]apman sold his interests to Chase for $40,000. The
[Wi]nter Park Company was then organized with a
[ca]pitalization of $300,000. F.L. Lyman and, later, Franklin
[Fa]irbanks served as presidents. One of the firm's first acts
[wa]s to contract with Francis B. Knowles to erect the
[Se]minole Hotel. Completed at a cost of $150,000 and
[bo]asting 150 rooms, the Seminole was opened on New
[Ye]ar's Day 1886, with 2,000 visitors attending the
[el]aborate ceremonies. The Virginia Inn was already open
[fo]r business by that time.

In 1887, the Orlando and Winter Park Railroad (later
[ca]lled the "Dinky Railroad") was begun, and, under the
[gu]idance of several prominent businessmen, was
[co]mpleted by 1889. The Town of Winter Park was
[in]corporated in 1887, with Robert White Jr. as the first
[m]ayor. Osceola and the black community of Hannibal
[Sq]uare were included, although Hannibal Square was
[lat]er detached in a stormy battle in 1893. With 850 acres
[of] orange groves and a population of 613, Winter Park
[se]emed to be realizing the goals of Chapman and Chase.
[Th]ere were 51 families from the South and 141 from the
[No]rth. With 57 Democrats and 133 Republicans
[re]gistered to vote, there was apparently "No North
[no] South."

SEPARATE AND UNEQUAL

There was, however, a division of society
developing. Blacks were generally regarded as a
servant class during the post-Civil War years,
[w]hen the central Florida communities were being
[se]ttled. After the Congressional efforts to incorporate
[bl]acks into the southern mainstream had failed, a
[ba]cklash developed. While blacks were regarded as

worthwhile as railroad laborers, domestic servants, and
occasionally as yeoman farmers, there was a growing
tendency to separate their residential areas from those of
whites. Hannibal Square was indeed physically distinct
from the white portion of Winter Park and was
developing a community of its own with churches,
schools, and a literary club, presided over by Gus C.
Henderson. Henderson was the second editor of the
Winter Park *Advocate,* a black newspaper started by S.A.
Williams. Henderson later moved to Orlando, where he
published the *Christian Advocate* and later the *Recorder*
until his death just before World War I. The bitter debate
in 1893, which ultimately led to the separation of
Hannibal Square from the Winter Park city limits, was
part of a general trend.

The same thing was happening in Orlando, although it
had as much to do with housing for blacks as with
segregation. James Magruder, one of Orlando's most
exuberant builders and owner of the Magruder Arcade,
built an "all-colored settlement" west of present-day
Greenwood Cemetery, which became known as
Jonestown. In later years, Orlando would zone residential
areas according to race, but that was not yet the case in
the 1880s. Milo Cooper operated a barber shop for
"whites only" during that era and built a fine two-story
home on Jackson and Lake streets in a fashionable white
neighborhood.

Maitland also had accomplished a separation similar to
that of Winter Park, but cast it in a much more desirable
veneer. Maitland blacks had built their homes around
Lake Lily, then known as St. John's Hole. John C. Eaton
and Isaac Vanderpool induced them to move by offering
to help establish the all-black town of Eatonville.
Incorporated in the mid-1880s, the town became a
source of stability for its citizens, even as it emphasized
the gradual separation of the races. J.E. Clark became the
leading merchant of the new town, and S.G. Moseley was

*Unidentified farmer
and family in central
Florida at the turn of
the century.*

A view of Orange Avenue in the late 1880s. The woman crossing the street is Mrs. Metcalfe, the beautiful and controversial wife of the local saloon keeper. C.A. Boone's Hardware is at right. Note the boardwalks and the animal skins hanging in front of Nicholson's Menagerie.

According to legend, author-anthropologist Zora Neale Hurston left Eatonville with a Gilbert and Sullivan opera company, eventually attended Columbia University, and did field work under Franz Boaz, the noted anthropologist. Hurston, whose novels often featured her hometown, was well-respected in literary circles across the nation, but was almost unknown in Orlando. Few people knew who she was when she died in poverty in 1960. The recent naming of the local federal building in her honor has at least placed her name before the public again.

Mahlon Gore was a leading newspaper editor of the 1890s, a prominent businessman, and one of Orlando's most enthusiastic boosters.

a long-time mayor. Eatonville became more important for central Florida blacks with the establishment of the Robert H. Hungerford Normal and Industrial School in 1897. On land donated by E.C. Hungerford, a winter resident of Maitland, and with donations from several white supporters as well as Booker T. Washington, the school was opened with R.C. Calhoun as president. For many years the school provided education not otherwise available to central Florida blacks.

Eatonville's best known resident was probably Zora Neale Hurston, the anthropologist and author, who had to leave home to rise in American society. Somewhat embittered by the lot of her people, Hurston once described her hometown as the place that began where the pavement ended on the west side of Maitland.

THE WEST ORANGE COUNTY TOWNS

Some of the communities around Lake Apopka have frequently emphasized their isolation from Orlando and the rest of the county, and Apopka was for many years the trading center of an extensive area. The recent growth of the metropolitan area, however, has begun to include them. Their diversity and independence in the early days have continued to the present, but more and more often their problems, accomplishments, hopes, and fears have become the same as those of the greater metropolitan area.

Older than either Sanford or Orlando, Apopka had evolved as the trading center of a sizable area around the Masonic lodge building, which was the meeting place for the entire county in its early days. Referred to simply as "the Lodge" until well into the 1870s, it was laid out and incorporated in 1882. Situated on high ground between the headwaters of the Wekiwa River and Lake Apopka, it was surrounded by some of the most desirable citrus land in the state. By the 1870s, such original settlers as the Stewarts, the Goolsbys, and the Buchans had been joined by Zelotes Mason, J.J. Combs, E.C. Morgan, and others to set out groves and to open stores. Page McKinney, E.R. Prince, and Joseph L. Guernsey — before the latter moved to Orlando — opened a bank. McKinney, Frank Davis, and others dealt in real estate. Apopka drew into its trading area the nearby communities of Clarcona, Lakeville, Piedmont, Clay Springs, Merrimac, McDonald, and Zellwood.

One of the first settlers along the south shore of Lake Apopka was W.C. Roper, who arrived in 1859. Shortly afterward, Dr. J.D. Starke settled near the lake that still bears his name. When Bluford M. Sims, after a short stay at Apopka, moved there in 1865, the place was known as Starke Lake, or South Apopka. These first settlers and a few neighbors grew winter vegetables, shipping them over sandy roads to Clay Springs until the railroad came through in the mid-1880s. T.J. Minor was an early storekeeper and J.R. Pounds ran the first of several sawmills. Experiencing considerable growth during the booming 1880s and anticipating arrival of the Florida Midland, the community was renamed Ocoee, an Indian word meaning "no cold." The town was laid out by a real-estate firm comprised of Dr. H.E. Clark, Charles J. Chun, and R.B.F. Roper. Ocoee remained a rural agricultural community until recent times.

Not far from Ocoee and claiming the allegiance of some of the same residents, Oakland was founded in the mid-1880s by Judge J.G. Speer and others. The railhead of the Orange Belt Railroad for a few years, the community boomed, with winter residents staying in several hotels, and permanent inhabitants planting and harvesting good crops of winter vegetables. Oakland gradually gave up its place in west Orange County to Winter Garden, which was emerging nearby.

A.B. Newton arrived from Mississippi in 1892 to become the first merchant at Winter Garden, which had grown out of an older community known as Beulah. There, Newton found a half dozen dwellings, a sawmill, and a tiny railroad station on the Orange Belt Railroad. post office was established in 1893, but the town was not incorporated until 1908.

Luther Fuller Tilden was one of Winter Garden's most influential boosters, although his residence was outside the community at Tildenville. Tilden had lived awhile at Apopka before purchasing extensive acreage on the

54

south shore of Lake Apopka, where he developed citrus groves and vegetable fields.

The area which became Gotha was, in the early 1870s, "an unbroken stretch of woods," with only three families living there. Then in 1878, H.A. Hempel of Buffalo, who had just received a large payment for his patented improvement of the printing press, decided to lay out a German town and name it for his birthplace in Germany. He was soon joined by B. Huppel, L. Hartman, Harry Moore, H.A. Regener, and L. Wichtendahl. Hempel opened a store, set up a sawmill, which supplied much of the lumber for the early buildings of Winter Park and Maitland, and began planting citrus trees. Charles Koehne came a little later and opened a store, which he operated for many years. Perhaps Gotha's most famous resident was Henry Nehrling, who came from Wisconsin in 1883. His ten-acre nursery became a showplace from the Orient. Nehrling developed new varieties of amaryllis

and caladiums in his nursery.

A social club, known as a *Turnverein,* was organized in 1886 with more than 30 members. In its hall, Gotha families gathered for such activities as dancing and bowling. Many of the local residents were employed as grove tenders for northerners from Chicago, Milwaukee, Louisville, and other midwestern cities who wintered at Gotha. Although the freezes of the mid-1890s were a serious setback, the groves were built back, and Gotha continued to be at the center of a growing citrus industry.

H. Wilkening arrived in the 1890s from Kansas and built a business block, which housed a grocery store and drug store. Later, a garage was added. Wilkening also established a water system for the community.

Jack Yates, Needham Bass, George Bass, and some of the Barbers were grazing cattle in the Kissimmee area when J.H. Allen built a store and sawmill on the shore of

An 1885 parade through downtown Orlando, featuring the Orlando Guards and the Cornet Band.

Gathering the crop at the David B. Stewart grove near Apopka, before the freezes of 1894-1895.

Lake Tohopekaliga. Called Allendale for several years, the settlement was later named Kissimmee, and was touted as "The Tropical City" when the railroad arrived in 1883. Some tourists were attracted there by the railroad and I.M. Mabbette's Tropical Hotel. After purchasing his four million acres in 1881, Hamilton Disston began draining land for sugar culture. Although Disston made his headquarters at St. Cloud, his dredging activity and construction of the Sugar Belt Railroad benefited Kissimmee. By 1884, a navigable waterway linked it to the Gulf of Mexico. With both railroad and surface transportation and a sizable boat-building facility, the town attracted settlers and enjoyed a brisk business for several years. Will Wallace Harney started the *Bitter Sweet,* Kissimmee's first newspaper, in 1885. Although its stormy existence was brief, other papers followed.

By the time the Midland Railroad was completed from Longwood through Apopka to Kissimmee in 1886, both the town and its surrounding area had grown enough that Osceola County was carved from southern Orange County, with Kissimmee as the seat of government. Steamboats continued to ply the Kissimmee River for years, but the sugar industry declined in the 1890s. Although Kissimmee grew to a population of nearly 5,000 before World War I, it declined to about 2,700 by 1920. It remained the center of an extensive open-range cattle industry until Walt Disney World altered that in the 1960s.

SLIPPING ON THE ORANGE PEEL

As more people came to the central Florida towns, citrus became increasingly important as a money crop. By the early 1890s, Orlando was an important marketing and supply center for the citrus industry. Several packing and shipping firms were organized, and the South Florida Railroad opened a new brick depot to handle the increased freight. Orlando was indeed being built "on the peel of an orange," but few recognized how slippery that stance could be.

The building boom of the past several years had strained the financial resources of central Florida, just as a comparable national program had done throughout the country. A money panic in the fall of 1893 brought on a national depression that bankrupted hundreds of railroads and industrial companies. In March 1893, the Orlando Citizens Bank consolidated with the older First National Bank, but in August the First National had to close its doors. When the Merchants Bank opened shortly afterward, Orlando seemed to have survived the money panic. But it had not counted on Mother Nature.

On Christmas Day 1894, the San Juan Hotel lobby was filled with commissioned merchants and citrus buyers from all over the nation, bidding for crops whose growers were not overly anxious to sell until the prices improved. But in the early afternoon the temperature began dropping. Growers hurried back into the lobby, but as the temperature fell, so did the prices. According to Karl Abbott, who lived with his parents at the San Juan, one man walked into the lobby, looked at the thermometer, groaned, and shot himself in the head. The freeze lasted several days, killing the fruit and damaging many trees. Some overextended growers gave up, but most decided to hang on until the next crop.

As the weather warmed, the trees put out new shoots. Then on February 7, 1895, the temperature plunged again to eighteen degrees and remained there for many hours. Sap froze in the trunks of the growing trees, causing them literally to explode with sounds similar to gunshots. Groves were left shattered, twisted, and blackened. Many people left Orlando and central Florida. Land values plummeted. In Winter Park, a home with 40 acres that would have sold for $40,000 in the late 1880s could be bought for $500 a decade later.

Farsighted men who could afford it purchased ruined groves, replanted, and eventually earned large profits, but many smaller owners were forced out of business. Some turned to celery production, and Sanford became the center of a burgeoning winter vegetable industry. Others went into the turpentine business and exploited the huge expanses of virgin pines in central Florida. At least two other severe freezes occurred before 1900, but the citrus industry gradually revived and expanded beyond the wildest expectations of the 1890s.

CHAPTER FIVE

OF THE MIND
AND SOUL
AND A LITTLE RECREATION

*John D. Burden and Carl Warfield
dressed for skating in 1885.*

A VERY SMALL BEGINNING

Born a slave, Doshia Greene lived for many years in Jonestown. She was a staunch member and supporter of Mt. Olive Colored Methodist Episcopal Church.

Before they had churches or regular ministers, central Floridians made "a very small beginning" toward ministering to the religious needs of the communities. A Union Free Church, built in Orlando in 1857, was shared on Sundays by Baptists, Methodists, Episcopalians, and later, Presbyterians. It doubled as a school during the week. Apopkans held services in the Masonic Lodge Building in the early years. Some churches had traveling ministers; others used laymen. Services also were frequently held in private homes, such as Francis Eppes' Pineloch and Arnold Court at Conway.

As the communities grew, so did the congregations, and the larger denominations began erecting buildings. By 1885, enough Catholics had moved into the Orlando area to form a church.

The churches not only looked after their congregations' spiritual needs, helped to educate their young, and gave aid to the poor and ill, but they also formed the nucleus for social and recreational functions. Orlandoans enjoyed picnic outings to Clay Springs (now Wekiwa) and other popular bathing places, and all-day singing and box lunches on the grounds.

Schools were established as soon as a few pupils could be assembled. One of the first schools was taught by Bluford Sims in 1865 in a vacant house near present-day Winter Garden. There were no certification requirements for teachers, and Sims' credentials apparently were that he was trusted enough to be hired by a few interested parents. Cassius A. Boone was probably the first teacher in Orlando, holding classes in the Union Free Church.

Education was an important matter for the settlers, however, and a public-school system gradually evolved from these individual efforts. The first board of public instruction was formed in 1869. It encouraged schools wherever they were desired, if the community could muster at least seven pupils. A school at Piedmont enrolled a 3-year-old in order to have seven students. Schools came and went rapidly as populations changed. The task of teaching was more and more often assumed by the women of the community. Mary and Emma Dart were just two of the dedicated women who devoted long

Orlando's first school building, constructed in 1870, shown here circa 1890.

lives to teaching, ultimately influencing both the children and the communities. James T. Beeks served several stormy years as a pioneer superintendent of public instruction. He was followed by Major William B. Lynch, who is generally credited with laying the foundation for a sound county school system.

The long tradition of private schools in central Florida began when Mrs. N.F. Abbott, a former teacher from Boston, opened a school in her home because the public school was too far away. The Cathedral School for Girls was opened in 1907 under the auspices of the Episcopal church. It enjoyed a long tenure in early Orlando. The church also supported St. John's Academy for black children.

Shortly after the Winter Park Congregational Church was formed, both the church and the community became interested in establishing a college. Several Florida towns were interested in the school, but Congregational authorities voted to locate the new facility at Winter Park because that town had offered the largest initial subscription — $114,000. Named for A.W. Rollins, whose $50,000 subscription decided the issue, Rollins College opened in the fall of 1885 with 43 students attending classes in the church. Knowles Hall was dedicated in March 1886 and gradually the college

campus took form. The church pastor, Dr. E.P. Hooker, was the first president, succeeded in 1892 by William F. Blackman. During Blackman's thirteen-year tenure, Rollins College emerged as *the* central Florida school, supported by both Winter Park and Orlando.

STEP RIGHT UP!

A popular and entertaining way to create a sense of community — as well as attract outside attention — was to hold an agricultural fair and livestock exposition. Orlando's first fair was held in a newly constructed building on Lake Eola in 1886. The adjacent racetrack was used for horse races and for ring tournaments patterned after medieval jousts. Despite heavy rains, the fair was a success. In 1892, several Orlandoans formed an association to promote and oversee future fairs. On an 80-acre tract on Division Street, they constructed new fair buildings and a racetrack. The annual fairs continued at that site until the 1894-95 freezes destroyed the local economy. The facility was then deeded to racing enthusiast Leslie Pell-Clarke, who had put up most of the money to build it.

The improving economy in the early 1900s revived enthusiasm for another fair. In 1909, several members of the Orlando Trotting Association formed an Orange County Fair association. They built yet another fairground and racetrack where Exposition Park is now located. They invited communities from all around to bring their exhibits and, to assure attendance at the 1910 fair, announced a flying demonstration and contest. The flyer who could stay aloft for five consecutive minutes would be awarded $1,500. Of the three flyers who participated, only Lincoln Beachy could stay up the required time, and continued to do so every day of the fair. Beachy enjoyed several years of fame as "the man without nerves" until, in 1913, his plane disintegrated over San Francisco Bay.

Beachy's feats helped ensure the success of the fair, which became an annual event as the Central Florida Exposition. In 1913, the Johnny J. Jones Shows brought carnival rides and games to the fair and decided to make its winter home at Orlando. The Jones Shows became an Orlando institution for many years.

While central Floridians were busily carving their livelihoods from Florida's abundant resources, some winter residents were concerned with what they believed to be a wasteful "carnage of Florida's plume birds for the adornment of women's hats." Hunters lay in

Students and faculty of the Apopka Union School in 1904.

The home of Lewis F. Dommerich at Maitland. This was the site of the founding of the Florida Audubon Society.

wait at the rookeries where thousands of wading birds gathered. Hundreds of the birds were killed with ease each night. Disturbed by these actions, Mr. and Mrs. Louis F. Dommerich and Mr. and Mrs. Isaac Vanderpool met with some of their Maitland neighbors at Dommerich's Hiawatha estate in 1900. They formed the Florida Audubon Society, with Bishop Henry B. Whipple as president and Mrs. Dommerich as secretary.

The Audubon Society hired patrolmen to watch the rookeries, but when a patrolman was murdered in 1906 by bird hunters, a national campaign was begun for restrictive legislation. Over the next two decades, satisfactory legislation was obtained — and women's

fashions changed as well. The Audubon Society continued to guard the birds and their natural habitats, and the group emerged as one of the most important advocates of conservation in the state and nation.

SHINE GUARDS, CORNET BANDS, AND SOCIAL CLUBS

Whenever an event in central Florida was important enough to warrant a parade, which was often, the local militia was immediately called out — not because trouble was expected, but because the militia was an important social institution in

A posture class at Rollins college in the early 1900s.

Early days at Rollins College. Above, Clara Guild, whose Boston-bred family was among Winter Park's earliest settlers. Her sister, Alice E., was the first woman to graduate from Rollins College. Right, the entire student body and most of the faculty of Rollins College poses for this 1901 photograph.

Automobile parade entering Fairgrounds in 1914.

"VICTOR HUGO OF THE NORTH"

*L*ike the men in his novels and movie scripts, Rex Beach was first and foremost an adventurer. Beach was born in Michigan in 1877, the son of an unsuccessful farmer who soon packed up his family and moved to Florida as a homesteader. At the age of 14, he was sent to the Rollins College prep department, and later became captain of the college baseball team. As a law student in Illinois, he distinguished himself not as a scholar, but as the winner of two Olympic swimming medals. He gave up his studies — probably without hesitation — to join the gold rush to the Klondike in 1900. Although Beach never made it to the Klondike, he spent many difficult years in Alaska, where he began to write about his experiences.

Beach also spent several years in the oil fields of America's Southwest, and some time in Central America, and it is in these places that he found the heroes and settings for his novels. Beach wrote 33 novels, several of which became popular movies, and was the first author to put a movie-rights clause in a book contract. The book — and later the movie — The Spoilers *earned him his first fortune.*

Late in life, Beach returned to Florida and settled in Sebring, where he made yet another fortune in flower and vegetable growing and cattle ranching. At the age of 72, suffering greatly from an incurable cancer, Beach took his own life. He was buried on the campus of Rollins College, where he had made significant contributions. Wrote a dear friend after his death, "[Beach] displayed in his strong character and modest manner the virtues of a great American . . . . He was the most amazing man I ever knew."

rural nineteenth century Florida. The Orlando Guards were organized by Captain Thomas J. Shine and were prominent in virtually all festive occasions.

In 1885, Shine, C.W. Arnold, and L.O. Garrett built the three-story brick armory near the Orange County courthouse. The Armory became a central part of the city. The first floor was leased by the city for a public market where produce, meat, and fish were sold. The second floor was used for professional offices. The third floor was used for the Orlando Guard's drills and exercises, but also served as an auditorium for club meetings, various entertainments, and the annual charity ball.

Renamed the Shine Guards after the premature death of the captain, the unit engaged in drill competitions around the state and helped to preserve the peace when local officials needed assistance.

The unit's finest moment came in February 1898 when the U.S. Battleship *Maine* was blown up in Havana harbor. The Shine Guard lined up at the armory one hundred strong and volunteered to go to Cuba. The exuberant patriots were called up and sent to Tampa. From there, however, they were reassigned to Huntsville, Alabama, where they sat out the war while Theodore Roosevelt and his Rough Riders made history in Cuba. When the Florida National Guard was established in 1900, the Shine Guard became Company C of the Second Florida Regiment. Under command of William Beardall, they were part of the famous Dixie Division in World War I.

Like the guard units, cornet bands were popular in all the parades and during festive occasions. Both Apopka and Orlando had cornet bands in the 1880s. Although members probably joined the bands more for the social intercourse and the chance to wear colorful uniforms than because of their playing skill, the Orlando band's performances on the veranda of Thomas Shine's Magnolia House were very popular.

Social clubs were also gaining in popularity. Orlando's venerable Rosalind Club got its start in 1894, when a group of women gave a ball "in appreciation of the many social courtesies" extended them by the Lucerne Club, a male social organization of the day. The club was organized that year with Mrs. Leslie Pell-Clarke as president and met at the armory for several years, before erecting its own building in 1901 at Orange and Wall. Patterned after the Jefferson Davis mansion at Biloxi, Mississippi, the new Rosalind Club became the center of social life for the next fifteen years. In 1916, the women moved to a new clubhouse on Lake Eola, and in 1919, West Street was renamed in the club's honor.

Central Floridians had long enjoyed such rural sports as hunting and fishing, but the English colony is generally credited with introducing modern sports to the area. H.B. Church founded the Conway Yacht Club, which held annual regattas to the delight of the entire community. Leslie Pell-Clarke introduced golf on a nine-hole course along the marshy shores of Lake Eola, and local residents watched with bemused curiosity as he chased a small white ball in and out of the water. Soon, many of them also were chasing golf balls, and improved courses were added. The British also brought tennis to Orlando, although it was gaining popularity across the country at about the same time. By the turn of the century, many of the fashionable homes were considered complete only when their grounds included a tennis court.

The three-story Armory became the social center of Orlando after the building's construction in 1885.

Entertainment for all. Far left, the original Whist Club of Orlando (whist was a popular parlor game). Left, the Dairy-maid's drill in 1896. Below, the Orlando Guards prepare for a parade.

Good times. Above, these Orlando women are posing in the attire they chose for a "tacky party." Right, a maypole dance at the Rosalind Club in 1910.

The Orlando High School football team, 1909-1910.

Tennis attire was very formal at the turn of the century. Dressed for the match were George R. Newell and his family. Newell was a major promoter of the Winter Park Railroad, and served as the company's attorney.

The famed Orlando Polo Club resulted from English intitiative. J.S. Swindler introduced the idea almost as soon as he arrived in 1886, and games were being played by 1888. When the Orlando club was organized in 1890, it attracted 100 members. Games were played on a small field near Conway (on the site of today's Dover Shores Shopping Center) until team member Isaac Hopper donated his racetrack on the East Winter Park Road. The racetrack was converted to a full-sized polo field.

The team became a local institution, and most of the town gathered for the games. Played on tough little Florida cow ponies whose size was limited to 14.5 hands, on a field 900 by 450 feet, the fast-moving game was a perfect spectator sport. The team played opponents from throughout central Florida and even as far away as North Carolina and South Carolina. On weekends when polo matches were scheduled, even the large San Juan Hotel boasted a full house.

Leslie Pell-Clarke built the first bicycle path in Orlando around Lake Eola, but the English were not solely responsible for the bicycle craze. Bicycling was a national activity and practically every community in America was caught up in it. Paths were laid out, in and between most central Florida communities. At one time a cyclist could leave Zellwood and travel through Apopka to Orlando on a hard-surfaced bicycle path. One observer declared it the "in" thing to ride a bicycle-built-for-two — over a path which Pell-Clarke had laid out — to the polo matches.

Bowlers at Van Brunt's Bowling Alley at the corner of Pine and Court streets, about 1910. August Wright and Beth Branham are preparing for their turns.

IF THEY COULD SEE US NOW

More than a half century before anyone would associate the name Disney with the city of Orlando, citrus industries were being intermingled with tourism and entertainment. Sometimes when one failed, it was superseded by the other. John B. Steinmetz, Clay Springs' most celebrated citizen, came from Pennsylvania to enter the citrus business. He set out a grove, built a packing house, and prepared for success. Instead, he encountered the freezes of 1894-95. Undaunted, Steinmetz converted his packing house into a skating rink, built a bath house, a toboggan slide into the springs, picnic facilities, and a dance pavilion. By the turn of the century, Clay Springs was an important destination for local as well as national visitors.

George Russell at Lake Ivanhoe followed a similar path. The first grower to use slatted sheds to protect his pineapples from the sun and cold, Russell enjoyed

The Orlando Polo Club engaged in a spirited contest in 1909.

67

Rest and recreation. Near right, young Orlando socialites enjoyed an outing to Clay Springs in 1898. Center, Carrie and Roy Hinson and Mabel Millard (McCulloch) at an 1899 picnic. Far right, a camping trip to Lake Butler included judges T. Picton Warlow and John M. Cheney. The black man is "Uncle Tom" Williams. Below, the Orlando Bicycle Club of 1892.

All owners of automobiles in Orlando were asked to assemble at Lake Lucerne for this picture around 1909, to demonstrate that Orlando was a progressive city. There were nine in all.

THE AUTOMOBILE CITY

*E*ver alert to promote their city, boosters began calling Orlando the "Automobile City" about 1915. To emphasize the new appellation, The Orlando Sentinel *published a special automobile edition that year. The advertisements in the edition reveal an amazing variety of manufacturers, most of which have long ceased to exist:*

W. Delaney Way sold Jeffery cars.
I.W. Phillips and Sons offered Dodges at $850.
The San Juan Garage advertised Studebakers from $885 to $1,050.
The Cook Company sold Buicks at costs ranging between $950 and $1,350.

Other automobile agencies and their products included:

Gordon and Schnarr — King cars.
Palms Automobile Company — Reos.
J.B. Magruder Jr. — Oaklands.
J.P. Holbrook — Hupmobiles.
F.G. Rush — Fords.

The Sentinel's special edition was particularly noteworthy because it demonstrated the changes that had taken place in only six years. In 1909, all city automobile owners were asked to assemble at Lake Lucerne to have their pictures taken with their cars, to prove that Orlando was a growing city. Total number of automobiles in the photograph: nine.

Dr. Joseph Rush, driving the first Ford in Orlando, about 1900.

success with his pinery until Cuban growers undersold him in the early 1900s. In 1910, he built a pavilion and dock with dressing rooms, a dance hall, and a picnic are with refreshment booths. Known as Russell's Point, and later as Joyland, it was a favorite spot for many years.

When Dr. R.L. Harris and a few neighbors purchased automobiles, they were regarded as curiosities rather than means of transportation. People lined up to pay ter cents for a ride down Orange Avenue, but the future wa fast approaching. In 1902, Orlando set a speed limit of five miles per hour and required "suitable gongs or alarms" on all cars. By 1905, John Cook, an enterprising wagon repairman, opened an automobile-repair shop an secured the agency for Cadillacs and Buicks. The 1910 fair not only featured the first air flight in Florida, but included a line of automobiles in the elaborate opening-day parade. The first brick road connected Orlando and Winter Park in 1896. The following year Orlando hosted the first International Good Roads Congress, which advocated the road system upon which automobiles would eventually transform central Florida. Orlando was soon to become the hub of the wheel.

CHAPTER SIX

A SMALL FARMING
AND CITRUS COMMUNITY

*A typical dwelling near Orlando at
the turn of the century.*

A wood turpentine still, located on the Orlando Water and Light Company property at Highland in 1909. Don Cheney is leaning against the post. Mr. Conway, in the white shirt, was the manager of the still.

A NEW CONFIDENCE

After the freezes of 1894-95, some growers turned to the forests to tide them over. Others went into lumber and naval stores permanently. These industries had been moving south from the Carolinas and were reaching central Florida in the 1890s. M.O. Overstreet and others acquired acreage in the Orlando area and built turpentine stills and sawmills, and numerous small operators supplied them with gum and lumber from the forests. Some of them moved on after awhile, but Orlando remained the center of an extensive forest-products industry for many years. In 1906, Overstreet purchased the Warnell crate mill at Lockhart and, with the Starbird mill at Apopka, merged the timber and citrus businesses by supplying growers with crates for shipping their fruit.

By the early 1900s, a new confidence in growing citrus was emerging. A 1910 visitor described Orlando as "a small farming and citrus community," but the town and its neighbors were on the brink of a dynamic period which would transform Orlando into the major inland city of the state. Between 1910 and 1917, the amount of central Florida citrus acreage would double.

The renewal of citrus culture brought with it improved methods of gathering and shipping the crops. Several new packing houses opened. One grower, Dr. P. Phillips, built an innovative processing plant and developed a successful method of canning single-strength juice. In 1913, newcomer Nick Belitz started one of the first fruit gift-packaging businesses. His successes with citrus growing in Orange and Lake counties eventually allowed him to build Belitz Plaza at Maitland. The Chase family of Sanford established large groves in the Windermere area and elsewhere, as well as winter-vegetable acreages. The Chases founded a business which now manufactures and distributes a wide range of agricultural products.

The increased production soon led to some problems with marketing. In the old days, growers had sometimes gathered and shipped their crops and sometimes sold them on the trees. Buyers would crowd the lobby of the San Juan Hotel each winter to bid on the crops. It was a risky way of disposing of such a time-consuming and expensive product. In 1903, the Florida Citrus Exchange was formed with W.C. Temple as its first manager. The exchange prompted growers' cooperatives in several communities. Gradually these associations developed marketing arrangements which made Florida citrus a more dependable and profitable enterprise.

Orange picking at the Minnehaha grove in Maitland in the early 1900s.

NO. 34 GATHERING AND PACKING ORANGES. MINNEHAHA GROVE, FLA.

The well-protected parent tree of the famous Temple orange.

Frank Johnson and Nero Pete were bellboys at the Empire Hotel in 1920.

Growers also began looking at ways to protect their crops. In 1905, the white fly became a serious problem. James B. Magruder, one of Orlando's most energetic businessmen and a large scale grower, offered the department of agriculture a place to conduct pesticide research. This brought Dr. W.W. Yothers to Orlando in 1906 to begin his long career in battling citrus diseases and pests such as the Mediterranean fruit fly, which threatened the state in the late 1920s.

About 1915, L.A. Hakes noticed some unusual fruit on one of the trees along his Winter Park driveway. He called it to the attention of W.C. Temple, who in turn showed it to a commercial nursery. The firm purchased the tree, built a padlocked fence around it, and budded thousands of new trees from it. The famous Temple Orange is now believed to have more than seven million descendants.

Another important contribution to citrus culture came in 1918 when Hoyle Pounds of Winter Garden developed a rubber-tired tractor which could work in sandy groves and travel the roads without damaging them.

Despite a severe freeze in 1917, citrus had become a permanent part of the central Florida economy by World War I.

THE CITY BEAUTIFUL

In 1908 city boosters held a contest for a new slogan to better describe Orlando's latest blossoming. When the judges announced the winning entry as "the City Beautiful," the slogan was adopted. It was a happy selection, for it reflected the city's appearance and stimulated residents further to beautify their streets. Azaleas and other shrubs were distributed by a committee headed by H.H. Dickson, with results similar to the tree plantings following A.G. Branham's activities in the 1880s. With its many lakes, tree-lined streets, "Honeymoon Row" — a line of fine homes on the shore of Lake Cherokee — and other beautiful houses surrounding Lake Lucerne, the city seemed to justify its new slogan.

About that time, Charles Lord, one of the English settlers, brought in two pairs of swans — one black and one white — and set them loose on Lake Lucerne. The original pairs reproduced, and swans were soon swimming on many of the city's lakes. Best remembered of all of them was Billy, often called the "Tyrant of Lake

WHICH WAY DID THEY GO?

The local fire departments developed their own forms of entertainment, but not always to the benefit of their communities. Fire companies from various towns would gather for tournaments. The company that could make the fastest run would win a silver cup, then all would settle in for an evening of merrymaking. The Orlando firemen were in Tampa for just such an event one day in 1906 when David Lockhart's huge lumber mill caught fire. When volunteers rushed to help, they found that the fire engine had also gone to Tampa. They helplessly watched $50,000 worth of lumber and milling equipment go up in flames, along with several freight cars.

The firemen had other difficulties. By 1907, the cowmen on Orlando's streets had ceased to be a problem, only to be replaced by workers from the turpentine stills. The rowdiness and disorder led to another wet-dry election in which the latter won by a scant two votes. Minutes after the results were announced, two Church Street saloons — which had especially raised the wrath of townsmen — were ablaze. The fire engine was present on that occasion, but upon reaching Orange Avenue where it was to turn left, the team went to the right. The driver refused to accept responsibility for his engine's late arrival, swearing someone had purposely crossed the reins.

A small boy feeding Billy the Swan, the tyrant of Lake Lucerne.

Lucerne," who became notorious for chasing Delaney school children, attacking passing automobiles, and especially for drowning his mate one spring when her eggs failed to hatch. Billy ultimately attained a sort of immortality when he was placed in stuffed splendor at the entrance of the Orange County Historical Museum. Although alligators, turtles, and dogs took a heavy toll on the swans, they continued to grace city lakes until the mid-fifties, ultimately succumbing to heavy automobile traffic.

A parade for any occasion. Above, a parade of flower and flag-bedecked automobiles, about 1909. The photo was taken from the courthouse, looking toward Lake Eola. Left, a parade float being prepared by the Routh and Caldwell Sheet Metal Company on Church Street.

Curry and Smith Cigar Company moved to its new building in 1914. The firm manufactured cigars in Orlando for more than 30 years, sometimes employing as many as 70 people. The first labor strike in Orlando occurred against Curry and Smith.

A fire in 1911 threatened most of Orlando and spurred city leaders to complete the transition which had followed the 1884 fire. The 1911 fire destroyed the Atlantic Coast Line Depot and the Walker Brothers and Citrus Exchange packing houses. The depot was rebuilt in brick and the packing houses were replaced with steel structures. All wooden buildings in a rectangle bordered by Orange, Central, Pine, and Court were ordered removed by 1913. A flurry of building followed.

The Dickson and Ives store underwent major alterations and a brick front was added; Joseph F. Ange built a new three-story brick building for the Yowell-Duckworth Company. Both were completed in 1914. The Baptists and Presbyterians built new churches downtown in 1913 and 1914. A new post office was dedicated in 1917.

By 1911, the Pastime Theatre was showing motion pictures. That same year James B. Magruder, already proprietor of the Magruder Arcade in the business district, completed a large opera house which shortly became the Lucerne Theatre. The Grand Theatre was opened in Winter Park in 1913, and in 1915 Mac Tillman became manager of both theatres and admitted blacks and whites to separate seating areas. The large, commodious Phillips Theatre was opened in 1916, becoming a longtime downtown landmark. The famous Beacham Theatre was not opened until 1920.

The city took full advantage of its new skyline for both advertising and entertainment. In late 1914, a roof garden was opened atop the Yowell-Duckworth Building for movies, dancing, and dinner. The gala opening celebration featured *The Queen's Jewels* as the first film. That same year the People's National Bank displayed a huge flag on top of its building. Hundreds of lights around the flag created a waving motion, beckoning viewers from miles around.

In 1915 W.J. Hamrick started the first city bus line. Soon, buses were running from Orlando to Ocoee, Winter Garden, and Oakland, as well as direct to Winter Park and Maitland. By 1917, traffic on Orlando's

THE GILES-DUCKWORTH FEUD

James L. Giles and Eugene G. Duckworth, like many prominent Orlando businessmen, believed that a close alignment between business and government would benefit the community's economic growth. Each, however, felt he was the one to lead the city. Giles, the incumbent in 1919, was backed by John Cheney and his Republican colleagues, while Duckworth was supported by Samuel Y. Way and the local Democrats. Way persuaded Duckworth to run even though he had to sell his interests in the Yowell-Duckworth department store to do so. The campaign was both grandiose and bitter. The candidates attacked each other fiercely, to the delight of the competing newpapers, but the debates split the town. A 100-car motorcade through Orlando on Duckworth's behalf climaxed the campaign and clinched Duckworth's election.

The hatchet was not buried, however. The two men assaulted each other on the Sentinel's front page for weeks afterward and in the council chamber for years. The verbal war accelerated to a more destructive level in early 1923 when G.H. Sutherland and J.G. Manuel, allies of Giles, won seats on the city commission. Constituting a two-thirds majority of the three-member commission, they set out to take control. Over Duckworth's opposition, they removed the police chief and replaced him with their appointee. They then ousted the city judge, city engineer, head of the parks, city physician (Hal Beardall), and the sanitary inspector. The impasse lasted more than a year, until Governor Cary A. Hardee ordered a recall election for commissioners Manuel and Sutherland. When both were reelected, Duckworth resigned. Giles was elected to succeed him.

Despite the vexations of his last year in office, Duckworth's administration was productive. With the city growing in all directions, he obtained a bond issue to buy and rebuild the water and light plant which the Cheney family had operated for a quarter of a century, and purchased a site for the new plant. More than 30 miles of sewers were laid, the Albertson Public Library was built, and more than 100 streets were paved. The city also acquired land for parks on lakes Cherokee, Lorna Doone, and Park. The fairgrounds was purchased, a municipal judgeship was created, and a city forestry department was established. The fire department became fully paid and the police went on a 24-hour schedule. Duckworth also had been instrumental in securing legislation creating the utilities commission. The city limits were expanded to Par Avenue on the north, Texas Avenue on the west, Grant Street on the south, and Bumby Avenue on the east.

Personal enmity did not deter Giles from continuing Duckworth's programs of civic improvement and development, and when the city experienced financial difficulty because of the recent public improvements, Giles' budgetary actions left all the programs intact. He employed Harland Bartholomew in 1925 as the first city planner in central Florida, and also approved the completion of the Winter Park highway in 1925 and the lighting of a white way along it. His administration negotiated the annexation of the old town of Formosa and 340 acres — including 80 acres relinquished by Winter Park — for additions to College Park and Walter Rose's Orwin Manor. He initiated the idea of a municipal auditorium and gained voter approval for its construction at the fairgrounds. It opened in early 1927 with the Grand Opera Company of Philadelphia performing Aida. Recently refurbished and opened as the Bob Carr Auditorium, it still offers entertainment for central Floridians.

This band played at a promotional program, featuring the sale of the first lots in the E. Frank Sperry subdivision, a large tract east of Lake Eola, in 1911.

owntown streets had increased so much that the onfederate monument — placed in the intersection of entral and Main — had to be moved to Eola Park. Orlando was growing out as well as up. New white migrants to Orlando found plenty of new housing dditions, with names like Highland Park, Rosearden, and olonial Park. In 1915, T.A. Yancey and J.F. Schumann pened Western Terrace, a 42-acre subdivision for blacks.

IE SUPER GARDEN SPOT OF THE UNIVERSE

'The man who started life as an infant and was born without a dollar in his pocket," H. Carl Dann was Orlando's preeminent builder — and romoter. A native Orlandoan, Dann developed 61 arcels of land from 1910 until the late 1920s, including oncord Park, Colonial Hills, Highland Grove, the ubsdread Country Club, and the Mt. Plymouth Club d Tourist Hotel in Lake County.

Dann's activities profited Orlando even when they most left him without a dollar in his pocket. In 1915, e became interested in the saw-grass land between ellwood and Lake Apopka. Several feet deep in rich uck, the land was most attractive to vegetable farmers. uring the previous three decades, several attempts to rain the land and make it arable had failed. Then, harles H. Jones of Zellwood, and other investors, rmed the Zellwood Produce Company and began edging again.

Things began to happen after Dann became interested. hen he determined to sell the "super garden spot of e Universe," people noticed. He organized a company ith branches in several northern cities, contracted with e Deluxe Bus Lines to provide service between rlando and Zellwood, and argued that "when the otatoes begin to grow" the farms would become a great

tourist attraction. He promoted potatoes because, by that time, World War I had started, and potatoes were scarce and high-priced. By early 1918, *The Orlando Sentinel* was proclaiming a "giant crop of spuds," and several Orlandoans had invested heavily in the crop.

Unfortunately, more than adept advertising was needed to tame the muck. The potatoes grew profusely, but were so saturated with water that as soon as they were taken from the ground, they rotted. (It was not until the 1940s, after much more was learned about muck farming in the Everglades, that the Zellwood lands began to produce their famous bonanza crops.) Dann's advertising, however, brought many visitors who found that citrus lands and winter residences in Florida could be highly desirable.

Dann wasn't the only developer whose promotional efforts were washed away by Florida's flat terrain. About 1903, Braxtom Beacham of Orlando and W.L. Van Duzor of Kissimmee had purchased 6,000 acres on which they planned to launch Prosper Colony. A misnomer if ever there was one, Prosper Colony lay about eight miles south of Orlando on the Kissimmee highway, on what was originally the site of a turpentine still. The purchasers laid out their Prosper Colony in lots suitable for small farms. Each parcel also included a building lot in the proposed town of Taft. More than 1,000 lots were sold, and several settlers built homes and began farming. Before the planned drainage could be completed, however, a storm in late 1910 flooded the area, forcing the discouraged settlers to abandon their investments. Beacham repurchased the land at a sheriff's sale and continued to promote it — but with little success. The few settlers who stayed incorporated the town of Taft in 1912. To reclaim their investments, the settlers formed the Taft Drainage District in 1913. A network of 67 miles of canals was completed, successfully draining 54,000 acres and finally making them suitable for farming.

E. Frank Sperry was one of Orlando's mayors during the progressive era just before World War I.

The town of Taft grew out of the unsuccessful Prosper Colony project. Above left, the Hotel Taft in 1919, after Prosper Colony had failed, but long before Orlando's growth over-ran the community. Above right, Duncan Pell (left) and Braxton Beacham in their San Juan Hotel office in 1908, just before launching the Prosper Colony venture.

MORE GROWTH IN THE COUNTRY

Several miles southwest of Orlando, near the Butler chain of lakes, is Windermere, ostensibly named by John H. Dawe, who lived there while building the Florida Midland Railroad from Longwood to Kissimmee. After the road failed, Dawe returned to New York, but the land was purchased by L.J. Griffin, a lumberman who had first moved to Conway from Gadsden County. Griffin operated sawmills at both places. His son, S.S. Griffin, a future state legislator, acquired the property about 1908 and built several houses, before selling out to J.C. Palmer and J.H. Johnson of Wauseon, Ohio. They organized the Windermere Improvement Company and began promoting the area. It remained mostly rural, however. Now one of the last comparatively undeveloped places in the Orlando metropolitan area, it is being subjected to intense pressure for development.

The distinguishing features of Windermere, until recently, have been its extensive groves. Both Dr. Phillips and the Chase Company of Sanford had hundreds of acres in oranges and grapefruit there.

Originally called Fish because of the plentiful supply of that species being taken from the Little Econlockahatchee River, Union Park came into existence as a post office in 1918. It remained a small community in the middle of an open-range cattle industry until recent years, when Orlando's growth toward the east and the opening of the University of Central Florida caused Union Park to expand into a substantial suburban area.

Founded primarily as a residential community for well-to-do winter residents, Winter Park experienced new growth in the early 1900s. In 1910, the town had 132 dwellings for whites, 76 of which were owned by permanent residents. A new Atlantic Coastline Railroad depot was opened in 1913, under the auspices of the board of trade, which billed its ground-breaking as "Town Improvement Day." C.H. Galloway installed his first telephone exchange at Maitland with ten lines. He ran a sideline grocery-delivery service, taking orders by telephone and having them delivered by his son on a bicycle. In 1912, he and B.A. Galloway obtained a franchise for the Winter Park Telephone Exchange, and the first instrument in town was installed in Dr. J.A. Trovillion's home. The following year, Galloway combined

THE WEEKS THAT WAS

Mr. Fred S. Weeks' (1839-1918) epitaph at Greenwood Cemetery is a classic example of a putdown, not only because of the furor it caused but because Weeks was around to see it achieve its end — sweet revenge.

Weeks' final resting place is within a large granite mausoleum, built by him around 1910, prior to his death. On the massive door is an epitaph from the Good Samaritan story (Luke 10:29): "A certain man went down from Jerusalem to Jericho and fell among thieves." Beneath it were the names of the three "thieves" whom he fancied had done him wrong. Today, only a black space is under the scripture where the names were originally.

As the story goes, Weeks claimed to have been swindled in a real estate deal by some of the leading lights of the community, pillars of the church. Weeks chose this way to get even. Although threatened law suits persuaded him to have the names chiseled from the door, he had already made his point.

Today, the curious come to see the epitaph and to scrutinize it from all angles in hopes of seeing a trace of the chiselers' names — long since chiseled off.

Weeks got his revenge and probably died laughing, proving once again, you can't take a man for granite.

Frederick A. Lewter was one of many developers who sold real estate in the areas surrounding Orlando.

Celery farming near Sanford in the 1930s. Celery became an important crop after the freezes of 1894-1895.

Lena Galloway at an early switchboard of the Winter Park Telephone Company.

the two exchanges to form the Winter Park Telephone Company, which operated as an independent firm until about 1980, when it was merged with the United Telephone Company. The Galloways were not the first to run telephone lines in Winter Park, however. J.B. Steinmetz had already done that about 1901, when he connected his Clay Springs home with Rollins College to keep in touch with his daughter, who was a student there.

OF FLYCATCHERS, PINE STRAW, AND PROGRESSIVISM

The city of Orlando adopted the commission form of government in 1914, in keeping with a national trend. Other central Florida communities followed suit within a few years. But progressivism also renewed civic pride and desires for even greater achievements. In 1918, the Winter Park City Council and the city's Board of Trade resolved to eliminate the flies from their community. A bounty of ten cents for every 100 flies was offered to anyone who brought his catch to the board of trade on Tuesday and Friday afternoons. The bounty only applied to victims of swatters or "comparable" weapons. Whether the efforts were successful has not been recorded, but the council certainly was determined. The battle was still being waged in 1921 when Moses Overstreet won second place in the fly campaign by turning in 150 carcasses.

Far more successful during those years were the effort to improve central Florida's roads. For years the town and county had used pine straw for road surfacing, but it did not last long enough to be worthwhile. They next turned to clay, but it was scarce. By about 1910, H.H. Dickson, an early leader in the good roads movement, advocated using bricks on the major roads. By 1914, Orlando had bricked North Orange Avenue and Lake Ivanhoe Boulevard, completing the first mile of a planned ten-mile project. In 1916, the communities along the north-south axis of present-day metropolitan

Convicts at work on a nine-foot brick road in 1916. Having tried to cover their roads with pine straw and then clay, central Floridians finally chose bricks as the best surface for automobile travel.

A 'gator hunt on the upper St. Johns, by J.P. Steinmetz and friends.

Gator Shooting on the Upper St. Johns, Florida.

Physicians and nurses of the Church and Home Hospital. The doctors are (left to right): W.C. Person, George Porter, J.S. McEwan, C.D. Christ, and S. McElroy. Nurses are: Mrs. Maude Cooper, Miss Meyers, Mabel Lewis, Miss Sallie Taylor, Mrs. Roy Daniels, Miss Napier, and Dorothy Best.

Boaters on Lake Estelle near the Florida Sanitarium, when hospital care was more leisurely than today.

rlando celebrated completion of 50 miles of brick road
etween Kissimmee and Sanford. That same year the
rlando and Indian River road was dedicated at a
eremony conducted by Senator Moses Overstreet.
Another Orange County brick-paving project was a
ad from Orlando to Lake County near Mount Dora.
hile it was still under construction, developer Carl
sher began promoting the Dixie Highway Association
attract attention to his Miami Beach project. Orlando
d other communities lobbied vigorously to have the
ad to Lake County designated as part of the Dixie
ighway. The association instead selected a winding
ute from Chattanooga through Tallahassee to
cksonville and down the east coast. But Dickson and
her Orlandoans continued their efforts. Finally, the
ixie Highway Association decided to have two routes
- the original one down the coast and a western route
hich included Apopka, Orlando, and Kissimmee. The
ixie Highway became a major thoroughfare along
hich motorists came to Orlando in their flivvers
the 1920s.
The progressive movement also led to demands for
etter health care. Orlando's first physicians treated their
atients in clinics in their homes or at the patients'
omes. In 1892, the Cottage Hospital Association was
stablished to care for dependent women. Acquired by
e Episcopal Church in 1895, the new Church and
ome Hospital was Orlando's only hospital until it ran
ut of money in 1916. When the hospital announced its
osing, local physicians John S. McEwan and C.D. Christ
d a subscription drive for funds to build Orlando
eneral Hospital. Opened in 1918, the hospital has
rved the central Florida area ever since.
In 1908, the Seventh-day Adventists, who had been in
entral Florida since the 1880s, took over a defunct
bercular sanitarium at Formosa and established the
lorida Sanitarium and Hospital. The sanitarium's two
hysicians began treating their four initial patients
ccording to the "Battle Creek" plan. The Adventist
ospital at Battle Creek, Michigan, had been successfully
eating patients with combinations of medicine and
rgery — and plenty of fresh air, sunshine, moderate
xercise, good food, and relaxation. This approach was
eally suited to Florida, which had long been acclaimed
a place where invalids could go to be cured of
eir maladies.
The Florida Sanitarium — the San — was an immediate
ccess and built a larger, modern building in 1912. After
addition in 1918, the hospital had 40 beds. That
ructure served for half a century, becoming the nucleus
f a fine system of hospitals which now provide care for
large area of central Florida.

NY WHICH WAY YOU CAN

n 1913, Sanford finally got its county seat. After the
Orange County seat was moved from Sanford (then
called Mellonville) in the 1850s, Sanford boosters
ad tried several schemes to get it back. Never
ccessful, they responded favorably when promoter
rrest Lake advocated the creation of a new county in
e territory near Lake Monroe. After a vigorous
xchange between those for and against the new county,
e 1913 legislature carved Seminole County from
range and designated Sanford the county seat.

Bert and Sophronia
Brooks of Jonestown,
with son Osborn.
Brooks, a longtime
employee of the South
Florida Foundry, did
the steel work for most
of the awnings on
downtown Orlando
businesses.

A BENIGN VOTING FRAUD

What must have been one of the least offensive
voting frauds in Florida history occurred in
Orlando in the early years of the twentieth
century. Hiram E. Calder had been a registered
voter who had repeatedly exercised that franchise
before his demise in 1914. When he died at the
county home in July of that year and it was
discovered that the body was that of a woman,
Orlando was duly surprised as a bizarre story
unfolded.

Early in life, "Hiram" had committed what was
delicately referred to as "an unfortunate misstep"
and had become an unwed mother at a time
when that was not condoned. To avoid
embarrassment, she had assumed the identity of a
man and passed the daughter off as "his" wife.

When the daughter died, "Hiram" provided a
distinctive monument at the local cemetery and
reserved a place beside her for himself. When all
this became known, a benevolent community
raised the necessary funds to have Hiram's body
removed from its pauper's grave and interred in
the proper place.

Getting there. Top, a wreck on the
Atlantic Coast Line Railroad near
Kissimmee in 1911. Above left, Carl
Kuhl, an Orlando native and Florida's
first licensed pilot, shown here in a
plane which he built about 1918. Right,
Judge Donald Cheney was driving his
Ford Runabout, "Hummingbird," when
he encountered a "pothole." The car
came to a stop in this position against a
convenient pine tree.

Inside view of the State Bank of Orlando, 1911.

The shelves were kept well stocked inside Mann's Grocery on East Pine Street in 1913.

Several Orlando and Orange County residents attended a rally in honor of Governor Napoleon Bonaparte Broward in front of the new school building in 1906.

Forrest Lake was a colorful mayor of Sanford, state legislator, and controversial banker who led the fight to carve Seminole County from Orange in 1913. After his bank closed in 1927, he was convicted of embezzlement.

William R. O'Neal was a prominent Orlando businessman in the early twentieth century, and one-time gubernatorial candidate for the minority Republican Party.

The Republican party had been on the decline in Florida since Reconstruction, and by the 1920s Florida was essentially a one-party state. That was not the case, however, in the Orlando-Winter Park area. Although Democrats won most of the elections, in Winter Park registered Republicans outnumbered Democrats until after World War I. Republican nominees for state offices were often chosen from the area. Edward R. Gunby, an Orlando attorney, ran for governor in 1896. In 1908, John M. Cheney was the Republican gubernatorial candidate, and in 1912 and 1924, W.R. O'Neal was the party standard bearer. Cheney also made a strong showing in 1920 against Duncan Fletcher, a popular incumbent United States senator.

In addition to the satisfaction of upholding their party principles, there were other compensations for carrying the banner of the minority party. When Republican presidents were in office — which was most of the time between 1897 and 1932 — there were important offices to be filled. John Cheney served as United States attorney for several years and established an excellent record defending the civil rights of workers at Gabriella and other turpentine camps. Alexander Akerman, Cheney's law partner, succeeded him and served during the 1920s.

Central Florida also differed from the majority of the state on women's suffrage. The Florida Equal Suffrage Association was founded in late 1913 by Dr. Mary A. Safford, a much-traveled Unitarian minister who settled in Orlando in 1911. Dr. Safford formed a fledgling Unitarian church in Magruder's hall, then launched her equal-suffrage campaign. In March 1914 a Men's Equal Suffrage Association was organized to help the women. E. Frank Sperry, Orlando's incumbent mayor, served as president. Perhaps because of these organizations, both Winter Park and Orlando permitted women to vote in municipal elections in 1919, shortly before the Nineteenth Amendment was ratified in time for the 1920 presidential election.

Mrs. A.B. Whitman, one of Dr. Safford's strongest supporters, was subsequently named to the influential Parks Board. The League of Women Voters succeeded the suffrage association in 1921, and was headed by Edna Giles Fuller. In 1928, Fuller became the first woman to be elected from Orlando to the state legislature, in a campaign which also sent Ruth Bryan Owen (daughter of William Jennings Bryan) to Washington as Florida's first female representative.

When Congress declared war on Germany in April 1917, Dr. Mary Safford addressed a huge crowd at the Lucerne Theatre about the ways Orlando could help wage the war. Orlandoans responded enthusiastically. Commanded by William Beardall, Company C began drilling in preparation for being called, a parade was held, and Liberty Bonds were being sold by May 5. On May 19, the blacks of both Orlando and Winter Park demonstrated their patriotism with their own parade.

Company C was soon ordered to northern Alabama, and a number of central Floridians eventually served in France. The Red Cross was organized, citizens observed meatless Tuesdays and made other efforts to conserve food for the armed forces. Each Liberty Loan drive was opened with an elaborate parade and the local newspapers kept tabulations of the contributions. Neighboring towns competed to see which would "go over the top" to fulfill the quota first. Every community exceeded its quotas, except for one drive which occurred after Armistice Day.

Floridians were patriotic, but they were also prospering — especially the farmers. Prices for syrup, sweet potatoes, and other crops grown in central Florida had skyrocketed. Costs of machinery and material goods had also gone up, but most Floridians, except those on fixed incomes, for once had money to spare.

Armistice Day brought an enormous celebration with huge crowd from all over the surrounding area. The soldiers returned slowly during the next few months, and Orlando was soon back to normal. From April 1917 to the end of 1918, the war was the dominant topic in town, but it did not slow the growth which had begun a decade earlier. Real-estate sales and construction continued at a brisk pace, and Orlando approached the 1920s with 10,282 citizens living within its boundaries.

Tom Shepherd, a former slave, was one of the first blacks to settle in central Florida.

View of Orange Avenue north from Church Street, circa 1920. Orlando once had its own White House, which was subsequently replaced by the First National Bank Building. The area is now the site of Valencia College's downtown campus.

A revenue agent destroys an illegal whiskey still.

Mayor Eugene G. Duckworth, whose political feud with Mayor James L. Giles did not deter the progress of Orlando in the early 1920s.

CONTRADICTIONS, CORRUPTION, AND CRIME

When William Jennings Bryan addressed an Orlando audience in April 1920, his topic, "Brother or Brute," filled the Delaney School auditorium to overflowing. It was little wonder. Postwar Florida, like the rest of the nation, was beset by contradictions. The great moral crusade against John Barleycorn had begun in 1919, but bathtub gin, speakeasies, and flapper attire flaunted both the law and traditional morality. Business profits soared while farmers struggled with plunging agricultural prices. The United States had emerged from the war as an international leader, but its people withdrew into isolationism and fear.

Bryan's denunciation of Charles Darwin's theories and his assurance that the world dated from 4004 B.C. comforted many confused fundamentalists. But they could not ignore their changing world for long.

Anticipating ratification of the Nineteenth Amendment, Florida Republicans decided to combine a women's voter-registration drive with a full-scale campaign in the 1920 elections. This, of course, included a drive to register blacks, who constituted the bulk of the potential Republican voters. Unfortunately, the nation was in an intolerant mood, having been aroused by the so-called Red Scare, by labor unrest, and by race riots in several northern cities. The American Legion was growing in Orlando and looking for ways to defend Americans against unnamed enemies and half-understood fears, and the Democratic party was anxious to preserve its dominant position as the white man's party in Florida.

Both sides were excited when Mose Norman, a black Ocoee farmer, was denied the right to vote at a local polling place. He registered a complaint and, followed by two white men, went to the home of July Perry, a respected and influential black landowner. An angry dispute grew into an all-day shooting and burning affray. When the smoke cleared the following morning, the entire black section of Ocoee had been leveled. Perry, an unknown number of other blacks, and two white men had died. The American Legion sprang into action, patrolling the streets to keep down further violence. Although no action was ever taken to determine

responsibility for the riot, tensions gradually subsided and things almost returned to normal — but not quite. There was no black section of Ocoee for many years, and citrus growers lamented a severe labor shortage that winter in west Orange County.

A postscript occurred in July 1922, when J.J. Wendler, editor of the Republican Winter Park *Post* was abducted from his home, tarred, feathered and flogged, before being ordered out of town. He complied after spending several weeks recuperating in bed.

Personal violence and crime continued to increase, perhaps as an aftermath of wartime, but certainly foretelling an adverse side of the city's future growth. In January 1919, Margaret Simmons Darling shot and killed her husband in a quarrel on an East Jackson Street sidewalk. Indicted and tried, she was defended by John M. Cheney, who won an acquittal to the applause of 200 female witnesses. In mayor's court in 1921, Leroy Hotaling shot and killed John Brown as Brown was standing in front of Mayor Duckworth for sentencing. Police Chief Ed Vestal and ex-sheriff Frank Gordon were watching. At Hotaling's trial, Cheney won an acquittal. Orlando had been scandalized in August 1920 when W.H. Miltmore, operator of the Arcade Restaurant, was found shot to death in a room at the San Juan Hotel. Two empty money bags from the West Palm Beach post office were found near his body. It turned out that Lena Clarke had stolen $32,000 from the bags and then killed Miltmore. At the trial, she was declared insane and spent most of her life in the asylum and prison. In late 1924, Napoleon P. Broward, nephew of the former governor, was killed in Hal Cady's home, and Mrs. Cady was wounded. Indicted for second-degree murder, Cady was quickly found innocent.

Sometimes the accused reached court in strange ways. J. Hopkins was charged by the Orlando Credit Association with passing worthless checks. An association representative told the judge that an intensive search for Hopkins had failed. And it was not surprising: He was

Mr. and Mrs. Sam Jones, for whom Jonestown was named. Jonestown was the first black housing development.

The booming twenties. Left, chamber of commerce members prepare to board an Orange Belt Auto Lines bus for an excursion. Below, an Orlando promotional vehicle advertised the city's qualities on a Tampa street. The claim of "No Insects" might best be attributed to "sales talk."

oon identified as a member of the jury which was to try ne case!

Prohibition brought on an era of daring bootlegging ith specially equipped cars carrying quantities of illegal ooze and "blind tigers" selling it in almost every ommunity. The sheriff and his deputies engaged in umerous high-speed chases and occasional shootouts ith the rum runners, but never seemed to have much iccess controlling the local outlets. The situation had ot improved much when, in 1929, Chief of Police L.G. ope was indicted for bribery, embezzlement, unlawful ossession of liquor, conspiracy, and other charges — nly to be fully acquitted.

When youngsters began to be more involved in local rimes, many alarmed Orlandoans blamed a new statute nat forbade teachers from punishing their students. The ity established a juvenile court to deal with the minors, nd Donald Cheney was appointed probation officer. Son f the highly respected John M. Cheney, he earned an xcellent reputation for his work with juveniles, and icceeded William Martin as judge for the juvenile court.

HE BOOM YEARS

The Florida land boom was part of a national phenomenon which accelerated the growth Orlando had been experiencing since the early 900s. On the periphery of the boom, Orlando enjoyed a eady growth, which permanently transformed it from ne "small farming and citrus community" it had been to ne largest inland city in the state. The city's population iore than doubled between 1910 and 1920, to over 0,000.

Although the railroads had contributed greatly to Orlando's growth in earlier decades, this time the "boom" was an automobile affair. Completion of the Cheney Highway in late 1924 made Orlando a hub of highway travel. Paved roads led to and from the city in all directions. Orlando and Winter Park had grown together — not without some difficulty — by 1925. This new metropolitan center began spreading tentacles along the highways — north to Maitland and beyond, south

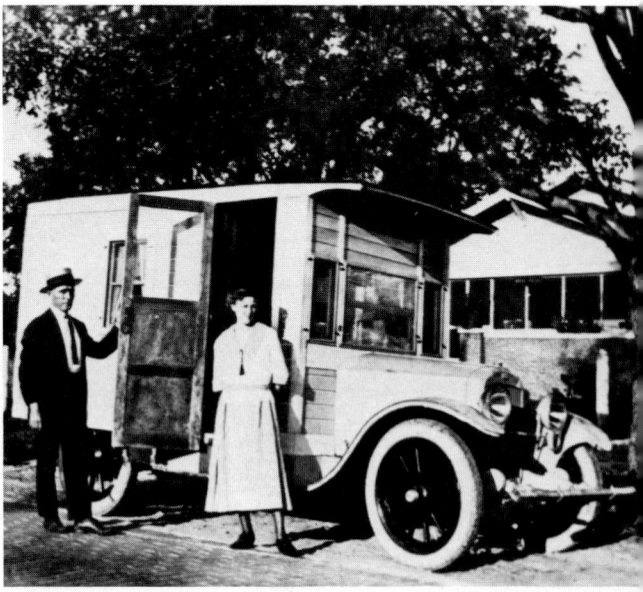

Twenties tourism. Above left, the Dixie Highway as it entered Apopka from the north. Now replaced by U.S. 441, at one time it was a major avenue into the Orlando area. Above right, "tin-can tourists" on Edgewater Drive in 1924.

through Fort Gatlin toward Pinecastle, east toward the coast, west toward Winter Garden, and northwest toward Lockhart and Apopka.

The Dixie Highway was the tourist run. Moms and dads packed up the children and the tents and headed for the Sunshine State. By 1925, Orlando had two tourist courts, offering tent space for the new "tin can tourists." Auto dealerships and service stations sprang up everywhere. In 1928, Harvey Firestone, hailing Orlando as the "most significant inland city in Florida," happily announced the construction of a "master station." The station, at Orange and Concord, has recently been restored.

As the "tin can tourists" rolled in, the real-estate boom was accelerating. The board of trade had reorganized in 1920 and had posted signs along the highways, pointing toward Orlando. Two years later the board changed its name to the Orange County Chamber of Commerce, with William Edwards of Zellwood as president and Karl Lehman as manager. Lehman advertised all of the Orange County communities and attracted favorable attention throughout the country. He also produced a movie about the county, which played to a large crowd at Madison Square Garden in 1924. Carl Dann's "Ask Carl Dann" information bureau was doing a brisk business. The annual construction rate was climbing toward a 1925 highpoint of $8,584,383.

In downtown Orlando, dozens of new businesses opened and skyscrapers stretched upward. The San Juan Hotel added eight stories in 1923, and the Angebilt topped out at eleven stories. When the State Bank of Orlando and Trust Company started its ten-story tower in 1922, the Orlando Bank and Trust followed immediately with one of equal size. Dickson and Ives had built a new four-story department store in 1920, and Yowell-Drew increased its building to five floors and added a three-story annex. The Negro Odd Fellows building on Church Street was sold for a premium price and replaced with a three-story store and apartment house. The Armory Arcade Market was refurbished and began advertising as "The Consolidated Little City" with twelve businesses. After a Pierson Company department store and an A&P store were opened on West Church Street, that business area boasted 126 stores and became known as "Hustler's Paradise."

Both the new department store and the A&P were part of the trend toward chain stores. The A&P Tea Company was a national concern with retail outlets all over the country, including two in Orlando. The new department store was the Pierson Company's fifteenth store. A Piggly-Wiggly store had opened on South Orange in 1921. V.W. Estes, an Orlando druggist, sold his pharmacy to the Elbre Drug Stores' chain in 1920, giving that firm 25 stores. A year later Estes and his brother bought the entire Elbre chain.

If the trend toward chain stores signaled that Orlando was growing out as well as up, it also demonstrated that the city was becoming a major marketplace for central Florida. Several new hotels were built to accommodate the increasing flow of travelers. In addition to the expanded San Juan and the new Angebilt, the Wyoming added three floors in 1923. The Orange Court, the Fort Gatlin, and the Avalon were all operating by 1925. The new Alabama Hotel joined several smaller establishment in Winter Park, and the Francis Marion was built on the Dixie Highway at Michigan Avenue.

Industrial construction kept pace. Dr. P. Phillips and Company built the world's largest citrus-packing house about ten miles southwest of Orlando in 1928. At that time, Phillips owned more citrus acreage than anyone in the state. To expand the market for his large grapefruit crop, he employed Edna Giles Fuller to give 25 lectures in northern cities. Kissam Builders Supply and Harry P. Leu, Inc., both expanded their operations during the mid-1920s, as did T.G. Lee. Lee started his dairying enterprise with two cows and a calf. He first grazed his small, but growing, herd on a pasture between Bumby and Primrose, but as Orlando spread eastward, he moved his herd to the Conway area. On the site of the old pasture, he built his processing and distribution center. Even after the main herd was moved to Conway, some cattle were kept at the "city pasture" until the 1950s, when that land became the Colonial Plaza Shopping Center.

The move to suburbia shifted into high gear. By 1921, Walter Rose was one of the largest residential developers of the area and a founder of the Orlando Realty Board. He paid $500,000 for the Wilkinson tract, a prime 360-acre parcel between Lakes Sue and Rowena and announced "Central Florida's first million-dollar

Winter Park's famed Park Avenue as it looked in 1920.

bdivision." This became Rose Isle, a beautiful sidential area wedged between Orlando and Winter rk. Carl Dann continued to build in Orlando, Winter rk, and as far away as Mt. Plymouth in Lake County. His bsdread Country Club was opened in the mid-1920s. ree additions to College Park were completed by)25. The Edgewater Heights, Lorna Doone Park, ring Lake Terrace, and Angebilt subdivisions were gun in 1924.

In 1925, Rose started Orwin Manor on land outside rlando's city limits, eventually including 80 acres of inter Park. After a lengthy controversy, Winter Park leased the land and Orwin Manor was incorporated to Orlando. The Tinker-McCracken Real Estate mpany began construction of Jamajo outside the city nits at the entrance to the Cheney Highway. Because of e Tinker's connection with the Cincinnati Reds baseball ub, many lots were sold to team members. And, in rly 1926, E.P. Beeman bought 282 acres on Lake Mann r a subdivision for blacks.

Winter Park, which had begun calling itself "The City Homes," also shared in the housing boom. Among the ore than 30 new subdivisions was Carl Dann's mstock Park with 325 lots. Winter Park Golf Estates, c., built the Aloma Golf Course and Country Club, rrounded by homes near the present-day Aloma opping Center.

GH SPIRITS AND THE CALICO KID

oe Tinker did more than build houses during the 1920s — he also built a baseball team for Orlando. Long popular, the sport was given a major boost hen Tinker, former star of the Chicago Cubs and anager of the Cincinnati Reds, agreed to manage the rlando team in the Florida State League. His team won

the 1921 championship and brought home the Temple Cup, formerly held by the Tampa Smokers. He later persuaded the Cincinnati Reds to sign a three-year contract to play in Orlando, and in 1923 Tinker Field was completed at a cost of $15,000. All businesses closed the day the field was dedicated, and 17,000 fans came to see the first game between the Orlando Bulldogs and the Lakeland Highlanders.

Demands for Sunday baseball and Sunday moving pictures brought on a struggle over local blue laws. In a spirited 1928 campaign, the "modernists" won out over the traditionalists, and repealed the blue laws with a 59-vote majority. It was a brief victory, however. The following year the traditionalists regrouped and once again made their Sundays safe from such activities.

Other popular activities, especially among the nearly 5,000 winter residents in Orlando, were croquet (and a

Guests played croquet on the lawn of the Wyoming Hotel, one of the last old-style luxury hotels.

A successful fishing trip to Mosquito Lagoon. The fishermen are Delaney Way, T.O. Brown, S. Kendrick Guernsey, and Leigh Newell.

Ed Nilson, a pioneer aviator and promoter of aviation at Orlando, at Buck Field west of the city.

A horseshoe pitching tournament at the original Sunshine Park at the corner of Main (Magnolia) and Central.

similar game, roque) and horseshoes. In 1920 the newly organized chamber of commerce installed croquet courts at the corner of Central and Main. Shortly afterward, the Orlando Tourist Club was organized to expand the facility. Roque courts and horseshoe rings were added, along with seats and lights for night play. Later moved to Livingston Street, these activities marked the beginning of Sunshine Park, a site for organized entertainment and social events for years.

In the mid-1920s, drug-store owners discovered that a newfangled invention — the radio — would do wonders for their soda-fountain business. People came to listen to election returns, prize fights and other events broadcast by Rollins College station WDBO. The station was later taken over by the Orlando Broadcasting Company and moved to the Fort Gatlin Hotel.

The Orlando black community remained segregated in recreation as well as in housing. Orlando blacks formed their own baseball teams and swam at their own beach on Lake Mann. The year 1928 saw an important fund-raising event for local blacks. A well-attended athletic carnival was staged at Tinker Field to raise funds for the black Hilton Sanitarium.

But perhaps the greatest attraction for Orlandoans in the 1920s was the airplane. In 1919, the board of trade turned a cow pasture into an airfield, organized the Orlando Aerial Company, and began to offer rides in its new plane, the Calico Kid. Herman Krouse and Ralph

Johnson bought the operation in 1920 and started a flying school.

Then in 1922, Ed Nilson moved his airplane service from Bartow to Orlando and opened Buck Field west of the city. Operating as Orlando Airlines, Inc., he conduct a flying school and a taxi service to most Florida cities. For many Orlandoans, however, Buck Field was a place relax for a few hours while waiting for one of the mysti flying machines to attempt a takeoff. That pastime was equally popular later on at Herndon Airport.

In 1927, the city bought a large parcel of land from Dr. P. Phillips on Lake Underhill. The purchase was intended to increase the city's water supply, but it wasn long before city leaders realized that the flat sands around the lake would make an ideal airport. On October 4, 1928, with little more to show off than one 2,000-foot runway and a single hangar, the city held its grand opening for the new Municipal Airport. Nearly 40,000 people attended the opening, lauded as the greatest municipal celebration in the city's history. Franklin O. King, Mayor Latta Autrey and even gubernatorial candidate Doyle Carlton presented the requisite speeches, followed by a grand parade, which featured four bands. Two weeks later Pan-American Airways approved the facility and announced plans to include it on a new route to Cuba and Puerto Rico. Th airport was a success, but the high-flying twenties were about to crash.

Charter members of Orlando University Club posed for this photo in 1930.

Charter members of the Rotary Club of Orlando in 1920.

*Looking east at Orange and Central
avenues in the 1920s. Note the police-
man directing traffic near the sign at the
middle of the intersection.*

*Orange Belt Auto Line Terminal on
West Central Avenue in 1924, with one
of the company's coaches preparing
for departure.*

Carl Dann and Clarke Robertson, portraying an old-time couple from the backwoods. The two repeated this act at the Mid-Winter Fair from about 1917 until 1940.

Auntie Meisterman, feeding chickens in her backyard at South and Rosalind streets in 1922.

Central Avenue westward from Main, showing the expansion of the Yowell-Drew Department Store in the twenties.

NOTHING MORE THAN A GAMBLING MACHINE

Carl Dann would comment later that by 1925, "It finally became nothing more than a gambling machine, each man buying on a shoestring, betting dollars a bigger fool would come along and buy his option." Dann was referring to the general situation in Florida, but Orlando was not far behind. The Bithlo Real Estate Company offered free lots in Bithlo, and a second lot free if the new owner would plant trees on both. Lots and a five-acre farm were offered for anyone who would actually build a house there. The Gentile grove near the Orlando Country Club sold for $250,000. Land auctions were held as extravaganzas, with expensive door prizes, brass bands, airplane rides, parades, and picnics to attract the crowds. Subdivisions were sold out almost immediately. One, Cherokee Park,

sold out in less than an hour. Exasperated by the frequent callers who wanted to buy his new home on East Central Avenue, C.S. Rybolt erected a sign in his front yard, saying "Not for Sale or Rent. Keep Out."

By 1926, speculative prices were so high on the southeast coast that many feared the end was near. Out-of-state newspapers began warning that Florida land was a high-risk investment. Some banks became reluctant to loan money for Florida land purchases. Then the devastating hurricane of September 1926 struck Miami and the adjacent areas, inflicting damage as far north as Winter Park. The central Florida towns rendered assistance to their stricken neighbors, then went right on with their own building plans. Many of the projects already in progress were completed. The Orlando Coliseum was launched amid good cheer and comparative optimism in December 1926, and construction continued on other projects. One of the last building projects of 1926 was the formation of the Golden Rod Corporation to build Suburban Homes, a tract of 158 lots on the dirt road between Winter Park and Oviedo. (The few lots sold before the stock-market crash in 1929 were all that existed of the Suburban Homes development for more than a decade.)

By 1928, hard times had arrived in Orlando. Loch Haven, site of the present-day cultural center, was only one of the subdivisions to be abandoned in the late twenties. By 1929, the annual value of new construction had declined to less than a million dollars. In July, Charles Rock Jr. became the first small businessman forced into bankruptcy. Many more would follow.

In April, an infestation of the dreaded Mediterranean fruit fly compounded Orlando's troubles. First discovered in an Orlando grove, the flies were later found in an area extending north to Maitland and northwestward almost to Apopka. The infestation spread to six other counties around Orlando. With $250,000 appropriated by the state legislature, state and national inspectors took to the

W.J. Barnes, C. Clifford, W.J. Biecker, and Golden, members of the Lafayette Development Company which built Spring Lake Terrace.

More parades. Above left, the famous Budweiser horses pulling a wagon in preparation for a 1927 parade. Above right, a 1930 parade on West Pine Street at Orange Avenue. Mayor James Giles is in the lead car.

One of the last meetings of the Pioneer Association, in 1928. The photo was taken in front of the Chamber of Commerce Building.

ORLANDO WHO?

*R*arely in history has the origin of a city's name been as confused or confusing as that of Orlando. One old account had it that Judge Speer insisted on the name because of his admiration for one of Shakespeare's characters. Another is that the town was named for a certain Mr. Orlando who was leading an ox caravan through central Florida when he had an attack of appendicitis, died, and was buried in the area. And several other stories were told to a Mrs. Willa Vick Griffin in 1923, when she was trying to prepare an article on the history of Orlando.

Most popular today, however, is that Orlando was named after a man whose name might have been Orlando Reeves or Jennings, but most likely was Rees. Originally thought to have been a Seminole War soldier, he is now believed to have been an early plantation owner. At any rate, he apparently was serving as sentinel for a small band of residents when he was attacked and killed by Indians. His body is said to have been buried near Lake Eola — then Sandy Beach Lake.

On a piece of wood laid upon his grave was scratched "Orlando R...s," the middle letters being illegible and thus leading to the belief that his name was Reeves. No records were ever found of a man by that name, however.

Then in 1975, librarian Eileen Willis uncovered records of a well-to-do Mosquito County plantation owner named Orlando J. (Jennings?) Rees. And, Rees did at one time have problems with Indians, evidenced by a letter he wrote to the federal government in 1837 complaining about the thefts of several of his slaves. This new material would seem to have solved the mystery once and for all, but for one small problem. By all other accounts, the man who was killed by Indians and buried at Lake Eola died in September 1835, two years before Orlando Rees wrote his letter.

Thus, we can only leave the story as Willa Vick Griffin did in 1923, with "I dared not ask another how Orlando got its name."

Two loaded trucks about to depart the American Fruit Growers packing house, about 1930.

100

Citrus survives. Above, Leon Kazanzas, "the Fruit Man," started out with a small local fruit stand and built it into this large enterprise, which shipped volumes of citrus all over the United States. Right, W.W. Yothers, an entomologist credited with stopping the Mediterranean Fruit Fly epidemic in 1929-1930. During his 25 years of work in the Orlando area, Yothers was instrumental in controlling many diseases which threatened the central Florida citrus industry.

field, quarantining large areas. No fruit was permitted to be shipped from affected groves, and four companies of the national guard had to be called in to enforce the quarantines. The fern and foliage industry was also hurt because plants had to be washed clean of all dirt before they could be shipped — a condition that made survival unlikely. W.W. Yothers of the Orlando experiment station supervised destruction of the infected fruit — nearly 600,000 boxes from 350,000 quarantined acres. By October 1929, the fruit fly ban was lifted and the citrus industry had been saved from possible collapse. The rest of the economy, however, had not.

While the battle with the fruit fly raged, the Orlando Commercial Bank — which had taken over the Bank of Orange and Trust Company when it failed — announced that it, too, was closing. The State Bank failed a few weeks later. The Orlando Chamber of Commerce placed a full-page advertisement in local papers stating that theirs was "a city that is unafraid...undaunted by disaster." But the next several years were grim ones for central Florida, reminiscent of the aftermath of the great freezes of 1894-95.

CHAPTER EIGHT

FROM DEPRESSION TO WORLD WAR AGAIN

The City of Orlando *was a 20 Air Force B-29, commanded and named by Lieutenant W.T. (Joe) Carroll of Kissimmee. He is shown here with Major J. Rocher Chappell, an Orlando doctor who named his hospital on Okinawa, "Orange Memorial."*

With tax delinquencies and business failures increasing, banks closing, and grass growing through the asphalt streets of failed subdivisions, Orlando was a depressed community in a depressed nation when Franklin D. Roosevelt was inaugurated in 1933. During the next few years, an array of innovative, audacious, and controversial programs known collectively as the New Deal permanently transformed the relationship between the national government and the state and local communities. Millions of dollars were spent through grants-in-aid for hundreds of civic projects in Orlando and surrounding towns, to ease the human suffering of an unprecedented national depression.

Orlandoans, however, did not wait for help from the federal government. In 1930, H.M. Voorhis and Raymer F. Maguire organized Florida Faith, Inc., to deal in real estate; three new Shell service stations were opened; the First National Bank opened its new building, and the Florida National Bank began operating. After discontinuing service for several months, Orlando Rapid Transit was back in business in early 1931 with a ten-year franchise. Both Sears, Roebuck and Lerner's opened stores in the same year. They were soon joined by S&H Kress, W.T. Grant and Walgreen's. George Stuart started his office-supply store in 1934.

Meanwhile, the city reduced tax millage and cut salaries by ten percent. An interracial committee began looking for ways to reduce black unemployment. The chamber of commerce asked merchants to give good prices to residents willing to undertake home-improvement projects to keep people working. A "Buy Now" campaign was launched with 10,000 residents marching from city hall to Lake Eola, while airplanes flew overhead to call attention to the event. To facilitate employment at a time when money was scarce, employers paid workers in scrip which local merchants accepted as payment for their goods.

Determined though they were, Orlandoans soon realized that traditional self-help efforts — which had brought them through hard times before — weren't going to be enough this time. The depression was simply too deep and too broad. By late 1933, 3,400 Orlandoans were on the relief rolls of the Civil Works Administration, with comparable numbers in surrounding towns.

One of the first New Deal projects was construction of a solarium on Lake Estelle, on property donated by Walter Rose. Some of the federally funded civic projects included the fencing of Tinker Field; construction of 1,000 seats at the fairgrounds; a new armory building; Dickson Azalea Park; and a 10,000-seat football stadium at Tinker Field. Also established were an artists' project to aid unemployed artists, a sewing room to provide jobs for women, and an agricultural-experiment station. Many streets were paved, including a portion of the Orange Blossom Trail.

Apopka built a new city hall and recreation facilities with federal funds. Winter Park shared with Orlando a project to widen Orange Avenue between the two cities, as well as construction of the Lake Estelle Solarium. Other important Winter Park projects included a municipal gymnasium, auditorium, fire station and jail, a

Orlando area judges, about 1930. Standing are Wilbur Tilden, Donald A. Cheney (to whom this book is dedicated), and W.A. Pattishall; seated are Frank A. Smith and Charles O. Andrews Sr.

Looking south on Orange Avenue, about 1940.

One of the major tourist courts along Orange Blossom Trail, Wigwam Village was built in the late 1930s. It was removed in 1973 to make way for the 8-Days Inn at the corner of Orange Blossom Trail and I-4. Inset, action of the national shuffleboard tournament at the Orlando Shuffleboard Club in 1933.

drainage sewer, a playground for blacks, and Mead Garden. These and numerous other undertakings provided useful civic facilities while putting people to work and priming the economic pump of the area. Several of the projects, under the auspices of the later Works Progress Administration, lasted until the early 1940s.

Businessmen who were still making it on their own were encouraged by the National Recovery Administration to make changes to help revive the economy. In Orlando, the Retail Merchants Association staged a parade to emphasize its support for the NRA. Grocers and other merchants agreed to limit their store hours and stabilize wages and prices. Participating stores displayed the "Blue Eagle," the NRA emblem, and buyers were asked to trade only with stores showing those signs.

The banking industry was still struggling to recover from the catastrophes of the late twenties and early thirties. When the Federal Deposit Insurance Corporation was created to insure individual bank deposits, bankers first hesitated, but then accepted the change.

By 1936, there were strong signs of recovery. In December 1935, an automobile show was held for the first time in several years. Deposits at the city's three banks showed more than a 50 percent increase. Bell Telephone had a fifteen percent increase in patrons, and other utilities reported similar gains. These signs of improvement were celebrated by a Festival of Progress, featuring a huge parade in 1936. Statewide, Orlando ranked second only to Miami in per-capita retail sales. Building permits exceeded a million dollars for the first time since 1928. At least one new subdivision and several new businesses opened. The First Federal Savings and Loan and the Orange County Building and Loan were reorganized as the First Federal Savings and Loan Association in 1937 by W.R. O'Neal, N.P. Yowell, and O.P. Swope.

Despite a wavering of the economy in 1938, the acceleration continued. In 1939, Wellborn Phillips announced plans for a hundred new homes in Colonial Gardens, a subdivision just east of Colonialtown. The Colonialtown business section had survived the worst of the Depression and was beginning to grow again by the late 1930s. The Great Southern Box Company opened a factory in Fairvilla Industrial Park, and the Crown Can Company built an even larger facility there. In 1940 R.N. Heintzelman expanded his Ford dealership, the first Publix Market opened, and the first Howard Johnson restaurant came to Orlando.

Although New Deal housing programs provided much-needed homes and jobs for Orlando, they also brought about increased racial segregation. Blacks had complained about congestion and deterioration of Jonestown for years. Finally, the Orlando Housing Authority agreed to use its first available housing funds to build Griffin Park, a 174-family complex for blacks. In 1941, 76 more units were added to Griffin Park. At Jonestown, the blacks' homes were demolished, and a new white subdivision was begun. Two years later, the city adopted a master housing plan designating black residential areas between Orange Blossom Trail and Hughey Street north of Central Avenue, and between the Trail and Division Street from South to Gore. The federal government leased the city's old Carter Street dump site

Dr. Gaston Edwards (standing) came to Orlando in 1914 and formed a partnership with Dr. John S. McEwan in the Orlando Clinic. Shown with him are (left to right) Mayor Samuel Y. Way, H.H. Dickson, and William R. O'Neal.

Sanlando Springs was a favorite watering place for local residents as well as tourists.

The Flamingo Cafe was located just outside the city limits on Highway 50 near Herndon Airport. It was frequently visited by the Orange County sheriff on business.

for housing black soldiers. Still, by 1946 black residential areas were again so congested that another area between Lake Mann and Clear Lake was bought and developed for blacks. Black neighborhoods continued to expand westward into one concentrated area. This would later add to Orlando's difficulties as it tried to desegregate its social, political, and economic institutions.

Although Orlando progressed more slowly during the Depression, it did not stagnate. Orlandoans were justifiably proud when hometowners Buddy and Vilma Ebsen began in 1931 a successful Broadway performance, which included roles in a Ziegfeld musical. A year later the two were welcomed as the headliners at the Beaux Arts Ball at the Orlando Country Club.

Horse racing had been discontinued at Exposition Park in 1928, the same year Ben White, a famous Canadian horse trainer, established his winter training headquarters in Orlando. Other racing enthusiasts soon joined him with their stables, and encouraged him to build Seminole Driving Park near present-day Casselberry. Horse racing would continue there for nearly twenty years.

Tinker Field was reacquired from the Cincinnati Reds in 1932. The field was refurbished and improved, with WPA assistance. Clark Griffith brought his Washington Nationals to train there in 1936, and liked Orlando so much that he spent the remaining eighteen winters of his life there.

R.D. Keene, exercising one of his fine trotters at Ben White Raceway. Keene was a self-made millionaire citrus grower and a generous benefactor of Orlando. He donated much of the land for the raceway.

IT RAINED ON THIS PARADE

In 1934, a group of about 60 civic leaders conceived the idea of a fair during the 1935-36 tourist season on a site which could later be converted to a permanent park. Intended to emphasize Florida's many and varied attributes, the proposed "Florida on Parade" was given statewide stature through a legislative resolution. Latin American nations were invited to participate as well. While the committee launched a bond sale to raise funds, the city looked for a suitable site. The Loch Haven subdivision, one of the casualties of the real estate collapse, already had streets and sewers in place. The city held several tax certificates on property there, and eventually secured title to about 80 acres.

Prospects were bright in early 1935. Over $100,000 had been raised from private sources, the national government was promising $750,000, and the citizens had approved a Special Park Commission to manage the impending fair and the park which was to follow it. But coordinating such a large undertaking proved impossible. Even after President Roosevelt declared his support, the project became embroiled in delays and the federal money was never made available. The grand plan for "Florida on Parade" expired, the victim of bureaucratic inertia. A small sum of money salvaged from the disaster was finally turned over to Mead Garden.

The effort was not a complete loss, however. In 1956 the city council aproved a master plan for Loch Haven Park as a science and cultural center. With the Orlando Science Center, the Orange County Historical Museum, Loch Haven Art Center, the Garden Center, Junior Achievement, and the Edyth Bush Theatre on that site, Lock Haven Park has become a valued part of Orlando and central Florida.

The bounty of the lakes. Far left, the catch, a large-mouth bass, is almost as large as the catcher. Above, fishing was a popular sport for women, as well. Left, Lake Apopka offered some of the best fishing anywhere during the 1930s, attracting tourists and locals alike.

A less universally welcomed change was the repeal of the Eighteenth Amendment in 1933. Senator Walter Rose was severely chastised by many central Florida women when he voted to authorize the sale of beer. Renewed sales of hard liquor aroused even greater acrimony. A ,000 tax charged to dealers in 1934 temporarily halted liquor sales. Then, in 1935, the sale of package liquor was approved, and Jack Sweetman of the Rausch Inn acquired the first license to sell it. Meanwhile, Sheriff Frank Karel closed down roadhouses and taverns which were defying the law. In 1937, he again closed Sam Warren's troublesome Flamingo Club, along with the Blarney Club, The Frolic, Little Orphan Annie's, and the Black Cat, as well as several Church Street "juke joints."

The city successfully dispelled unwelcome changes in other areas. When the recently organized Congress for Industrial Organizations — much more militant than the older American Federation of Labor — attempted to organize central Florida citrus workers, grove owners and citrus processors were alarmed and outraged. Mayor Samuel Y. Way spoke for a majority of Orlandoans when he campaigned to keep the CIO out of the area, while assuring the AFL that it was welcome. Addressing a group of local blacks, Mayor Way warned them to stay away from the "Communist International Organization." Through their spokesman, Dr. C.E. Eccleston, the blacks agreed to cooperate in keeping the controversial union out of the city.

The Jehovah's Witnesses were equally unpopular. They met in Orlando in the late 1930s and angered local residents by refusing to salute the American flag. The outraged American Legion called on the city council to pass a resolution making it a crime for anyone to encourage others not to salute the flag. Despite a protest by a prominent Jacksonville resident, the mayor declared any group that wouldn't salute the flag was "definitely not worthy of existence," and the ordinance passed.

In 1940, when Sheriff Karel arrested an outspoken pro-Nazi, a clamor against "aliens and saboteurs" arose. The American Legion formed a home-defense plan to assist authorities in observing suspected persons. All aliens were required to register with the police department and to be fingerprinted. About twenty aliens, several of whom had once been officers in the German army, registered. One German spy was apprehended at the Orlando air base when he demonstrated too much flying skill for one who was supposedly just learning.

ADVENT OF THE AUTOMOBILE AGE

Many of the greatest changes of the thirties arose from Americans' new mobility. Increasing ownership of automobiles even created new forms of entertainment. In 1934, W.J. Goodbread of Macon, Georgia, opened Orlando's first drive-in

The Orlando Lawn Bowling Club gathered for a competitive event at the corner of Garland and Livingston streets in 1930.

A cockfight at Orla Vista, where world-championship tournaments were held for many years. Cockfighting was legal, but gambling on them was not. The two were exceedingly difficult to separate.

*The Miami Elks Club motored to their
annual convention in Columbus, Ohio,
in 1935, and stopped along the way
at the Orlando lodge.*

*The Antiquarian Society's antique exhibi-
tion in 1934. This is the Chippendale
Room, featuring many historic pieces
owned by Floridians.*

Golfers and their caddies beneath the wing of an early tri-motored aircraft at Mt. Plymouth Golf and Country Club in the late 1930s.

restaurant on North Orange Avenue. Advertising T-bone steak dinners for 35 cents, he offered 24-hour curbside service. Goodbread's soon became the hangout for the younger set, who parked their cars on both sides of Orange Avenue, sipped soft drinks, and mingled with friends. Older Orlandoans, however, did not appreciate the increased noise and congestion. When they complained, the city enacted an ordinance declaring Orange Avenue a "heavy-traffic zone." Curbside service was permitted only directly in front of Goodbread's and only until midnight. With these restrictions, Goodbread's continued to be the hot spot for Orlando night life, and drive-in restaurants proliferated.

Another portent of the automobile age came in 1937

Advertising of an earlier time.

when the old signal tower at the intersection of Orange and Central was replaced with overhead traffic lights. And in 1940, Orlando's first drive-in theatre opened at Gore Avenue and Orange Blossom Trail.

Municipal Airport, Orlando's proud new baby in 1928, was in such wretched condition eight years later that the government threatened to discontinue mail flights. City Commissioner G. Wayne Gray and several colleagues reactivated the Florida Aviation Association and persuaded the city to do something about the situation. The city agreed to add 200 acres to the airport and obtained WPA assistance to resurface the crumbling runways and add more buildings and hangars.

The response was swift and positive. Eastern Air Lines began regular flights to and from the city almost as soon as the new asphalt hardened. A tenth-anniversary celebration in 1938 brought Eastern's president, Eddie Rickenbacker, to Orlando to address the huge crowd which gathered for a two-day celebration. By 1940, the airport boasted three paved runways of about 2,500 feet. Again, the government took notice. This time, it was not the post office that was interested, but the military. The newly renovated airport became a prime prospect for a military flying facility as the nation began preparing for the possibility of yet another war.

Within months, the Army Air Corps Center was established at Orlando Municipal Airport, and the Army took a 25-year lease on land west of the field for barracks and family housing. A second military airfield was announced in early 1941, to be located seven miles south of the city between the Dixie Highway and the Narcoosee Road.

The aviation industry followed on the heels of the
[ar]my. The Monocoupe Airplane and Engine Company of
[St.] Louis moved to Orlando in 1940 and built about 50
[pla]nes before the nation entered World War II. The
[Ae]ronautical Supply Company purchased the recently
[bu]ilt Cannon-Mills Airport and began to distribute and
[ma]intain its Aeronta planes there. As military operations
[ex]panded, most of the nation's aircraft companies
[op]ened facilities in Orlando. By 1944, the city was
[to]uting itself as "Florida's Air Capital," with more flying
[da]ys per year than any other location, two of the nation's
[lar]gest airports, outlets for most aircraft firms, and what
[see]med to be a permanent AAF center.

[AL]L-OUT VENTURE FOR VICTORY

Having published *The Orlando Sentinel* since the
early 1930s, Martin Andersen was a major
opinion leader of the community by 1940. He
[ur]ged his readers to recognize that "this is an all-out
[ven]ture for victory. Whatever we make, buy, or sell will
[be] made, bought and sold only for victory. Nothing else
[co]unts until we achieve that." He called on everyone to
[fol]low the example of Henry Land of Apopka, who had
[alr]eady signed a government contract to produce crates
[for] fuel cans at his Consumers Lumber Company plant.
[No]t only did Land make a million crates for use in the
[No]rth Africa campaign, but the $100,000 loan he
[rec]eived from First National Bank of Orlando became the
[pat]tern for financing the many government-funded
[pro]jects which followed.

In October 1940 men between the ages of 21 and 36
were required to sign up for the draft. They expected to
be called for only one year of active duty, but were
obliged to remain in service for "the duration and six
months" after the Japanese bombed Pearl Harbor. The
Orlando National Guard was activated at about the
same time.

When President Roosevelt called for a declaration of
war following the Pearl Harbor attack, central Floridians
enthusiastically responded. Blackout drills were held,
many more men volunteered for service, scrap drives
were launched, war bonds and stamps were purchased,
scarce commodities were rationed, and some 5,000
victory gardens were soon growing in Orlando
backyards.

The war inadvertently stimulated the new town of
Casselberry. A sizable fern industry had developed in the
1920s at Fern Park, and a major grower, Hibbard
Casselberry, incorporated Casselberry in 1940 as a "tax-
free town." But when ferneries were classified by the
government as unessential to the war effort, Casselberry
was obliged to find a more "essential industry." He
sought and received government contracts to produce
ammunition bandoliers and parachutes for fragmentation
bombs. Employing women in his defense plant,
Casselberry became a contributor to the war effort and
his newly founded town grew as a result.

Several other Orlando-area companies participated in
important wartime industries. The American Machinery
Corporation and Madewell Company were cited for their
vital roles in producing equipment for landing craft, and
by 1945, the American Machinery Corporation was also

*Eastern Airlines was
the first major
company to include
Orlando on its
scheduled flights.*

*William C. Lazarus,
Nancy Carroll, Quentin
Reynolds, and Dewitt
Miller at Orlando
Municipal Airport in
the late 1930s. Lazarus
was an aviation leader
in Orlando and
Florida. His* Wings in
the Sun *is a history of
early aviation in the
state.*

The Orlando Morning Sentinel's *front window in 1940, long before two major expansions of its facilities were conceived. It appears that Lucky Strike cigarette manufacturers were major advertisers in the newspaper at the time.*

making 500-pound bombs. The Pine Castle Boat and Construction Company made assault boats and related equipment, and the Florida Aircraft Corporation rebuilt and repaired aircraft for the Air Corps. A large plant was built at Zellwood to prepare and ship dehydrated foods for the armed forces. An experimental plant at Plymouth worked to develop a method of preserving fruit juices for shipment. From this experiment came the Minute Maid Company, which eventually became an enormous branch of the Coca-Cola Bottling Company, with processing plants and huge groves in Florida. A Department of Agriculture experiment in Orlando led to development of DDT. Although it was later found to be a dangerous toxin, DDT was used widely during the war to control mosquitoes and other insects.

Still, Florida's major contribution to the war was from the vegetable fields and citrus groves. But acute labor shortages caused Mayor William Beardall at one point to annonce that "zoot-suited loafers" would not be tolerated in Orlando, and idle men were sometimes ordered to the fields. The CIO once again came under attack when 438 blacks were shipped out of Orlando on a train bound for a Campbell Soup plant in New Jersey. Citrus and vegetable farmers were outraged at this "labor pirating." The War Manpower Commission, which was responsible for placing workers were they were needed most, eventually promised to allow no more raids. Otis G. Nation, business agent of the Citrus and Allied Workers' Union, was found guilty of recruiting labor without a license.

The war overshadowed Orlando's centennial celebration. The three-day event in 1942 noted the 100th anniversary of Aaron Jernigan's arrival in central Florida. It would be three more years before any real celebrating would begin — first on May 7, 1945, when the Germans surrendered, and again in August, when the Japanese surrendered and the war was officially over.

Referred to as the "red-brick" courthouse, this edifice was built in 1892 and served the county until it was replaced in the 1920s.

SAVING THE OLD COURTHOUSE

A plan to sell the old red-brick Orange County courthouse in 1944 met with much opposition, but none quite as colorful as a letter to the Orlando Reporter Star. The letter was signed, "Beulah Backwoods," a pseudonym for a pioneer who occasionally wrote to the newspaper, commenting on the events of the day.

"But that old COURTHOUSE wuz bilt so elegant it aint needed thing one done to it, and it sets there jest as proud and haughty of its looks as it did when we wuz all childern and passed it with awe and respeck on our way to school . . . .

"And them fireplaces. I kin see my pappy now, asettin ther awaitin to see Cap. Ben Robison in his office, and spittin clean across the room and always hittin the flame smack in the middle. My pappy shore loved his Brown Mule and he were a expert expecterater.

"One halloween we stoled chalk frum Miss Noon Delaney's room, in the old wood

schoolhouse and rit on the COURTHOUSE steps and all over the sidewalk. 'Hal Beardall loves Ethel Starkey' and Chief Carter and Sheriff Vick wuz mad as wet roosters and sed if they ever found out who did it theyd put em in the caliboos, and we wuz scared plenty.

"I see where the Roslind Club is in favor of keepin the buildin. Thems the silk-stockin crowd, and I dont no but one lady in it, an thats Miss Agnes Person. O yes I no Miss Bell Howselt too. Miss Bell and her ma used to run the old Summerlin Hotel down in the holler, and she had a feller thet wuz of considerable importence around that old COURTHOUSE, and I no she would agree with me, that the old clock rings out the struggles of the PINEERS, the joys of all the weddins and births and the sorrows of all the mourners. I aint tryin to say whut to do with the inside except, SAVE THEM FIREPLACES, and leave the outside be . . . ."

The air force in Orlando. Left, Mayor William Beardall (in the colorful tie), General Leo A. Walton, and a group of military and civilian officials at the Orlando AFB Officers Club in 1942. Above, the first military aircraft assigned to Orlando Air Base. Photo was taken by James Clyde King from aboard the second plane to arrive.

These Orlando women were among the many who prepared "Bundles for Britain" during World War II.

Inside view of a modern citrus packing house, around 1950.

Winter Park resident parking his mule in front of Bumby Hardware (the Winter Park branch), during the centennial celebration in 1942.

A Pepsi-Cola delivery truck with empty racks at the end of the day. Prices were much more favorable to the consumer in the 1940s.

CHAPTER NINE

INTO THE SPACE AGE AND THE AGE OF DIMINISHING SPACE

By the early 1960s, the space program was accelerating the growth of Orlando, and residents were being treated to scenes such as this. Space shots were usually visible from anywhere in the city.

THE BEGINNINGS OF SUBURBAN SPRAWL

Returning servicemen found the central Florida communities much as they had left them — but not for long. Thousands of airmen who had passed through Orlando during the war liked what they saw and decided to make their homes there. The GI Bill helped make that possible by providing money for education and home loans, fueling the local economy, and causing yet another boom in residential housing, public facilities, and business.

International affairs helped to sustain that growth, even as they caused doubts and uncertainties for most Americans. Both the Orlando and Pine Castle air bases had been placed on standby status after the war, but they were soon back in full operation as the Cold War worsened and fighting began in Korea. By the early 1950s, the bases were pouring millions of dollars into the local economy through payrolls and new construction. Orlando Air Force Base outgrew its facilities and moved across Colonial Drive to larger quarters on Bennett Road.

When the United States Missile Test Center opened at Cape Canaveral in 1955, many of its employees decided to live in Orlando, adding to housing demands. Azalea Park, with 1,100 houses and a shopping center, was the largest of several housing projects stimulated by the reactivated bases. Lakewood Homes was built west of the air base, and Dover Shores, which also housed many Air Force families, was brought into the city in 1955. When Highway 50 was completed early in the decade, Pine Hills became the first subdivision to be constructed so far outside the city. Other additions followed rapidly, heralding the age of suburbia.

For a while at least, Orlando's downtown business district expanded as well. It was still business as usual when Morrison's Cafeteria relocated in downtown Orlando in 1949. Then a rush of building projects began, including construction of the new *Sentinel-Star* facilities on North Orange, the Eola Plaza Hotel (later Cherry and now Park Plaza), and several other hotels and banks. In response to the city's tremendous growth, the voters approved a new city hall, which was begun in 1956. Several churches expanded their downtown buildings.

Some of the new building projects occurred at the expense of city landmarks. Duke Hall, a famous old boarding house dating from the late nineteenth century, was removed to make room for expansion of the First Baptist Church.

In the early 1960s, however, it became apparent that downtown Orlando was becoming the victim of suburbanization. By the mid-1950s, shopping centers were operating at Bumby and South streets, in Azalea Park, Pine Hills, and Washington Shores. The Western Way Shopping Center and Parkwood Plaza opened in 1955 and 1956, respectively. Montgomery Ward announced its new store on West Colonial Drive in 1960. Even the downtown post office had been supplemented by "miniature post offices" in Colonialtown, College Park, and on South Orange Blossom Trail in 1952.

The first direct raid on the central business district came in 1956 when Walgreen's Drug Store left downtown and moved to the new $3.5 million Colonial Plaza. Gibbs-Louis and Rutland's kept their downtown

Even as the city spread out, urban still mixed pleasantly with rural, as this 1950s aerial photo demonstrates.

William H. (Billy) Dial, a prominent Orlando civic leader and county attorney who played a major role on the city's phenomenal growth after World War II.

A household name. Above left, T.G. Lee's dairy supplied Orlandoans with milk products for decades. Shown here is the "milking parlor," about 1950. Above right, Colonial Plaza, shortly after being converted from T.G. Lee's dairy pasture and before Jordan Marsh was added.

THE TREMONT HOTEL

The Tremont Hotel — an architectural collage.

A familiar landmark in downtown Orlando from 1895 to 1956, the Tremont Hotel at Main and Church streets was built by James Walle Wilmott, an English sea captain who settled in the city in 1883. The hotel was an eclectic structure consisting of parts of three older buildings. The southern face of the Tremont was actually Orange County's last wooden courthouse, a three-story building which was moved in 1891 to make room for the county's first brick courthouse. The northern end of Wilmott's hotel was part of the old Charleston House. The rear of the hotel was formed from an old building which had belonged to the Methodist church.

Completed in 1895, the Tremont was a major hostelry for winter visitors for many years, thriving even after the hotel-building era of the 1920s. Orlando residents also continued to frequent the Tremont, where they could expect excellent fare from the dining room and comfortable accommodations for guests.

A good reason for the hotel's continued popularity was its management after 1926 by Mrs. Blanche Mallett, Captain Wilmott's daughter. A native of Orlando, she had traveled extensively throughout the country advertising the nutritional value of citrus fruit before returning to take over the hotel. Her sister Lillian remained in Orlando, married D.E. Fishback, and raised a family, members of which are still prominent in the community.

The Tremont fell victim to modernity in 1956, when it was razed to make room for a parking lot. That lowly role was ended in 1962, however, when the First Federal Savings and Loan Association built a handsome five-story office building on the site.

cations but added second stores at the plaza in 1962. Downtown Orlando's future became even more precarious when J.C. Penney and Ivey's (successor to Yowell-Drew) opened second stores at the new Winter Park Mall.

New subdivisions led to new shopping centers, drawing businesses away from downtown and replacing neighborhood groceries with new "supermarkets." In 1956, Winn-Lovett Food Stores, which had bought the Margaret-Ann Chain in 1949, was reorganized by A.D. Davis as Winn-Dixie Stores, Inc. An aggressive businessman, Davis expanded his chain while aiding the construction of still more shopping centers. Publix supermarkets and Food Fair also joined in the shopping center movement. The arrival of the 7-11 Food Stores in 1958 struck the deathblow to most of the remaining neighborhood groceries.

Unable to compete with the suburban stores, the once-supreme Dickson and Ives Department Store closed its doors in 1965. By that time, Mayor Robert Carr had appointed a Downtown Orlando committee to find ways to revitalize the shrinking central business district and to locate a site for a convention hall. An option was taken on the old San Juan Hotel for the proposed hall, but the idea soon became embroiled in controversy. Much discussion but little action resulted.

GOBBLING UP THE FARMLAND

When Milton Blank of the Orlando Industrial Board announced that Tupperware Home Parties, with a $250,000 payroll, was moving its headquarters near Orlando, there was a round of applause, but little notice that the firm had purchased 1,000 acres of farmland between Orlando and Kissimmee on the Dixie Highway. There was still enormous open space in central Florida in 1952.

Four years later, however, quite a few people noticed when the Martin Company paid nearly $2 million for 7,300 acres in southwest Orange County. Most of the land had been used as a pasture for Clarence Zeigler's dairy herd. Even before the Martin plant was completed, Cushman Radebaugh sold an adjacent 2,750 acres to L.B. McLeod for an unheard-of $850 per acre. Those transactions changed central Floridians' perspective of agricultural land values. Suddenly, they saw that their farming and grazing acres would be far more valuable if sold for urban or industrial use.

The Martin Company transformed Orlando in other ways. With a work force that has varied in size (usually

Mayor Bob Carr viewing the city in 1965.

Orlando's new city hall in 1958. The building just beyond it was the McElroy apartments.

125

Participants in the National Orange Picking Contest in 1951. Heller Bros. of Winter Garden and other central Florida firms were promoting Florida citrus.

Modern citrus. Far left, groves in the ridge district near Orlando in the 1950s. Although urbanization has removed many acres of groves, scenes such as this are still common in west Orange County. Left, central Florida grove owners and citrus packers had many colorful labels, which were attached to the ends of citrus boxes.

upward) from about 8,000, Martin (later Martin-Marietta) became by far the area's largest employer. By 1970, the firm had put more than $1 billion into the local economy in payroll alone. In only two years, its presence spawned at least 72 other new businesses. Martin employees settled all over town, but especially in Pine Hills, Sky Lake, Rio Piñar, and Dommerich Estates in Maitland. The company's success in obtaining and fulfilling defense contracts has made it a prominent addition to metropolitan Orlando.

Looking east on Central Avenue in the early 1960s (far left).

Martin-Marietta's contributions also made Orlandoans more hospitable to other light industries. Under the direction of the Orlando Industrial Board, five industrial parks were opened throughout Orlando and more were added in surrounding towns.

SOCIETY IN TRANSITION

Central Floridians entered the dynamic second half of the twentieth century with optimism over the growing economy and anxiety about national security and social change. The same international events that had stimulated growth also brought doubts about security, as Russia exploded an atom bomb and tightened its Iron Curtain across Europe. The two oceans, which had been America's defensive bastions for over a century, no longer seemed adequate. When Joseph McCarthy suggested that communists, or at least "fellow travelers," had infiltrated the national government, he caused a "Red hysteria."

Concomitant revelations that "organized crime" was rampant in Florida, coupled with accelerated demands by black Americans for equality, added to the frustration. Lake County Sheriff Willis McCall's sensational handling

Z.L. Riley, a prominent black leader of Orlando, conferring with Bob Hayes, a Florida A&M football player and Olympic gold-medal winner who went on to a professional career with the Dallas Cowboys.

BRICK BY BRICK

The bell tower of First Methodist Church creates a striking contrast with the Barnett Bank.

The battle to save Orlando's old brick courthouse finally ended in 1957. That it was a beloved part of Orlando's history was made clear by a eulogy in The Orlando Sentinel, *written by Jean Yothers:*

"The Old Orange County Courthouse, well known pioneer, died yesterday after a lingering illness at its home on the corner of Main St. and Central Ave.

"Death was attributed to natural causes brought on by the inevitable march of progress.

"It was 66 years old.

"A native Orlandoan, the Old Courthouse was the city's most famous landmark and was prominently identified with the life of the community throughout its existence.

"Born Jan. 15, 1892, of sturdy, red-brick stock, it first served with distinction as a house dedicated to courts, lawmaking and public meetings. Later, it was used as offices for the county welfare department and also housed the Orange County Museum. Its lawn was a favorite spot for ticket selling and its benches popular for basking in the sun.

"Up until the denouncement of its usefulness, it faithfully boomed out the hours from its tower clock and proudly showed the correct and/or incorrect time on each of its four faces.

"The Old Courthouse became incurably ill last summer when it began to crumble and falling bricks narrowly missed hitting Juvenile Judge Mattie Farmer. Prior to that time, its frame had undergone constant care and doctoring in an effort to keep it safe for occupancy. It had also been wounded by the barbs of being called 'an eyesore' and 'a monstrosity.'

"The end became near as plans were fomented for a new courthouse annex to be built in its place.

"Pioneers mourned.

"They had fought valiantly for the structure's historical preservation. They now realized it was only a matter of time before the city's last remaining link with pioneer Orlando returned to dust.

"Gradually as though suffering from a malignancy, the building faded into a nothingness. Brick by brick, it was dismantled, and a wall built around it to make the pain of death seem private.

"Final arrangements were in charge of a Jacksonville wrecking firm.

"Final rites will be held in the hearts of those who held it dear. There, its memory will rest in peace.

"There are no immediate survivors. Only progress!"

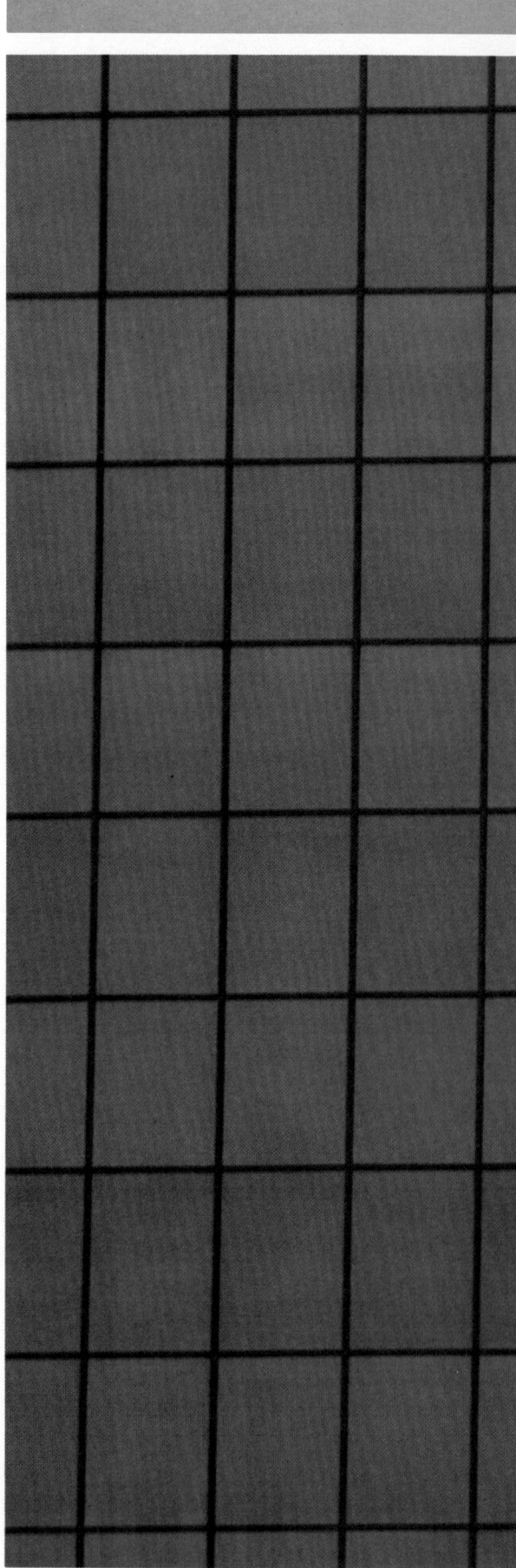

Construction boom. Above, the construction site of the Sun Bank Building on Orange Avenue, 1958. Right, view of downtown Orlando from Lake Eola, featuring the construction site of the Robert Meyer Hotel in 1958. Later renamed Kahler Plaza, the hotel is presently operating as the Harley Hotel, a luxury accommodation overlooking the lake.

four blacks accused of rape, an ugly riot at Groveland,
d publicity resulting from the trials of the alleged
pists excited passions at the very time that cool heads
d calm deliberation were most needed. Central
oridians' anxieties were further exacerbated by
collections of their encounters with the radical labor
ions in the 1930s.

The Ku Klux Klan began marching all over central
orida. The "invisible empire" even compromised its
isibility in exchange for permission to rally in Eola
rk. With the approval of Mayor William Beardall's
ministration, a Klan meeting was held in the park, but
e city forbade Klan parades, masks, and cross burnings.
osses were burned at other locations in the city, and
nners with the slogans, "Let's Practice Americanism"
d "Wipe Out the Blackburn Gang," were conspicuously
t nearby. The latter was a reference to Harlan
ackburn, suspected of controlling gambling interests in
ntral Florida.

While the Klan expostulated, more responsible people
ted, albeit somewhat reluctantly. The only city in
orida in 1950 still excluding blacks from voting in
emocratic primaries, Orlando finally abolished the
hite Voters' Executive Committee. Mayor Beardall
dered a citywide primary election permitting blacks
vote.

It was a modest beginning. Since blacks comprised a
arter of the city's population — occupying less than a
th of its space — it was nearly impossible for a black
rson to win a citywide election. But as enforcement of
e Voting Rights Act accelerated in the late 1970s,
lando voluntarily adopted a single-member districting
stem for city-council elections, and black
presentation on that body has become commonplace.

School desegregation followed a similar path. At first
ite reluctant to comply with the celebrated Brown
cision of 1954, Orlando and other central Florida
mmunities have now accepted integrated schools as
rmal. The path from total segregation to substantial
tegration was stormy, but perhaps made somewhat
sier by the need for major expansion of the school
stem to provide for a growing population. After serving
Orlando's high school since the late 1920s, the school
East Robinson was changed to a junior high in 1953.
dgewater and Boone high schools were built, along
th numerous elementary facilities. The first school to
tegrate was Durrance Elementary where many Air
rce children — already accustomed to integration —
tended. That was not until 1962, but by the following
ar, only Oak Ridge and Winter Park high schools were
ll all-white, apparently because no qualified blacks had
plied there. Some of the outlying communities did not
tegrate until 1969, when the federal government
plied additional pressure.

While the school situation was still unresolved, civil-
ghts activists began arguing for black admission to
her public facilities as well. Mayor Carr named a ten-
ember interracial council in 1957, and it helped to
se tensions somewhat. "Sit-in" demonstrations
curred in the early 1960s, at downtown lunch
unters and other public places where black admittance
as prohibited. After the tense summer of 1963, the
terracial council moved to integrate all public places.

As mayor from 1941 through 1952, William Beardall
d served in that office longer than any of his
edecessors. An amiable person with a ready wit, he

Ground breaking for
the new Orlando Util-
ities Commission
Building in 1966.

This burial occurred on
the courthouse lawn in
1948. Representative
Tyn Cobb and pub-
lisher Martin Andersen
wanted to consolidate
the tax collector's
offices, simplify the
election process, and
employ a county man-
ager. Their legislation
was defeated in 1948,
but all three measures
passed during the next
quarter-century.

had been quite popular while leading the city through World War II and the periods of readjustment and growth afterward. His plans to retire in 1952 brought swift reaction from prominent business leaders. They were especially concerned because of a stormy battle between Beardall and three commissioners, E.B. Moses, Walter Bass, and William James. The debate centered on the mayor's authority to handle personnel and budgetary matters according to long-accepted practices. Beardall's supporters hastily formed the "Better Government Committee" to induce the mayor to seek a fifth term. When Beardall declined to run again, the committee tried to draft J. Stanley Bumby to succeed him, but Bumby also declined.

At the same time, the West Church Street Improvement Association, a group of leading businessmen, circulated a petition to recall the three dissident commissioners. The recall election was never held, but when E.B. Moses was defeated in the 1952 election, matters quieted down. J. Rolfe Davis was elected mayor, polling a majority of 10,391 votes, the largest turnout in city history to that time. Davis served until 1956, during which time Orange Avenue was extended southward across a causeway over Lake Lucerne to Kuhl Avenue. Kuhl Avenue became a part of Orange, and the causeway was named in honor of Mayor Davis.

Robert S. Carr succeeded Davis, serving from 1956 until his death in 1967. A moderate man of great patience, he presided over a city which was undergoing enormous physical and social changes. His leadership won the respect of both white and black leaders who cooperated with him to make the transition much less difficult than it might have been. In 1977, the restored municipal auditorium was named the Bob Carr Performing Arts Center in his honor. (In 1973, a beautiful park was built on the site of the old police building at the corner of Orange and South streets. The park was named in honor of former Mayor Beardall who, at 83, was present at the dedication ceremony.)

BROTHER JACOB

A familiar site on Orlando streets in the 1950s was "Brother" Jacob Mueller, whose patriarchal beard, colorful garb, and cryptic commentary earned him a place as the city's genuine eccentric. A Russian immigrant who arrived in New York in 1892, he made his home in Orlando from 1950 until his death in 1965 at the venerable age of 93. A staunch individualist who refused private charity or official "old-age assistance," he was supported by his five children — who were probably pleased that he subsisted on vegetables and rainwater.

Building renovation details, Central at Orange.

136

CNA Building from Beardall Park.

A VERY UN-LADYLIKE LADY

In 1960, natural disaster visited Orlando twice. First, excessive rainfall — more than ten inches in four days — caused serious flooding in some of the new subdivisions. Westside Manor residents had to be evacuated by boat, and many never returned. Frustrated residents and more fortunate neighbors soon renamed the subdivision "Wetside Manor."

Then in September, Hurricane Donna swept through central Florida, inflicting more damage on Orlando than any hurricane before her. Donna caught the city by surprise. No one had even considered leaving the area. They simply bought extra food, boarded up their windows, and filled their tubs with water for drinking — just in case. They were soon grateful they had done so. Donna pounded the city with fierce winds and heavy rain, uprooting many beautiful oaks and snapping power lines. When the power went out, many startled residents, who were watching television, wondered what had

happened to the Miss America Pageant, and whether t[hey] soon would have more serious concerns. About 20,00[0] families were left without power for several days, and many couldn't even leave their homes. Streets were either flooded or blocked by crackling power lines, th[e] sewer system backed up in some areas, and property damage was severe. Fortunately, the hurricane took relatively few lives, and most deaths occurred closer t[o] the center of the storm.

Neither physical disasters nor social controversy interfered with the phenomenal growth of the area. When President John F. Kennedy announced in 1961 t[hat] the United States would put a man on the moon withi[n] ten years, Brevard County declared itself the "Gatewa[y to] the Moon." The announcement dismayed Orlando leaders, who interpreted it as a threat to their city's preeminence in central Florida. They reacted by changing their "City Beautiful" to the "Action Center [of] Florida," and then tried to figure out how to put substance behind the new slogan. First they had to bolster the city's position as a transportation center. Herndon Airport, formerly the Municipal Airport, was [no] longer adequate because the runways were too short [for] modern jetliners. But there didn't seem to be enough time — and possibly enough money — to replace it.

Civic leaders instead proposed a bold plan to share space with the Air Force at McCoy Air Force Base (formerly Pine Castle). The base had been expanded t[o] handle B-47 jet bombers, and had three runways. Afte[r] extended negotiations, Orlando obtained the unusual privilege of using an active military base for landing civilian jet aircraft. The city was granted the use of a 12,500-foot runway, taxi ramps, and land on which to build a terminal. On October 29, 1961, members of th[e] Orlando Chamber of Commerce watched a Delta Airli[ne] Convair 880 inaugurate jet service from Orlando to L[os] Angeles. Eastern Air Lines initiated jet service to easte[rn] seaboard cities in early 1962.

Conventional commercial aircraft continued to land [at] Herndon until late 1965, when the Air Force granted [for] joint use of McCoy AFB for commercial aviation. The[n] in 1968, Mayor Carl Langford signed a long-term lease with the Air Force, giving the city full control of civili[an] air traffic at McCoy. The cost to the city — one dollar.

Community leaders. Right, Dr. James R. Smith (1918-1977) was a prominent black physician and leader of the Washington Shores community. Far right, S. David Starr was Orange County sheriff from 1948 to 1971. One of the most colorful personalities to hold that office, he is shown here with Mrs. Starr campaigning for reelection.

Grace Smith (1884-1962) came to the Orlando area in the early 1900s when her husband, Charles F. Mather-Smith, retired with a fortune from his Chicago paper manufacturing business. The two built a 22-room home overlooking Lake Apopka near Oakland, and enriched the social life of Orlando and central Florida while scandalizing their neighbors. Their lavish parties were the "talk of the town."

One of the legends which still circulates about Mrs. Smith involves a party that was about to begin when she suddenly had to make a hurried trip to Orlando. Stopped by a constable and fined ten dollars as she sped through Ocoee, she hastily handed him a twenty-dollar bill and told him to keep the change because she would be "coming back through here flying like hell in a few minutes."

Mrs. Smith was responsible for several personal and public projects. Dissatisfied with the golfing facilities of west Orange County, Mrs. Smith had her own country club built. She was also interested in the theater, and sponsored a series of vaudeville acts, skits featuring local talent, and a chorus at the old Orlando opera house. A beautiful woman, she posed for photographs to be used on the citrus labels of local packing houses.

Despite her generosity, Mrs. Smith's style was too much for the Oakland community, and she remained an outsider and subject of social outrage until her death.

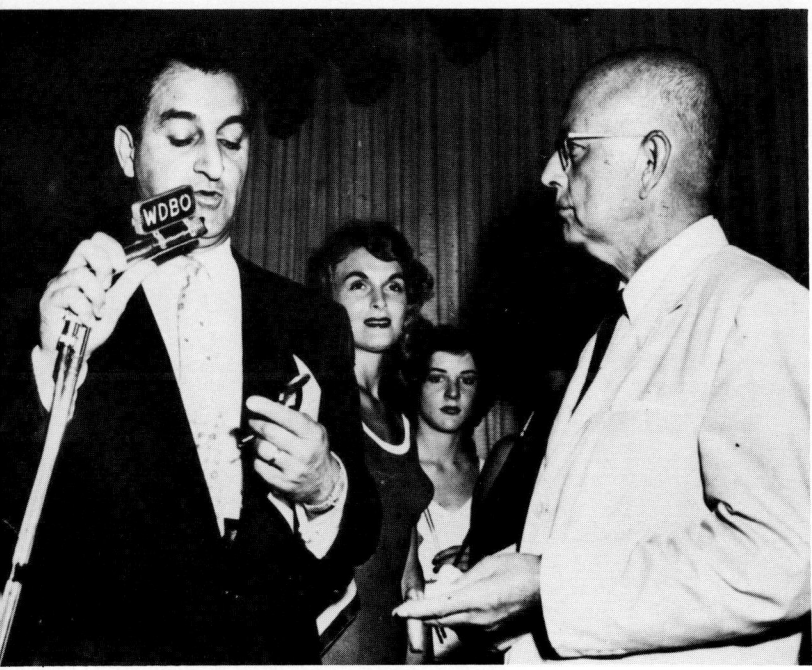

Mayor Bob Carr, giving the key of the city to Danny Thomas, during a 1958 fashion show at the Cherry Plaza Hotel.

Ben F. White was a prominent horse trainer who wintered in Orlando and spearheaded plans to make the area a winter training center for trotters.

Windows on Park Avenue.

*Hub of the wheel.
Right, when the Orange
Blossom Trail was the
major north-south
artery through central
Florida, a business dis-
trict developed along
that route. This sign
was erected to ensure
that tourists did not
miss downtown
Orlando. Below left,
directions to the
Beeline Expressway, a
toll road which opened
in the late 1960s to
facilitate travel
between McCoy Airport
and Cape Canaveral.
Below right, the inter-
section of I-4 and the
Florida Turnpike, early
in the development of
Florida Center.*

ALL ROADS SHOULD LEAD TO ORLANDO

Civic leaders were also determined to keep Orlando the hub of highway travel, as it had been since the 1920s. Highway 50 and Orange Blossom Trail (U.S. 441) were both widened in the city limits. And as the state added new limited-access highways to attract more tourists, city boosters made sure their town was included on the new routes. The Sunshine Parkway (subsequently the Florida Turnpike) was opened in 1963. It connected Orlando with I-75 at Wildwood and with the lower east coast through Fort Pierce. Interchanges at Highway 50 near Winter Garden, I-4 near the Martin plant, and U.S. 17-92 between Orlando and Kissimmee assured increasing commercial development all around the city.

The completion in 1965 of Interstate-4 connected Orlando with Daytona Beach and Tampa, but did not end the controversy about the road. A bitter battle over its routing through the city had begun in 1957. Downtown Orlando merchants supported the state's plan to run the new road along Orange Avenue through both Winter Park and Orlando. Several citizens, however, were concerned that the route would damage the downtown and Lake Ivanhoe areas. They formed a Citizens' Expressway Association, and argued for a new route through the western part of the city. The two sides finally agreed to compromise. I-4 was routed along the western edge of Winter Park, but then crossed Lake Ivanhoe and wound precariously through the heart of Orlando. The city continued to be the hub of central Florida's highway system, but the accident rate on I-4 through the downtown area was — and remains — quite high.

There was yet one missing link. None of Orlando's new roads had brought the McCoy Jetport any closer to Cape Canaveral. If McCoy was to be the airport for the space center, another high-speed road seemed necessary. At a cost of more than $3 million, a seventeen-mile road was built by Hubbard Construction Company, connecting McCoy to State Road 520 to Cocoa. Named the Martin Andersen Beeline in honor of *The Orlando Sentinel's* retiring publisher and longtime advocate of good roads, it was the final link in fulfilling Orlando's claim as the Action Center of Florida.

CHAPTER TEN

THE CITY BEAUTIFUL

*White on white — the St. James Cath-
olic Cathedral and Pan American Bank.*

Something was happening to Orlando in 1965. Something big. The rumors rumbled out of the citrus groves, through the diners and offices, and over the backyard fences. Somebody, somewhere, for some reason, was buying land in southwest Orange and Osceola counties at prices remarkable even for central Florida. Five thousand acres here, then another 10,000 acres over there. But why? What was the "mystery industry" that needed so much space and had so much money?

Some said it must be a gigantic nuclear power plant. Others said only Howard Hughes would move so clandestinely. The more practical ones thought it might have something to do with aviation — possibly McDonnell Aircraft or Lockheed. For months, *Orlando Sentinel* reporters badgered Florida Ranchlands, Inc., for tidbits of information about its client. In mid-May, when reporters were finally given information about the 47 sales transactions, the name Walt Disney joined the mystery list. Store owners on the fringes of the 30,000-acre tract reported that Californians were always visiting their stores — but they were closemouthed. Then Disney himself flew to Cape Kennedy — ostensibly to research a movie about space — and the *Sentinel* learned that he had also rented a helicopter and toured the mystery tract. Still, the *Sentinel* pieced the story together only weeks ahead of Disney's official announcement on November 15, 1965.

The project would be twofold, said Disney. The $100 million Walt Disney World would be similar to California's Disneyland, but "bigger and better," offering total entertainment for the millions of Americans it was sure to attract. The second phase, an Environmental Prototype Community of Tomorrow (EPCOT), would be constructed later.

As Henry Swanson later wrote in *Countdown for Agriculture*, "the Disney thunderbolt struck and set off a wave of speculation which few seemed to comprehend." Land values in Osceola, Orange, and Seminole counties soared. A 1,500-acre parcel of swampland near the Disney buildings — which had sold in 1964 for

Architectural excitement at EPCOT. Left, Spaceship Earth at night. Below, the French Pavilion.

Inspecting the balloons at Walt Disney World.

Main Street at dusk, Walt Disney World.

A wild ride on the water slide at River Country, Walt Disney World.

$168,000 — was resold in 1966 for over $2 million. Multimillion-dollar transactions became commonplace as investors, anticipating the flood of tourists, purchased sites deemed suitable for hotels and motels, service stations, restaurants, and other tourist attractions.

The promise of thousands of new jobs magnified the population boom. More than 4,000 workers were needed to build the Disney theme park alone, and thousands more would be needed to operate it later. By the time Walt Disney World opened in October 1971, the Orlando area was growing much faster than the rest of the state, which was itself exceeding the national growth rate. In its first two years, Walt Disney World entertained more than 20 million visitors, had gross sales of $3.2 billion, and employed 13,000 people with an annual payroll of $365 million.

Sea World, the largest of the numerous attractions built in the wake of Walt Disney World, opened in late 1973. A $20 million sea-life park, it entertained as many as 20,000 visitors a day by early 1974. During peak periods these facilities caused long traffic jams along Interstate-4, and despite the furious rate at which motels were being built, many visitors had to stay as far as 50 miles away.

One of the larger commercial developments was Major Center (now Florida Center), on 3,000 acres around the intersection of I-4 and the Florida Turnpike. Major Realty Corporation, the project developers, envisioned five villages, each with its own commercial or industrial center. Its elaborate Cypress Creek Golf Club was completed in the mid-1970s. Howard Johnson soon erected a ten-story motor lodge with a restaurant. An even larger project was a Sheraton Inn with twin, twenty-story towers that have become a landmark visible from both the interstate highway and the turnpike. The huge concentration of tourist facilities along International Drive is an outgrowth of the Major Center undertaking.

The frenzied building boom was not limited to the Walt Disney World area. All along the interstate for 30 miles to the northeast, along the Kissimmee highway, and at crucial interchanges with other highways, tourist-related businesses cropped up with amazing speed. The cost of land reached such a premium that residential builders turned away from the traditional single-family homes. Instead, they constructed apartment complexes

"Worlds" of fun. Left, children enjoy a close-up view of Shamu at Sea World. Below, a Circus World visitor clowns around with the regulars.

The Central Florida Fair brings out the daredevil in just about everyone.

An electrifying halftime program at the Florida Citrus Bowl.

Orlando is host to the USTA Junior Championship Tournament every July.

and condominiums, often in the form of high-rise buildings to maximize the use of now-precious space.

By the late 1960s, it was becoming increasingly difficult to distinguish between once-separate communities. Semoran Boulevard (State Road 436), conceived as an outer loop connecting the communities of Orange and south Seminole counties, was nearing completion in 1969. Within a few years, it was engulfed by the growing suburbs. Goldenrod sprawled along and to the east of Semoran. Casselberry filled up the open space on both sides of the highway as it spread eastward from U.S. 17-92. Both Winter Park and Maitland built out to Semoran on the east and spread westward.

Few towns were unaffected. Altamonte Springs had been for decades a small rural community with a two-lane, tree-lined main street surrounded by citrus groves. Then, in the late 1960s, Mayor Lawrence Swofford, an enthusiastic advocate of economic development and city expansion, presided over the sleepy community's transformation. Apartment complexes, new businesses, and shopping malls — including the massive Altamonte Mall — replaced citrus groves. The city limits were expanded until Altamonte Springs abutted Forest City on the west and Longwood on the north. The flow of commuters and shoppers brought the city some unwelcome fame as the site of central Florida's most congested interchange at I-4 and S.R. 436.

Near the western end of S.R. 436 Forest City, a quiet community noted for its Seventh-day Adventist Academy and a citrus processing plant, began filling up as well. Only Apopka remained a clearly identifiable town, but it was also being drawn into metropolitan Orlando by the 1970s.

Wispy clouds reflect off the gleaming window-walls of Southeast Bank.

THE GOOD LIFE IN THE COUNTRY

Even while the existing communities were interlocking, plans were underway for luxury developments beyond the suburbs. More than two miles northwest of Apopka, Richard L. Marks developed Errol Estates, a country-club community featuring golf courses and beautiful homes. Near the old Clay Springs community, Everett Huskey built Sweetwater Oaks, a community of fashionable homes for the very wealthy, or at least the definitely upper-middle class. Sweetwater Oaks rapidly became a bedroom community for executives of companies moving into Orlando. Other luxury developments included the Springs, Tuscawilla, and Rio Piñar. To the southwest amid the citrus groves near Windermere, Arnold Palmer started his exclusive Bay Hill development. Each of the expensive new developments had its own golf course and country club. Most have sponsored golf tournaments capable of drawing the best of touring golfers, attracting even more national attention to the area.

Construction of commercial and professional office space was also proceeding at near-warp speed. The most spectacular of these was the nineteen-story CNA tower,

Performing arts. Top, the Florida Symphony Orchestra in concert with the Bach Festival Choir and visiting artists. The Bach Festival was founded at Rollins College in 1936 by Isabel Sprague-Smith.

Right and above, the past and present homes of the Florida Symphony Orchestra, a major regional orchestra with 70 musicians performing classical, popular, and educational concerts throughout the state. The revival of the orchestra, after World War II, was made possible by the support and initiative of John Tiedtke, Mayor Robert S. Carr (for whom the new facility is named), and Helen E. Ryan, a local business woman.

lt by the Connecticut National Assurance Company at ange Avenue and Jackson Street. Others included the ger Center near Colonial Plaza and Crane's Roost in amonte Springs.

By 1973, however, a mismatch between supply and mand began to reveal itself. Although the boom had ught its share of high-salaried executives into the a, the majority of metropolitan Orlando's 250,000 rkers were not of that stature. Thousands worked at tourist attractions and in tourist-related services. Very v developers had provided affordable homes for the derate-income families. They had, however, provided nty of apartment and office space — far more, they n realized, than was needed.

At the same time, the national economy began fering from the oil shortage, a general recession, and precedented inflation. The national recession and local erbuilding stagnated parts of the Orlando economy. nstruction workers had to find new jobs or leave the rket. Rising interest rates and inflation further dened the gap between the price of housing and the lity of home-seekers to pay. But with woeful dictions that increased oil prices would end the age the automobile, it seemed that many people were termined to have one more vacation. The tourist lustry held up, and in turn sustained the community, using less disruption in central Florida than in the tion as a whole.

BEYOND TOURISM

The arrival of Walt Disney World in the mid-1960s had shifted Orlando's economy heavily toward tourism, but military and space activities remained important to the area. When the mission of Orlando AFB diminished early in the decade, local leaders sought a new role for the installation. After lengthy negotiations, it was announced that the Navy's basic-training activities at Bainbridge, Maryland, would be transferred to Orlando. The Orlando Naval Training Center opened in mid-1968. With nearly 6,000 permanent employees and several thousand recruits, the base remains an important part of the local economy.

The growing population brought changes in higher education. Rollins College continued its role as a private liberal arts institution, but the private Orlando Junior College gave way to Valencia Community College in 1967. Seminole Community College near Lake Mary opened at about the same time.

The state university system was also expanding. Central Floridians convinced the legislature to provide them with a senior institution. Florida Technological University (now the University of Central Florida) was approved in 1965. The Apopka Sportsmen's Club offered to donate a 1,000-acre building site — where Wekiwa State Park is now located — but the school was built

Naval personnel from the Navy Training Center, at Church Street Center.

instead on 1,200 acres of pine barrens in east Orange County. Because of the extensive space program on the coast, the state reasoned that FTU should be so located to make it a strong engineering school. There was some concern in the early 1970s when much of the space program was moved to Houston, Texas. But the school continued along its original path, and by the mid-1970s was an important reason for the influx of high-technology industries into central Florida.

In 1981 and 1982, nearly 100 firms announced plans to relocate or expand their businesses in the area. Westinghouse opened a large research and development facility in east Orange County near UCF. The U.S. Navy is planning a large facility in the university's new research park. Several other firms are already planning to build there. Martin-Marietta is building a second plant in east Orange County. AT&T's recently completed data center and J.C. Penney's planned credit office are examples of numerous small additions to the area economy. And Harcourt Brace Jovanovich, Inc., a major publishing firm which also owns Sea World, is nearing completion of its headquarters in southwest Orlando.

For most of Orlando's history, its prosperity has come from its abundant natural resources — a clean, warm, and sunny environment, plentiful fish and game in the undeveloped countryside, and land suitable for citrus and vegetable agriculture. But the recent changes have dramatically shifted the delicate balance of nature. Former county agent Henry Swanson recently lamented the "countdown for agriculture," as dairy pastures became manufacturing plants and orange groves became shopping centers and residential developments.

Agriculture still plays a major, if diminishing, role in the central Florida economy. Citrus Central, Inc., near

Relaxing moments. Above, a University of Central Florida student ponders the newspaper. Right, a serene moment at the monument at Kraft Gardens.

*The Confederate Soldier Memorial at
Eola Park.*

*Downtown workers enjoy the results of
Orlando's downtown Streetscape
project.*

Modern dance. Above, a dancer in
costume at the Strawberry Spring Festival, Leu Gardens. Below, a Southern
Ballet Theater dancer rests at rehearsal.

Arts, past and present. Above, visitors to Lake Eola admire the artwork at Festival in the Park. Right, members of the Orlando Art Association gather at the Lee Tieman home in Merrit Park in 1927.

Water fun. Above, canoeing is a popular pastime on the Wekiva River. Right, boating was also popular at Clay Springs in the 1890s, but it is difficult to imagine that the people posing in the picture are dressed for it.

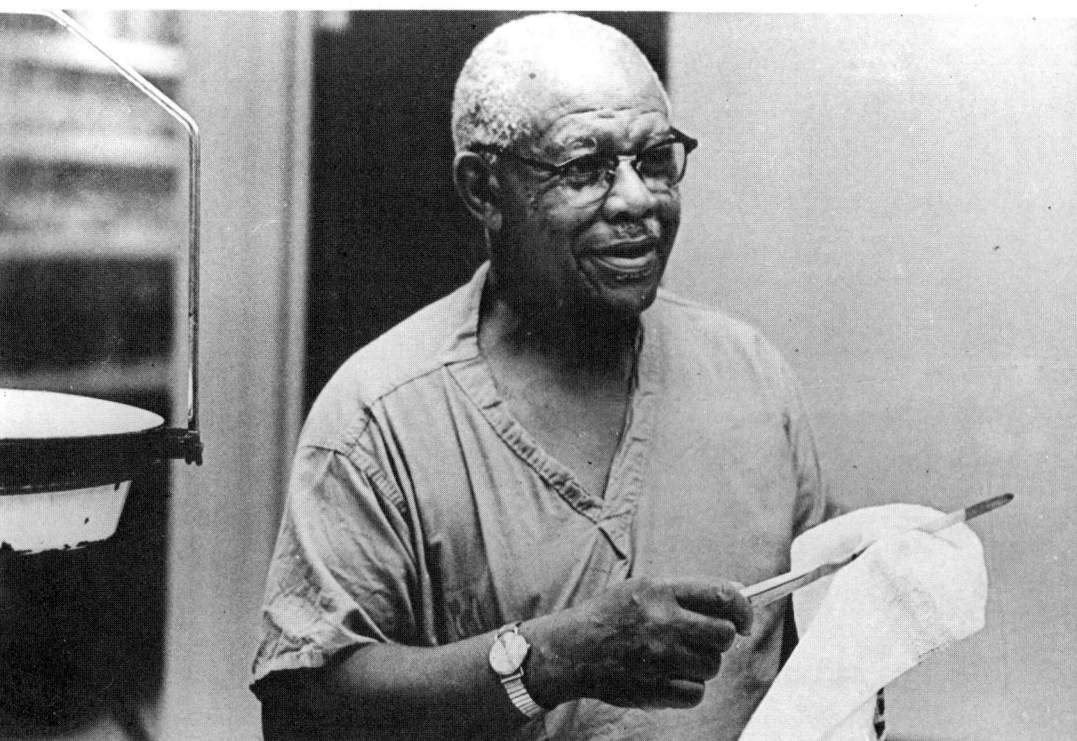

Tim Hale, one of the oldest employees of the Orlando Regional Medical Center, joined the staff in 1922.

A PLACE TO LEARN, A FUTURE TO BUILD

What remains of the old Callahan School at Parramore Avenue and Washington Street is important to Orlando's history, and is symbolic of days when education was prized and, for some, difficult to acquire.

Heralded as a black community landmark, Callahan's history is of a fiber that weaves throughout the educational history of blacks in central Florida. Education for Orlando's black schoolchildren formally was established in November 1882, when the Orange County School Board approved a petition to open the Orlando Colored School.

Located in a frame building at Garland and Church streets, the school first was headed by principal I.S. Hankins. Before 1900, the school moved to Jefferson and Chatham streets and was renamed Johnson Academy, in honor of its second prinicpal, L.C. Johnson.

Johnson Academy's third principal, L.C Jones, came to the school in 1912 and helped build what is now known as Callahan School. Jones' family donated land at Parramore and Washington for the school, which opened in 1921 as Jones High School, with grades six through ten. Elementary students remained at Johnson Academy until additional wings were built at Jones.

The first high-school commencement was held for graduating seniors in 1931.

For years, Jones High School and Hungerford Normal and Industrial School in Eatonville offered the only formal education to blacks in central Florida.

Hungerford, on the site of what is now Wymore

Career Educational Center, opened in 1899 as a private boarding school for black high-school students. In the 1930s, the Florida Circuit Court and Florida Supreme Court declared Hungerford an esential part of the "Negro Education System" and ordered it protected as a "high-class private school." Prior to 1939, when Hungerford became a public school, blacks throughout south Seminole County and the Winter Park area traveled to Jones for high school classes.

Because there were few high schools in the state that would admit black students, blacks from as far away as Miami traveled to Jones and Hungerford. Hungerford students lived on campus, and students who attended Jones lived with families in the Orlando area.

Although the Jones High School building was a modern facility, built by community men and women with donated materials, classroom teachers had to rely on used and sometimes outdated schoolbooks and equipment handed down from white schools. Still, achievement was emphasized, and portraits of outstanding black scholars, educators, and scientists were focal points in school hallways. A majority of Jones High School students went on to black colleges across the country. Several graduates have achieved local and national acclaim.

Among the notables are Orlando City Councilman Nap Ford; Wilbur Gary, of Orlando's Downtown Development Board and head of the Orlando Vocational-Technical Center; Abraham Peterson, head of dentistry at Meharry Medical College in Tennessee; Dr. Joseph Bruton, a

Arthur R. "Pappy" Kennedy became
Orlando's first black city commissioner
when he was elected in 1972.

An Alpha Phi Alpha
fraternity meeting at
the St. Mark AME
Church in 1978.

biochemist and medical researcher at Walter Reed Army Hospital; Dr. Maxie C. Maultsby, a nationally known psychiatrist; Albert Nelson, head of Orlando's human relations department; and Elijah Rogers, city administrator of Washington, D.C. All these people graduated before Jones moved to its current location.

Burgeoning school enrollment in the early 1950s made it necessary to build a new and larger facility. When Jones High School moved to its current site at 1400 West Cypress Street in 1952, Orange County School Board officials created Callahan Elementary at Jones' former location.

Callahan, named for Orlando physician Dr. J.B. Callahan, served as an all-black elementary until 1970, when the school system was integrated. The school was closed, and the building was used for storage and offices until it was sold to the city of Orlando in 1976.

The city planned to demolish the building to expand and landscape Callahan Park. Plans called for the addition of lighting to existing tennis courts and construction of new basketball and handball courts. Planners also hoped to save about 8,000 bricks from the original school to refurbish or rebuild the playground's recreation building, and to create a historic museum of Callahan neighborhood artifacts. The proposed changes would have cost about $318,000.

Neighborhood residents and former school students, however, fought heartily against plans to raze the school. After a series of compromises, the city was persuaded to keep part of the school

intact. Early in 1984, the city agreed to spend up to $500,000 to rebuild the dilapidated landmark. Orange County commissioners also allocated $100,000 to the project.

Because of the building's extreme deterioration from weather and water damage, builders will save only portions of the front wall and entrance, to capture and preserve Callahan's image. The rest of the building will be demolished. A 10,606-square-foot community building, designed by Tampa architect Robert Wilson, will be constructed, incorporating the original facade and using bricks from the old school.

Included in the facility — which will be about one-fourth the size of the original school — will be classrooms, a community/game room, an exhibition hall, offices, and storage space. The city plans to use the reconstructed building for neighborhood and community service programs, arts and crafts classes, and meetings. The new Callahan Neighborhood Center is expected to be finished by April 1985.

Orlando also plans to develop the park — adding a field for soccer or football, picnic grills and shelters, and basketball, baseball, and racquetball courts — and to build low-income housing in the neighborhood. When the projects are completed, this important part of the city's heritage will have been both preserved and revitalized.

Julie Johnson,
Orlando Sentinel

163

Orange County has had a strong League of Women Voters chapter since the 1920s. Here, Mrs. George Anderson, president of the local branch, is shown with Mrs. Henry Killen and state president Margaret Piper.

Lockhart, and the Winter Garden Citrus Products Cooperative are the largest of the central Florida firms which still sell hundreds of millions of dollars' worth of fresh fruit and citrus products annually. A wide variety of winter vegetables are still grown in the extensive lowlands, which are less suited to development. Many growers have turned to production of foliage plants — ferns and ornamentals that require much less space because of intensive growing methods. Their cultivation is so important that Apopka now calls itself the "Indoor Foliage Capital."

The loss of farmland to development, however, has increased the problems of flood control and waste-water runoff. The runoff from the many parking lots and streets is making it impossible for the city lakes to continue to serve as catch basins. And with the population now crossing the borders of three counties, it is no longer acceptable for one political entity to dump its sewage

into streams that run into its neighbors' terrain. While many of the lakes and streams still offer excellent fishi others, like Lake Apopka, are no longer producing thei previous bounty. And perhaps most crucial of all, the growing population cannot continue to increase its us of water from a subsurface honeycombed with limesto that can and does collapse when the water table drops

Without the fields to separate the towns, local governments have found themselves increasingly overlapping one another. There is a compelling need f these groups to cooperate to solve the problems they now share. A glaring example is the highly visible decline of the Orange Blossom Trail business district, now congested with flesh-peddling businesses and wit individuals who purvey their wares in neon-lit audacity That it lies partly within the city's jurisdiction and par in Orange County, increases the difficulty of reviving – or at least controlling — the area.

THE WORLD'S MOST FAMOUS SINKHOLE

On May 9, 1981, after an extended drought — 70 days without a drop of rain — central Florida gained a new and unexpected tourist attraction when "the World's Most Famous Sinkhole" appeared in downtown Winter Park. Immediately consuming several expensive Porsche cars, Mae Owens' home, a large corner of a public swimming pool, and a portion of a city street, it spread several hundred feet across, threatening eventually to consume the Porsche agency and other businesses on Fairbanks Avenue.

News of the calamity spread across the nation and the world, and central Florida tourists added the sinkhole to the list of attractions they wished to see. Equal to the occasion, local entrepreneurs

made the most of the situation. Roger Holler's Chevrolet dealership, just across Fairbanks Avenue from the sinkhole, was soon advertising its "sinkhole sale," and the usual T-shirts and assorted trinkets were hawked by peddlers at the site. A Sinkhole Institute was quickly established at the University of Central Florida amid visions of lucrative research grants. Meanwhile, the city of Winter Park was trying to decide what to do with its new hole in the ground. Nature probably had more to do with that, however, than any political entity. After several days of uncertainty, the crater stabilized and began to fill with water. The man who lost his Porsches was even able to retrieve some of his lost property.

While central Florida has benefited mightily from the sinkholes which have produced many beautiful lakes, no one was sure about how to handle the gaping crater until it, too, could be transformed into a lake. As the sinkhole neared its third birthday, it seemed to be developing a split personality. The side of the hole on which the public park was situated was landscaped into a lake — but the side adjacent to the Fairbanks Avenue businesses was a morass of broken concrete and rubble dumped by the owners to prevent the hole from spreading and consuming their establishments. Rob Morse, an Orlando Sentinel columnist who recently joined the central Florida "worlds" with his "Column World," wrote that the phenomenon is no longer a sinkhole, but rather a "sinkhalf," looking very much like a natural calamity on one side and a piece of desirable lakefront property on the other.

The story of the Winter Park sinkhole has not ended. As more and more people come to live or visit the area, some are wondering if the sinkhole's appearance was a unique event — or a portent of things to come.

By the time Ivey's closed its downtown store in 1976, the shopping malls had virtually replaced the central business district. At the same time, ge commercial parks such as Maitland Center and thland Executive Park were competing with wntown for new tenants.

But the downtown business district did not die. In 72, the voters approved a downtown taxing district, d the Orlando Central City Neighborhood Board (now wntown Orlando, Inc.) was formed to help city ders save downtown. One of its first downtown jects was Bob Snow's purchase and restoration of the mons Department Store on West Church Street. It on opened to a rousing reception as Rosie O'Grady's od Time Emporium. Snow has since added three other ilities. Other individuals, such as Mack Meiner, have ned him in opening successful downtown restaurants d specialty shops.

In the mid-1970s, the Downtown Orlando velopment Corporation purchased several empty wntown buildings with the intention of restoring and

SQUEEZING OUT THE ORANGE GROVES

By 1977, it was hardly an uncommon occurrence. An old citrus grove, which once belonged to Miss Mary Compton, an Orlandoan well-known throughout Florida for her garden club activities, was bulldozed and replaced with a supermarket and an assortment of commercial establishments.

But this time it was different. For this time, the grove was on Orange Avenue, a street once named for the abundance of groves lining its path — and this was the avenue's last grove. People had become so accustomed to it that they rarely thought about it, and many were surprised when the trees were bulldozed to reveal a once stately 50-year-old home. It, too, was bulldozed to make way for a Publix Market expansion and an Albertson food store, and by 1978, Orange Avenue was orange in name only.

Bob Snow's Rosie O'Grady's Good Time Emporium in downtown Orlando.

selling them. Although that enterprise foundered, some of the buildings were sold. Maguire, Voorhis, and Wells — one of the city's major law firms since 1921 — acquired the old Dickson and Ives Building and converted it into a handsome office facility now known as Two South Orange. Across the street the old Yowell-Drew-Ivey Building has also been restored and enlarged as the downtown branch of Freedom Bank (formerly ComBanks).

Recent changes in tax legislation favoring preservation of historic buildings have contributed greatly to the revival of downtown. With assistance from the city's community development department, many investors have begun to refurbish landmark buildings. The Kuhl-Delaney Building, the first brick building erected after the 1884 fire; the James L. Giles Building, dating from 1885; and the Rogers Building (the English Club), built in 1887, have all been restored. An entire block of small buildings along Pine Street is now being refurbished. The Dr. Phillips Theatre Building and the Beacham Theatre have both been restored.

New construction is resuming as well, partly because of consolidation of independent banks into large holding companies. Some of the largest of these firms have constructed impressive towers in the downtown area, providing expanses of attractive office space and helping

to convert downtown Orlando from a state of impendi decay to one of vibrant daytime activity.

Efforts are now being made to balance that trend w an active night life. The recently modernized Centropl with its Bob Carr Performing Arts Center is expected be augmented soon by a large hotel. A downtown spor arena is also planned for the Centroplex. Emphasis is a being placed on residential development. When about 15,000 people showed up for a recent evening promotional event, there was increased confidence tha downtown Orlando can become a round-the-clock cen once again.

THE CRITICAL ISSUE

The survival of the agriculture industry and the revival of downtown have assured that at least some of the essence of old Orlando will remain But Orlando today is a tourist-based metropolis, and it survival as such depends more on adequate transportation than any other issue.

The need for a new international airport was recognized more than a decade ago. By the early 1970 the McCoy Jetport was being taxed to its limits to keej up with the increasing flow of passengers. In 1973, 3.2

PIONEERING AVIATORS

Orlando's long association with aviation began with Lincoln Beachey's successful flights at the 1910 fair. Numerous area residents became interested in flying as a result. While some used their official positions to bring civilian as well as military aviation facilities to the city, others pioneered in the air.

Carl Kuhl, the son of a pioneer Orlando family, was so impressed by Beachey's aerial demonstrations in 1910 that he soon learned to fly and became Florida's first licensed pilot. Within a few years it was Kuhl who was captivating Orlando crowds by his stunt flying at the midwinter fairs. In an empty warehouse in Jacksonville in 1915, Kuhl also constructed the second airplane to be built in the state. During World War I he trained pilots for the balloon corps before pursuing a career with United Airlines.

Helen McBride of Apopka received her pilot's license in the mid-1930s and went on to become a cross-country racer and World War II flying instructor. In January 1939, she flew to Miami and Havana in national competition, and in June she was the only woman in a 100-plane "aircade" sponsored by the Florida Branch of the National Aeronautical Association during the New York World's Fair. When World War II began, Mrs. McBride first taught in the Civilian Pilot's Training Course at Stetson University before establishing her own flying school. With four airplanes in 1942, she offered primary training to military pilots at Ryan Field at Apopka. She

continued her flying school at Ryan Field until 1952.

Joseph Kittinger Jr. brought notice to Orlando in 1957 when he established an altitude record in lighter-than-air craft by taking a balloon to 95,000 feet. Three years later he jumped from a balloon at 103,000 feet over New Mexico and walked away safely. Shot down and imprisoned during his third tour in Vietnam, he was one of five Orlandoans to be released and returned home in 1977.

John Young, of College Park, was a football star and honor graduate of Edgewater High School who went on to become one of the first to volunteer for the space program. He made two orbital flights around the earth in 1965 and 1966, and walked on the moon in 1972. He was the chief astronaut for the Apollo-Soyuz flight, and participated in many other space projects.

Orlando-born astronaut John Young, who made two trips to the moon, was honored on John Young Day at the Cherry Plaza Hotel in 1965.

illion people passed through the terminal. At the same ne, the Air Force was ending its long tenure at McCoy. ayor Carl Langford, whose "cracker" demeanor ncealed a brilliant mind, led the way to a mutually tisfactory use of the land on which McCoy was situated. ter the Air Force left in 1974, the $61 million base and out 2,500 acres were transferred to the city, giving it out 6,300 acres on which to build a new airport.

A Greater Orlando Aviation Authority was created in 75, and the commercial airlines serving Orlando reed to help underwrite a bond issue to fund nstruction. After a lengthy controversy over the size of e new facility, a $400 million airport — designed to be sily expanded — was agreed upon. The result was a autiful and convenient international airport, which by 082 was serving six million passengers, many coming om abroad.

Automobile transportation, especially inside the etropolis, was a different matter. The problem was rticularly compounded by the major tourist attractions d by the shopping centers which cater to vacationers. tamonte Mall, the largest in central Florida, with 168 ores, has been a delight for residents and tourists alike, t it has also caused Semoran Boulevard near I-4 to gain e derisive appellation of "the world's longest parking t." A widening project now underway will do little to neliorate the problem. A concentraton of business and tail activity east of downtown has caused similar roblems on East Colonial Drive. Planned construction of e massive Florida Mall at the intersection of Sand Lake ad and South Orange Blossom Trail will compound an already serious situation there.

The opening of EPCOT Center in October 1982, while sustaining Orlando's tourist industry at a time when it might otherwise have lagged, has also added to the transportation problem. This "community of tomorrow" has received an amazingly favorable reception, attracting visitors from all over the world. Other attractions have followed, adding markedly to central Florida's tourist appeal — but also adding to the crowds. One regional planner has predicted that highways of twelve to fourteen lanes would be needed to handle the traffic of the '80s. Financial and logistic difficulties make that possibility unrealistic.

Most planners and public officials agree that some form of mass transportation is essential for the bustling metropolitan complex. By the early 1980s, the tri-county transportation authority (OSOTA) was transporting about 3.5 million passengers per year, and the number of patrons was increasing. Shuttle buses run between distant parking lots and the various centers of downtown activity. But much more is needed.

The questions now being discussed are whether a new rapid-transit system should be publicly or privately financed, what kind of vehicle should be used, and where it should go. The critical areas, most planners agree, are between the airport, downtown Orlando, and the attractions southwest of the city, with the likelihood of a subsequent expansion into south Seminole County. Completion of this most desperately needed long-term project should assure Orlando's prosperity as a tourist and trade center well into the twenty-first century.

The intersection of I-4 and Colonial Drive is busy even at night.

RETROSPECT AND PROSPECT

When the Florida Heights League was formed in 1902 to revive "the freeze devastated areas between Altamonte, Fairview, Lake Conway, and Gabriella," its members probably had in mind something quite different from what has happened there. Metropolitan Orlando has spread to and beyond all of the communities mentioned, with the exception of Gabriella — then a huge turpentine camp at the site of present-day Jamestown — and Goldenrod is rapidly growing in that direction. The tourist attractions of the past two decades have stretched the metropolitan area to the west until it now encompasses most western Orange County as well as significant portions of Osceola and Seminole. Perhaps stimulated by the presence of the University of Central Florida, industrial and residential construction are now extending greater Orlando even further to the east in both Orange and Seminole counties.

As the city crossed over county barriers, problems have arisen among the various governments. But recent improvements in communications among those concerned with Orlando's future show much promise. Cooperation and common effort enabled construction of a convention center in southwest Orlando, and similar efforts are funding the long-anticipated sports arena in the downtown Centroplex.

And Orlando, by all accounts, will continue to grow. As it does, special efforts are being made to preserve and enrich the Orlando of the past. Park Avenue, downtown Winter Park's business district, has successfully battled all efforts to destroy its ambience, and has emerged as one of the city's most popular shopping areas. The much larger downtown Orlando is thriving, with the present blending of large office complexes, smaller restored buildings, shopping and entertainment facilities, and residences.

The tourist industry is healthy, but Orlando is no longer a one-industry town. Its central location has made it a major distribution center for retail firms as well as headquarters

for others. The presence of Martin-Marietta and other space-related firms has meant a substantial industrial payroll for Orlando for years, but that has been vastly augmented by the growth of the nearby Harris Corporation and the opening of the Westinghouse plant, as well as numerous electronics firms of varying sizes. As the focal point of central Florida, Orlando also has a substantial commitment to human services. Its hospitals and schools serve a large surrounding area, and the various services offered by both state and

168

national governments are administered here. And, finally, the very presence of 750,000 people creates a large service industry with an extensive work force. Just as any thriving modern city, Orlando has a mixed economy which seems likely to expand during the remainder of the twentieth century and beyond.

But where will the people live? In December 1983, 47 acres of residential land on the Sweetwater Golf Course were sold for $13.5 million. Obviously most of the suitable land has been developed, and what remains is extremely expensive. It is entirely likely that Orlando workers in future years will be commuting to their jobs from Volusia and Lake counties. When that occurs, the isolated town which was served in the 1870s by the "Bumby Express" — lumbering its daylong journey from Orlando to Sanford and back — will have been succeeded by a metropolitan complex where daily commuters routinely travel far greater distances through a far different land.

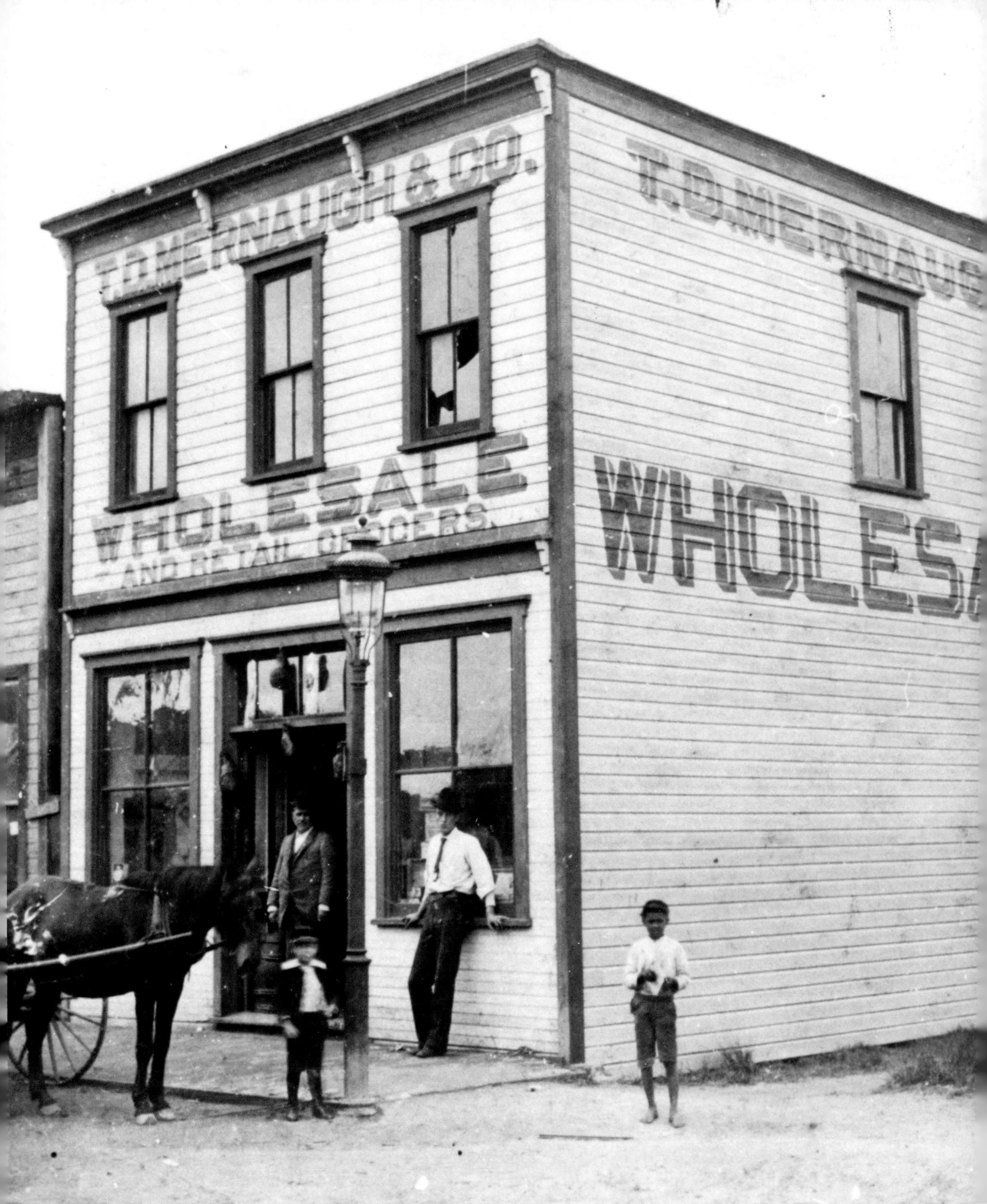

T. D. Mernaugh with a store and warehouse on Church Street at Garland was a major wholesaler of groceries in the 1890s.

PARTNERS IN PROGRESS

Orlando area's partner in progress

Since its beginning in 1913, the Greater Orlando Chamber of Commerce has served as a spark for community and business development and has played a major role in making the Orlando area one of the finest places in this country to live, work, and play.

When incorporated in its initial year, the Chamber represented a small but thriving business community. The organization's first president, J.N. Bradshaw, was one of more than 50 presidents to shape the Chamber's growth until the early 1960s when a "new" Chamber of Commerce emerged.

In October 1964, through the efforts of then President J. Rolfe Davis and President-elect Curtis Stanton, the Chamber steered a new course which would bring that newly energized business organization in line with its community's phenomenal growth over the next decades. Under Stanton's direction, a Fair Share Investment schedule was inaugurated, which was later dubbed the "Orlando Plan" and copied by more than 600 other chambers. Volunteer committees were called into service for the first time, and over 450 Chamber members responded.

Those early years of the newly reorganized and reincorporated Chamber of Commerce saw several "firsts" which were to become Chamber tradition. Events and programs such as the Orange Juice Forum, annual Hob Nob Barbecue, monthly Area Beautification awards, and the annual presentation of the John Young Award continue

The Greater Orlando Chamber of Commerce building, 1968 to the present, located at 75 East Ivanhoe Boulevard.

Orlando's Chamber of Commerce headquarters on Central Avenue housed an active organization until 1968 when its new building was dedicated.

today. Later years would introduce others, such as the Mayors' Prayer Breakfast, Small Business Weekend, Airline Day, the Annual Community Recognition Awards Luncheon, and Leadership Orlando.

By 1966, the Orlando area had grown from a turn-of-the-century population of just under 3,000 to a thriving 372,000. As a prime mover and leader, the Chamber had continued to firmly solidify strong recognition and base support. Coveted accreditation from the

Chamber of Commerce of the United States was awarded to Orlando's Chamber, one of only 100 to earn that status.

Recognizing its new place in the community and wishing to maintain the momentum, the Chamber coined "Action Center" as its slogan and actively promoted itself as well as the entire Orlando area to prospective visitors and industries. The 1960s brought support for the county "resort tax concept," and a four-year effort climaxed in the state's agreement to develop Wekiva State Park. The Chamber assisted in and supported the efforts to secure the U.S. Naval Recruit Training Center in Orlando.

During the 1960s and 1970s, the Chamber continued to be a major catalyst for congressional action and economic understanding. A blue-ribbon Committee of 200 was formed to promote new industry for the area and subsequently helped to bring in such major companies as Stromberg-Carlson and Westinghouse Electric. The Committee merged outside the Chamber in 1977 with the Orlando/Orange County Industrial Board.

The opening of Walt Disney World in 1971 ignited growth unprecedented in the Orlando area. Mail inquiries to the Chamber jumped 50 percent (to more than 60,000), and lobby visitor traffic increased 20 percent. The tourism industry was fast becoming the area's largest employer, touching off growth throughout the entire area. A Travelling Action Team was formed to spread the "Orlando word," and in 1976 logged 500,000 miles visiting 25,000 travel agents nationwide.

On the threshhold of the eighties, the Chamber was in strong position to voice issues of concern of its growing membership. Transportation funding, environmental quality, and education are among areas of primary thrust. The opening of Orlando's new International Airport brought quick Chamber response to new foreign trade and visitor needs.

Since its beginning, the Greater Orlando Chamber of Commerce has had a keen eye to progress. With membership numbering only a handful in 1913, the Chamber has grown to nearly 3,500 business members who participate in shaping the dynamic urban and industrial growth of the Orlando area. The Chamber and the greater Orlando area it serves are partners in progress and together will assure that the Orlando area is the best place to live, work, and play.

Over 60 years of serving Orlando's business community

Akerman, Senterfitt & Eidson is the largest law firm in central Florida, and one of the oldest. With over 60 attorneys and a statewide practice, the firm has long been recognized as a leader among Florida law firms, especially in finance and banking. Akerman, Senterfitt & Eidson has continually expanded its practice areas and is now also a leader in real-estate development, litigation, taxation, securities, environmental law, labor law, and governmental affairs.

The firm was founded in 1922 as Akerman & Akerman by Alexander and Hugh Akerman. Although the firm's practice originally consisted primarily of litigation, it quickly developed a reputation for its aggressive representation of clients. In a short time, the firm represented such clients as the Florida East Coast Railroad and the Dr. Phillips Company, at that time one of the largest citrus growers in central Florida. Following the 1929 appointment of Alexander Akerman as judge of the United States District Court, the firm began broadening its areas of practice as its clients grew with the central Florida economy. In 1933, with all but one of the banks in Orlando closed, the firm's members joined other community leaders in establishing a new bank, The First National Bank At Orlando, which today is Sun Bank, N.A. The new bank retained the Akerman firm to represent its commercial department, and the firm's historic ties to Florida banking began. During this period, William H. "Billy" Dial assumed the lead in the firm's banking practice, and William Y. Akerman joined the firm, developing its real-estate practice.

In the 1940s and 1950s, Akerman, Dial and Akerman developed a pattern of steady growth, fueled by a commitment to serve new businesses relocating to Orlando. During this time, Billy Dial became a leader in the development of central Florida, serving on the Board of Control of Florida in 1953, the Florida State Road Board from 1955 to 1958 and the Florida Development Commission in 1958 to 1959. His many accomplishments include having Interstate 4 and the Florida Turnpike routed through the Orlando area, making Orlando the crossroads which has attracted many new business ventures, including Walt Disney World.

In 1958, a new generation of leadership came to the fore. In that year, Billy Dial resigned from the firm to become president of The First National Bank At Orlando, where he created the holding company which is now Sun Banks, Inc. (He would return to the firm in 1977, upon his retirement from banking, to serve as counsel to the firm.) Upon Dial's departure, the firm merged with a rising Orlando firm, Turnbull & Senterfitt. In the following years, under the leadership of William Y. Akerman, Donald T. Senterfitt, and George T. Eidson Jr., the firm committed itself to a course of expansion to serve the full needs of its clients.

As the Orlando economy moved into the space age, new industries located in the area

In 1947, Akerman, Dial & Akerman moved its offices from the Tinker Building to the second floor of what was then the First Federal Building.

and existing businesses expanded. The firm rapidly became a leader in providing legal services to a clientele with statewide and national interests. By the 1970s, the firm had become the largest law firm in central Florida. The continuing expansion of the firm resulted in the 1979 opening of offices in Tallahassee.

In 1980, Don Senterfitt resigned from the firm to become vice-chairman of Sun Banks,

Inc. A third generation of leadership has since continued upon the charted course of expansion. Offices were opened in Miami in 1983, and the firm has continued broadening its areas of practice. Committed to the twin goals of excellence and service to clients, Akerman, Senterfitt & Eidson will continue to serve the businesses attracted by Orlando's position at the center of Florida's dynamic economy.

The November 10, 1954 closing of the sale of several thousand acres of citrus groves by Dr. Phillips, Inc. to Minute Maid Corporation provided the oranges for the world's first frozen concentrate plant. (L. to R.) William H. "Billy" Dial, Caywood Whitley, J. Thomas Gurney Sr., Holman Cloud, William Y. Akerman, Howard Phillips, and William Speller.

A united approach for cultural Orlando

Life in Orlando is rich with cultural opportunities. Despite its youth, the Orlando community has developed a colorful and dynamic cultural history, leading to the formation of Arts, Inc., in 1982. With the support and cooperation of the following cultural organizations and the foresight of James Fenner and the business community, Orlando can proudly say it has the only united arts fund in Florida. Operating as a division of Arts, Inc., the Arts United Fund raised over $2 million in its first two campaigns in support of the following funded organizations:

The Loch Haven Art Center has grown from a small, dedicated group of art lovers organized in 1924 to a professional organization accredited by the American Association of Museums. Originally a place for only local artists to exhibit and attend classes, the Art Center has assumed a much larger role. Now the thrust in the Art Center's programming is to showcase major exhibitions, establish a permanent art collection, and offer a wide variety of educational opportunities. Located in Loch Haven Park in a 31,698-square-foot facility, the Art Center is a vital hub of cultural activities with the goal of helping people enrich their lives through participation in and awareness of the visual arts.

The Central Florida Civic Theatre, originally called the Orlando Little Theatre and later the Orlando Players, started in 1926 as a movement to provide more activities for young people and was later developed by the City Recreation Board. The Orlando Little Theatre was well organized and independent by 1930, and it was incorporated in 1934. The Civic Theatre steadily progressed to a six-play season in 1949, and the players moved to a renovated house on Montana Avenue where they produced plays from 1959 to 1973 and added Junior Theatre and a Drama School. The establishment of the Theatre Guild in 1969 followed a final name change in 1967. New facilities in 1973 and an expansion in 1979 now support the theater's eleven-show season.

The Florida Symphony Orchestra was organized following World War II, filling a void left by the demise of an Orlando orchestra that operated during the 1930s. Led by John Tiedtke, former Mayor Robert S. Carr and Helen E. Ryan, the Central Florida Symphony Society was organized in 1950 and achieved full professional status in 1952.

Originally a group of 40 musicians, conducted by Yves Chardon and performing a six-concert series, the Florida Symphony continued to develop under the direction of

conductors Frank Miller in 1954, Henry Mazer in 1959, Herman Hertz in 1967, Pavle Despalj in 1970, and then Sidney Rothstein in 1982. Associate conductor Alfred Savia joined the orchestra in 1978. In 1980, James Fenner and the new general manager, Robert S. Gross, led a new board of directors toward an amazing financial recovery. The Florida Symphony now performs throughout the state, presenting varied musical programs to over 150,000 people annually.

The Bach Festival Society, Central Florida's most renowned choral program, marked its beginning in March 1935 on the 250th birthday of Johann Sebastian Bach. In 1985, the Bach Festival Society of Winter Park will mark the 50th in its uninterrupted series of two- and three-day annual festivals in the Knowles Memorial Chapel of Rollins College.

Maestro Sidney Rothstein, Florida Symphony Orchestra.

A professionally trained choir with over 120 voices presents programs of music by the entire Bach family and other master composers. The society also sponsors a Festival Concert Series under the direction of conductor Ward Woodbury.

The Maitland Art Center was created in 1937 when founder Andre Smith designed and executed what was then known as The Research Studio. Beginning in the early 1930s with a studio near Lake Sybelia, Andre Smith received a gift from Mrs. Bok to develop a "laboratory" studio. More studios and living quarters were added, along with courtyards and gardens, all constructed or supervised by Smith until his death in 1959. The

Edyth Bush Theatre.

Maitland Art Center.

Orlando Opera Company's production of Turandot.

buildings are highly decorated with murals, bas-reliefs, and carvings done in an Aztec-Mayan motif. The nonprofit Maitland Art Association reopened the Center in 1971.

The Morse Gallery of Art was originally founded in 1942 as part of Rollins College. Since 1976, it has been a separate institution owned and operated by the Charles Hosmer Morse Foundation. Essentially a museum of American paintings, sculpture, and decorative arts, it is best known for its collection of the work of Louis Comfort Tiffany. The Tiffany collection was assembled in 1955 by the founder of the gallery, Jeanette Genius McKean, and it includes most of the leaded windows designed personally by Tiffany.

The Osceola Art and Culture Center is a multidisciplinary arts council organization and center for the arts. Its five member organizations include: The Osceola Players theater group; The Osceola Art Association featuring classes, seminars, and monthly exhibits; The Osceola Historical Society as the official County Museum; The Choral Society; and The Civic Orchestra. The Center also houses the Sweet Adelines female singing group. Beginning in 1947 with the founding of the Osceola County Historical Society, the Footlight Theatre Guild was added in 1960 to form the Center in 1962.

The Orlando Science Center formally

began in 1955 as the Central Florida Museum, Inc., and operated for several years as a "museum without walls." The first building was completed in March 1960 and included the first planetarium, featuring a Spitz Model A-1 instrument. The Shatteen Blalock Memorial Room was added and an expanded planetarium featured a Minolta MX-10 projector. By 1975, the Edyth Bush addition was completed, providing an auditorium, exhibit hall, laboratory, and other facilities. The center has offered participatory exhibits, films, lectures, trips, and planetarium shows to thousands of school children, with thousands more attending "suitcase lectures." A new natural and physical science facility broke ground in May 1984.

The Orlando Opera Company traces its beginnings to a concert of operatic arias featuring four members of the Metropolitan Opera in 1958, sponsored by the Junior League and the Florida Symphony Orchestra. The Junior League continued to sponsor those concerts annually, with increasingly elaborate sets and opera performers of national recognition, including Robert Merrill, Beverly Sills, and Placido Domingo. Full-length operas began with Puccini's *La Boheme* in 1963 and education programs for youth were added with the production of *Carmen* in 1964. *Tosca* was the first full production of the Orlando Opera Guild in 1959, and by 1971, the Guild was producing two operas a season. The 1983 season saw *Porgy And Bess* as the finale of the first three-opera season.

The Pine Castle Center of the Arts began as a dream of Florence Fishback and developed into the Southern Garden Arts Center in 1965. An old Orange County home extension building was purchased and renovated for a cultural center. Classes, a choral and theater group, a children's summer arts camp, and a drama group developed, requiring expansion of the facility across the street and the addition of a director and full-fledged music department. In 1976, the Pine Castle Arts League was formed. The Pioneer Days folk festival was organized in 1974 and remains a trademark for this living museum.

The Council of Arts & Sciences was established in 1967 as a central coordinating agency for cultural affairs in central Florida. Initially an all volunteer organization, the

Council has developed into a full-time, full-service community arts agency with professional staff. Affiliated with the council are over 90 member organizations and scores of individual artists, as well as individuals and businesses interested in the the development of all the arts. The Council has provided information and referrals, developed publications such as calendars and directories, offered technical assistance and training, coordinated management services and administrative support for the Arts United Fund, and produced festivals and outreach programs which develop new audiences.

The Southern Ballet Theatre was founded in 1974 as *the* company to provide performing experience for area dancers. In 1976, the company gained recognition through its involvement with the nationally aired environmental movie, *Dance At Dawn.* In 1978, the Company became the Southern Ballet Theatre and presented *Cinderella* at the Bob Carr Auditorium. By 1980, the Ballet had initiated a subscription series at the Bob Carr. In 1982, the Ballet's school opened to the public, allowing progression from the youth program to the full-scholarship apprentice program to the professional company. The Southern Ballet Theatre has produced over 40 ballets, danced for over one million people and done over 500 performances; it is an official State Touring Company.

Crealde Arts, Inc., was founded in 1975 by William S. Jenkins and has become a vital force for hands-on-arts education. The two divisions of Crealde Arts include the Crealde School of Art in Winter Park and ArtReach, which services Orlando's cultural community in a variety of settings. Serving over 1,000 children and adults annually, the Crealde School's professional staff and featured artist workshops work to develop each student at his own level. ArtReach offers the only art therapy program in Florida, and it serves primarily elderly and handicapped individuals in greater Orlando.

Center Stage is a nonprofit monthly publication devoted to reflecting artists' efforts in central Florida. Started in 1979 by Grapefruit Productions, *Center Stage* was a 4-page tabloid, intended to serve the area's theater interests. Now independent and under the supervision of Mary A. Johnston, the journal now covers all of the arts with a 16-to 20-page color magazine and a circulation of 20,000. Through *Center Stage,* the arts community has a forum for ideas and a medium for the promotion of the arts.

A half century of service and tradition

Anderson & Rush is a mature, old-line, business law firm that provides the whole range of legal services for a wide variety of individuals and institutions involved in all fields of business with emphasis on financing, land acquisition, development, building, and related activities. As a full-service law firm, it has departments specializing in wills, estates, trusts, probate, tax, business organization and planning, and commercial litigation. It is staffed by seasoned attorneys having an unusual number of academic degrees in accounting, business, taxation, and related fields. It is also highly computerized and has the distinctive feature of its own internal real property abstracting and title division. The lawyers are supported by an experienced paralegal staff, averaging three for each attorney. The firm routinely handles matters on a day to day basis throughout Florida.

The firm performs major legal work for such diversified interests as Alliance Mortgage Company, AmeriFirst Federal Savings and Loan Association, Connecticut General Life Insurance Company, Coral Gables Federal Savings and Loan Association, The Housing Authority of the City of Orlando, The LeTourneau Foundation, Mutual Life of New York, Regal Hotel Corporation, Southeast Bank, N.A., Southeast Mortgage Company, Toy King Distributors, Inc., and Tucker & Branham, Inc.

Anderson & Rush has always been a downtown Orlando law firm. Since 1960, it has occupied the renovated McCraney home, the distinctive Georgian landmark on the south shore of Lake Eola.

The firm was founded by Robert T. Anderson in 1937. Its first clients during the early FHA/VA days were the builders, developers, and mortgage bankers of Jacksonville, Tampa, and Orlando. Many have remained clients of the firm. Prior to the date of the creation of the Attorneys' Title Insurance Fund, Anderson pioneered the concept of attorneys issuing title insurance. In 1938, Anderson, at the request of Mayor Samuel Yulee Way, formed the Orlando Housing Authority, which the firm continues to represent as general counsel. Recognized nationally as a model Authority, it now serves more than 3,000 low income families.

In 1942, World War II interrupted Robert Anderson's law practice. He became a lieutenant colonel in the infantry and graduated from the Command and General Staff College. He designed, built, and operated the battle courses at Fort McClellan, Alabama. After the War, he served as the first president of the Orlando Reserve Officer's Association.

In 1949, Anderson was joined in the law practice he had resumed by James K. Rush, who shortly thereafter became a partner, and the firm became Anderson & Rush. Rush had

also seen duty in World War II as a combat officer in the Pacific Theater. His roots in the community were deep. His family had lived in Orlando since 1880. Rush's paternal grandfather, Joseph D. Rush, was one of Orlando's first physicians and was the first president of the Orange County Medical Association. Today, Rush is acknowledged in *The Best Lawyers in America* (Woodward/White, 1983) as one of the twelve best real estate attorneys in Florida.

In the early 1960s, the firm built and operated Land Title & Abstract Company, which later became the abstract plant in Orange County for Attorneys' Title Insurance Fund.

Members of the law firm have contributed over the years significantly to the civic, cultural, religious, and social life of the community. While serving on numerous local, statewide, and national insurance and financial institution boards, Anderson also found time to serve as president of the Florida Symphony Orchestra, Florida's oldest. Taking the reins when the symphony was at its lowest ebb, he restructured its leadership. Anderson and the late Helen Ryan obtained a $500,000 grant from the Ford Foundation, which was later matched by the community. Anderson was one of only two symphony presidents in the nation invited to the First Festival of the Arts at the White House. He also served as president of Loch Haven Art Center and on the Board of Trustees of the University of the South. He was the president of the University Club for two terms, during which time the club's present building was constructed and equipped and its administration overhauled. Rush has served as president of the University Club and for many years as an officer and board member of the Orange County Historical Society. In 1980, he hosted the National Conference of Pro Athletes Outreach and has served as a director on numerous local boards.

Harry H. Marvel has served as president of the Maitland Art Center. Vernon Swartsel has served as president of the Council of Arts & Sciences when it created the Arts United Fund and on the boards of a variety of local service and political organizations. H. Richard Bates founded the Christian Conciliation Service in central Florida and has served as its president.

The firm has had a reputation for 30 years of recruiting attorneys from leading law schools throughout the nation. It has brought many outstanding young lawyers to Orlando. Over the years, lawyers from the firm have gone on to become county and circuit judges, law school professors, authors, city attorneys, presidents, and governors of bar associations. A dozen former members now head other major central Florida law firms.

This distinctive Georgian home, built in the 1920s, has been the office of Anderson & Rush since 1960.

A tradition of growth to keep pace with customer needs

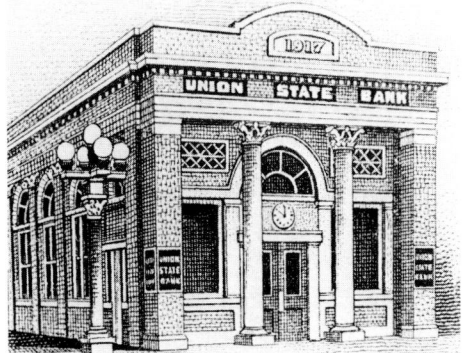

Union State Bank, established in Winter Park in 1917, was the forerunner of what is today Barnett Bank of Central Florida, N.A.

Although always considered a leader in the financial industry, Barnett Bank of Central Florida truly had modest beginnings by today's standards. In 1917, the small state bank opened its doors on Park Avenue in Winter Park as Union State Bank. At that time, total assets of $30,000 gave the founding fathers good reason to firmly believe in the future of central Florida. Yet, little did then-President Dr. C. D. Christ realize that that offspring of Union State Bank would one day be part of the largest banking group in Florida, with assets far exceeding $11 billion.

In 1922, Ray Rosenfelt joined the firm as a stenographer, bookkeeper, and teller, and eight years later Union State Bank reorganized to become Florida Bank at Winter Park. Capital stock was $50,000 and $337,000 was on deposit. This relatively small institution was one of only two banks in the area to survive the Depression. In early 1945, Florida Bank of Winter Park was granted trust powers and renamed the Florida Bank & Trust Company to reflect the added scope of services. Mr. Rosenfelt had risen to the presidency by this time, and in 1951 the bank moved across the street to its present location at the corner of Park and New England avenues in Winter Park. Five years later it became the First National Bank of Winter Park with a quarter-million dollars in stock and deposits totaling $16,750,000.

In 1966, Barnett National Securities Corporation, now Barnett Banks of Florida, Inc., purchased First National Bank of Winter Park, subsequently renaming it Barnett First National Bank of Winter Park. In 1967, Mr. Rosenfelt was named chairman of the board and, at the age of 32, Charles E. Rice was named president. Rice subsequently became chairman, president, and chief executive officer of Barnett Banks of Florida, Inc., a position he currently occupies.

Exceptional growth coupled with foresight resulted in plans for the bank's physical expansion, and a 100,000-square-foot structure was built in two stages from 1969 to 1971. This building — the same one which today houses Barnett Bank of Central Florida's Winter Park office — became Winter Park's largest financial institution, as well as the physical realization of the founding father's commitment to central Florida.

With a receptive community and room to grow, Barnett Bank introduced a number of firsts to central Florida. BankAmericard opened its doors to central Florida out of third-floor quarters in Barnett's Winter Park office. The Winter Park bank also provided central Florida its largest vault, the door of which weighs in excess of seven tons. The only vault built underground, it serves a double function as an air-raid shelter for area residents.

The 1970s and 1980s brought additional growth and changes for Barnett Bank. A new president, Charles K. "Pete" Cross, came to what was then Barnett Bank of Winter Park in 1974. Three years later, branch banking

was permitted in Florida, opening the door for Barnett Bank of Winter Park to become Barnett Bank of Orlando/Winter Park. Four banks in the Orlando/Winter Park area became branches of Winter Park, increasing assets by $44 million to $181 million.

Barnett continued its accelerated growth

Since 1982, Barnett Plaza has provided Barnett Bank of Central Florida, N.A. a major downtown Orlando presence.

pace and merged in 1981 with Seminole and Brevard counties to become Barnett Bank of Central Florida, N.A. Assets once again increased, this time by $200 million. In late 1982, the desire for a major Orlando presence and corporate banking location saw to fruition Barnett Plaza, a 275,000-square-foot structure in the heart of downtown. The same month, Barnett Bank of Central Florida acquired Century Bank of Orange County in Apopka, expanding the bank's geographic boundaries and increasing assets by $70 million.

Two years later, Barnett Bank of Central Florida welcomed Flagship Bank of Kissimmee into its fold and expanded to its present four-county area of Orange, Seminole, Brevard, and Osceola counties. The second-largest bank in the Barnett system, Barnett Bank of Central Florida was serving its community with 30 offices and approximately 1,000 employees. By April 1984, its assets had surpassed $1 billion.

Today, R. Michael Strickland serves as president of Barnett Bank of Central Florida, and Charles K. "Pete" Cross is chairman of the board and chief executive officer.

Quality care with a personal touch

Brookwood Community Hospital, a health care center of American Medical International (AMI), is a 153-bed JCAH (Joint Commission on Accreditation of Hospitals) accredited full-service acute-care facility located on 32 acres in Orlando, Florida.

Dedicated to quality care, Brookwood believes in providing its patients with the personal touch not often found in large facilities.

Servicing West Orlando and surrounding communities, Brookwood provides a 24-hour physician-staffed emergency department; state-of-the-art diagnostics (including CT Scan, ultrasound, and nuclear medicine); obstetrics; a top-calibre critical-care unit equipped with individual pressure and cardiac monitoring systems; 24-hour respiratory therapy; a same-day personalized out-patient surgery suite; fully equipped operating and recovery surgical department; in-house lab; pediatric unit for 20 children; labor and delivery facility; complete diagnostic breast scanner; the latest neuro-diagnostic lab; and the most up-to-date emergency ear, nose, and throat treatment room.

Brookwood Community Hospital was first opened in 1965 as Mercy Hospital by the Catholic Diocese of Orlando. Thirteen years later, Brookwood Health Services, Inc. purchased the hospital and changed the name to Brookwood Community Hospital. A multihospital corporation, the company then merged with American Medical International, and on July 1, 1981, AMI began operations at Brookwood.

In keeping with its commitment to quality care, AMI is updating equipment and expanding the facility to meet the ever-changing needs of quality patient care.

Since 1981, AMI has invested almost $5.5 million into the expansion of Brookwood. An additional $15 million update is currently underway.

State-of-the-art medical equipment is being used throughout the facility and is continually upgraded to meet the needs of the community. Renovations to admissions, emergency room, and intensive critical-care areas of the hospital have been significant.

Technologically advanced computers, monitoring systems, and the latest diagnostic equipment complement every care unit.

In the area of diagnostic and vascular monitoring, Brookwood offers the highest quality of equipment . . . with its Computer Tomography (CT) Scanner capable of detecting the slightest body tissue variations . . . with its vascular monitor to detect stroke and potential stroke victims . . . and with the hospital's digital vascular imaging for advanced arterial diagnosis.

Brookwood is also equipped with a graphic stress telethermometry (GST) unit (the only one in central Florida) used to check breasts for disorders without x-rays. The electroencephalogram (EEG) equipment at Brookwood, used to detect such dis-

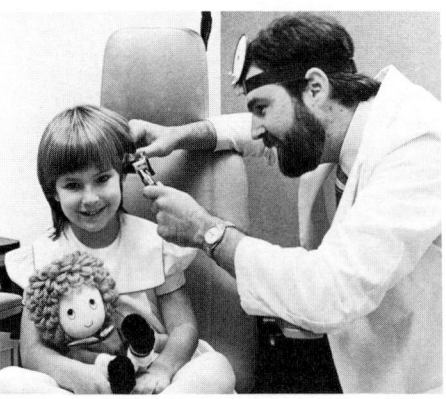

Brookwood has one of the best-equipped ear, nose, and throat (ENT) emergency rooms in the city, handling such ENT procedures as minor ear surgery, nasal fracture reduction, and other head and neck traumas.

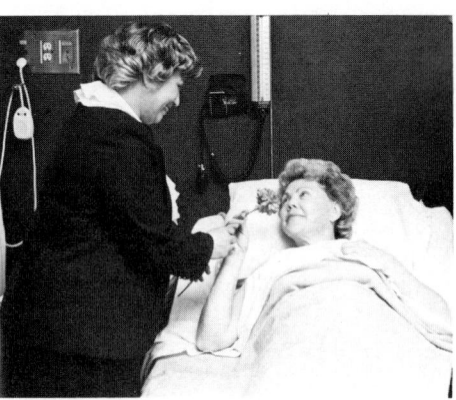

Quality care with a personal touch is delivered every day to patients at AMI's Brookwood Community Hospital in Orlando.

Brookwood Community Hospital, an American Medical International (AMI) facility, has undergone an extensive renovation program with an additional $15 million update currently underway.

orders as tumors, epilepsy, and hypoglycemia, is the first of its kind installed in central Florida.

Nestled in a pine-lined lake setting, Brookwood has a flowering landscaped boulevard entrance way with parking close to the facility. This is especially helpful to elderly patients and visitors who find walking long distances a hardship. The relaxing setting also offers ambulatory patients a beautiful campus where staff can wheel them in the sunshine to help aid in their recovery.

At Brookwood Community Hospital, nearly 400 special nurses, technicians, and other trained personnel join 150 top physicians to produce the finest care team in central Florida.

In a pledge to quality care with a personal touch, the staff at Brookwood is dedicated to seeing that each patient's stay is the best possible. A complimentary flower upon arrival, a morning paper every day, the latest state-of-

the-art phone system, free television service, along with a nurse's caring smile, are all a part of Brookwood's patients' days.

American Medical International (AMI), Brookwood's parent company, was founded in 1960 and is the first company of its kind, leading the way for what is now known as the public-owned hospital industry.

Today, AMI is a leader in the delivery of health care services, both domestically and internationally, with more than 500 communities receiving its services.

Drawing on more than 20 years of experience and a broad base of hospital operations, AMI has constructed, equipped, renovated, and re-equipped more than 100 full-care hospitals in the United States and ten countries around the world.

AMI has proven experience to determine the equipment and hospital systems which operate most effectively and economically in any given location or situation . . . always keeping in mind the quality care, personal touch aspect emphasized in every AMI facility . . . like Orlando's Brookwood Community Hospital.

The nation's largest manufacturer of modular housing

Perhaps no company will have a greater impact on the future of the country's shelter industry than Cardinal Industries Incorporated, which has been involved in manufactured housing since 1954 and has emerged as the nation's largest manufacturer of modular housing.

With assembly-line production facilities in Sanford, Florida; Columbus, Ohio (two plants); Atlanta, Georgia; and a fifth opening in mid-1985 in Baltimore, Maryland, Cardinal has come a long way from those early days in 1954 when it produced roof trusses and wall panels in a small shop. Since the company's founding by Austin Guirlinger, Cardinal's assembly lines have produced thousands of nearly identical 12' x 24' modules which have been the basic building blocks of a diverse product line including rental apartments, motels, single-family homes, commercial office parks, adult retirement villages, and courtyard condominiums. By the end of this decade, Cardinal will be capable of producing 100,000 modules annually.

Most of Cardinal's growth has occurred in a relatively short time — since 1970, when it decided to phase out the building-component business and channel its energies to producing 3-dimensional modules full-time. By the end of 1983, Cardinal had built and developed nearly 600 properties and managed nearly 23,000 apartments throughout the Southeast and Midwest, as well as a chain of 50 Knights Inn motels, which it owns and operates. And every year since 1970, when Cardinal began modular production, the company has enjoyed an annual growth in excess of 20 percent a year. In 1983, it registered a record $381 million and ranked number 15 in *Professional Builder* magazine's annual national-industry rankings.

By the end of 1983, Cardinal employed more than 3,500 people and housed more than a half-million square feet of production space, with 4 of the nation's longest continuous housing assembly lines. Already, these assembly lines have continually produced more quality-controlled modular living units than any other manufacturer — ever — and the gap is getting wider.

Cardinal's assembly lines have dozens of housing modules in production at all times. By standardizing its product and building in such high volume, Cardinal takes advantage of the many technological benefits and techniques such volume affords. As a result, Cardinal not only is a leader in manufacturing techniques, but also is producing housing at a rate which vastly exceeds industry averages. Its products are 95 percent completed on the assembly line, including plumbing and wiring for power, telephone, and television; walls have been covered, floors carpeted, and bookcases built in; even drapes have been hung and light bulbs are in the fixtures. Cardinal can manufacture a 60- to 80-unit apartment complex in approximately two days, while related on-site construction can

be completed in about 90 days.

Cardinal's Sanford facility opened in October 1976. It has completed and opened more than 130 developments throughout Florida and south Georgia. At any given time, the Sanford facility has 5 to 7 projects under construction, with 15 to 20 more being planned.

Public acceptance of Cardinal's modular units — from apartments to single-family homes — has been just as spectacular as its production, transportation, and installation

Building living units in a totally controlled work environment enables Cardinal Industries to maximize quality control at every step of the assembly process, to eliminate delays associated with conventional-site construction, and to deliver a quality product in a fraction of the time.

techniques. When Cardinal opens a new development, it usually is rented within 30 to 60 days; in some instances, developments are rented before they are completed and opened. Overall occupancy rates of Cardinal communities are 97 percent, higher than the national average for apartments.

Yes, Cardinal has come a long way in a relatively short time. But for a company whose long-range goal is to become the country's number one builder, the journey is just beginning.

Each 12' x 24' module weighs about 5 tons and is lifted by its roof when placed on its foundation, attesting to the strength and durability of modular construction.

Rental apartments represent just one example of Cardinal's diverse product line. All Cardinal's apartment communities are characterized by open green areas and generous landscaping.

A quest for excellence

Carlton, Fields, Ward, Emmanuel, Smith & Cutler, P.A., one of the oldest and largest law firms in the state of Florida, has maintained an office in Orlando since 1968. The firm was established in 1901 when Giddings E. Mabry commenced the practice of law in Tampa. Mabry was joined in 1904 by his father, Milton H. Mabry, a former lieutenant governor of Florida, who also served as chief justice of the Supreme Court of Florida. Doyle E. Carlton, who joined the firm in 1912, was governor of Florida from 1929 to 1933 and served as a member of the first U.S. Commission on Civil Rights. O.K. Reaves became a member of the firm in 1921 after having served in the Florida legislature and as a circuit judge. The firm name included Mabry, Reaves, and Carlton for over 40 years. Throughout this time, especially, these founders of the firm were leaders in public, religious, and civic activities.

During the first half-century of its existence, the firm primarily served Tampa citizens and businesses. D. Wallace Fields and David E. Ward became prominent in firm and community affairs during the latter half of this period.

Responding to Florida's economic progress, the firm grew rapidly after World War II, and its practice expanded throughout the state. Numbering twelve lawyers in 1960 and 38 in 1970, the firm now numbers over 100 lawyers and maintains offices in four cities. In addition to the Orlando office established in 1968, offices were established in Pensacola in 1971 and in Tallahassee in 1977.

The firm name was changed in 1963 to include the names of Michel G. Emmanuel,

Milton H. Mabry, 1857–1919.

Wm. Reece Smith Jr., and Edward I. Cutler. Emmanuel joined the firm in 1949 as one of Tampa's first tax specialists. Smith became a member of the firm in 1953 and has since served as president of the University of South Florida, The Florida Bar, and the American Bar Association. Cutler, a commercial law specialist, practiced in Philadelphia and in Tampa as a sole practitioner before joining the firm in 1961.

Other senior members now include Davisson F. Dunlap, a prominent trial lawyer; James A. Urban, a past president of the Orange County Bar Association, The Florida Bar, and the Florida Bar Foundation; Lawrence M. Watson Jr., a trial lawyer specializing in construction litigation; A. Broaddus Livingston,

currently president of the firm; Paul A. Saad, active in the affairs of the Republican Party; Leonard H. Gilbert, a past president of The Florida Bar; Jacob D. Varn, formerly both chairman of the Department of Environmental Regulation and the Department of Transportation of the state of Florida; Alan C. Sundberg, formerly chief justice of the Supreme Court of Florida; and Sylvia H. Walbolt, the third woman to become a fellow of the American College of Trial Lawyers.

The firm has sought to follow the example of its founders in public, professional, and community service. Over the years, members of the firm have served as appellate and trial judges, state legislators and cabinet officers, city council members, governmental authority members, public counsel, county attorneys, city attorneys, college presidents and trustees and presidents of religious groups, bar associations, and civic and social clubs.

Likewise, it has sought to be progressive in firm development. Carlton, Fields was the first major law firm in Florida to employ women and members of minority groups as lawyers, and it is a leader in the provision of free legal services to the poor and the disadvantaged. It has also been progressive in firm management and was one of the first firms in Florida to become a professional association, to employ a director of administration, and to use computers and data processing techniques in its work.

Carlton, Fields, Ward, Emmanuel, Smith & Cutler, P.A. is proud of its history, its tradition, and its capacity for progress. Its ranks now include men and women of varied origins and interests who remain dedicated to the welfare of the communities they serve and to the continuity and improvement of the firm.

Doyle E. Carlton, 1885–1972.

Giddings E. Mabry, 1877–1968.

O.K. Reaves, 1877–1970.

Out of decay an urban renaissance . . . and the good times roll again

In 1972, at least one section of downtown Orlando, the 100 block of West Church Street, was in danger of becoming a "ghost town." That was the year entertainment entrepreneur Robert J.S. Snow happened to be looking for a location to build his second Rosie O'Grady's. Snow's dreams became reality and the "ghost town" became Church Street Station.

In Orlando during the early 1970s, there was little talk of restoration. The popular building trend was to tear down and build anew. Snow was one of the few who spoke of restoring instead of starting from scratch. After a successful renovation of Seville Quarter in Pensacola, Florida, where Snow opened his first Rosie O'Grady's in 1969, he looked for a place to open another, this time in central Florida. He was looking for someplace "old," but initially found nothing to his liking.

On the way back to the local airport for his return trip to Pensacola, Snow was told by his cab driver about an old railroad station in downtown Orlando. He immediately asked to be taken there. What he saw was an area of derelict structures replete with broken bottles on the sidewalks. The renovation of the Slemons Department Store (circa 1924) did indeed become the second Rosie O'Grady's Goodtime Emporium in 1974. Growth has been continuous throughout the past 10 years, with expenditures of more than $25 million. Included in these costs

The south side of West Church Street. Forefront is old Bumby Building down to end of street where the Cheyenne Saloon and Opera House now stand.

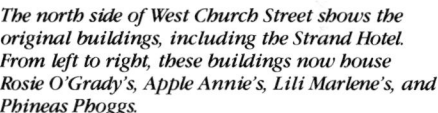

have been the restoration of the Leon Building (circa 1919) to make Apple Annie's Courtyard, the Strand Hotel (circa 1922) which became Lili Marlene's Aviators Pub and Restaurant and the Teele Building (circa 1924) which became Phineas Phogg's Balloon Works.

On the other side of Church Street stood the Purcell Building (circa 1920) which became the Cheyenne Saloon and Opera House, taking two years and $5 million to complete. The opposite end of the block was occupied by the old Joseph Bumby Hardware

The north side of West Church Street shows the original buildings, including the Strand Hotel. From left to right, these buildings now house Rosie O'Grady's, Apple Annie's, Lili Marlene's, and Phineas Phoggs.

Company, the second-oldest business in Orlando at the time. The original building, constructed in 1886, has been scheduled for renovation as an arcade reflecting the Victorian era. The original inspiration of Bob Snow's Orlando dream, the old brick railroad station built in 1890, has become the visual and thematic focal point of the entire complex.

Snow's continuous worldwide travels have nurtured the acquisition of significant antiques and artifacts which include vintage trains, planes, and architectural relics. These have been used in each renovation and contribute to the unique character and theming of the complex.

Almost 500 employees, known as the Goodtime Gang, host more than 2.5 million guests annually. In addition, Snow and his staff have donated much time and consideration to benefit charitable organizations within the community.

Church Street Station's continuing success as historic downtown Orlando's complete entertainment, dining, and shopping complex attests to a consistent eye for quality, attention to detail, and enthusiasm. What was once a derelict downtown area with a failing economy has been revitalized as a result of the entrepreneurial insight and perseverance of owner Bob Snow.

Orlando's first mall leads retailing renaissance

It was born in 1956 out of dairy pasture lands amidst a small but quickly growing metropolis called Orlando. Colonial Plaza Mall offered central Florida residents their first shopping center, and the tradition it has set as a pacesetter in retailing is still evident today.

The Mall has a heritage, one that breeds great loyalty among its customers who have traditionally treated the Mall as much more than a "string of shops." Instead, it was a community gathering place, a reputation the Mall still strives to maintain through extensive community service and involvement. Even its "Grand Reopening" in 1983 was a community affair, including a black-tie evening, drawing more than 1,000 people to benefit a popular local cultural organization. This gala event was followed by a week of special events, including a festive ribbon-cutting ceremony attended by some 1,500 local residents and led by Orlando's mayor.

Over the years as Orlando prospered, customers came to expect a growing sophistication in the atmosphere of the Mall as well as in its merchandise. For this reason, the Mall has always led the renaissance of retailing in central Florida, pacing the changing desires of an emerging city.

Colonial Plaza Mall was originally considered to be located at the northern perimeter of the Orlando metropolitan area, just three miles from downtown. Downtown is still just three miles to the east, but the metro area's northern border has expanded to include several burgeoning and popular residential "bedroom communities." Progress and growth in the area meant the Mall must progress as well.

An ambitious and comprehensive renovation project was undertaken in 1982, which, when completed a year later, proved to be the most striking facelift the historic Mall had ever seen. Among the most noticeable of changes was the new ceiling and interior design created to bring more of outdoors Florida — indoors. The roof was vastly changed, with new structural steel, extensive use of skylights, additional clerestory, and a new fire sprinkler system. The installation of special acoustical ceilings help keep Mall traffic noise to a minimum — just one more subtle renovation that makes the shopping experience pleasurable.

New storefronts were installed. Lighting fixtures and signage were updated. Lots of tropical plants and large green trees were installed around new, sleek, wooden seating areas, creating the kind of inviting "people places" so important to the eighties life-style.

It wasn't the Mall's first facelift. In 1962, the original Plaza was enlarged with the addition of Jordan Marsh, and in 1973 another major addition was made with the arrival of Belk Lindsey. This meant Colonial Plaza Mall again offered Orlando residents a first in retailing — it was the area's first enclosed

Orlando residents have traditionally visited Colonial Plaza Mall for more than shopping. It has been known as a community gathering place since it became Orlando's first mall in 1956.

shopping mall, adding yet another chapter to Orlando's retailing history. Shoppers embraced this new style of shopping with even greater patronage.

Now, with its three major anchor department stores, including Ivey's, added during the renovations of 1982, the Plaza has more than 110 stores encompassing a million square feet of space. The major impetus to the constant updating of the Mall is its owner since 1980, The Prudential Insurance Company of America.

Dedicated to maintaining Colonial Plaza Mall's position as a leader in retailing, Prudential has effectively provided loyal customers with the cutting edge of shopping experiences. Upon its purchase of the Mall, Prudential hired the experienced mall management firm of J.J. Gumberg Co. of Pittsburgh to constantly work with tenants on merchandise mix, renovation, and new tenant prospecting.

Sleek mirrors, black marble, and cosmopolitan merchandise displays flavor Ivey's and long-time Mall stores. Skylights and extensive landscaping dot the interior of the Mall. Additional parking has been added over the years, and even the original facade has been updated to reflect the bright new freshness of

Colonial Plaza Mall has kept pace with the changing Orlando market over the years with facelistings that add sleek, updated interiors and merchandise to the Mall's heritage.

Orlando. The Mall remains at the top of technology, with state-of-the-art computer videostore directories installed in each concourse.

The ingredients for retailing success have been established, and it's a recipe that works. Being the first shopping center and the first enclosed Mall in Orlando created a heritage for Colonial Plaza — a heritage that has now adapted itself to the changing needs and tastes of a growing market. The renaissance is evident and will continue.

They changed the course of central Florida history

The Public Broadcast Center is 36,000 square feet of state-of-the-art communications technology surrounding a subtropical courtyard, east Orange County's landmark liaison with the twenty-first century, home base of Community Communications Incorporated.

Known for the public broadcasting stations Channel 24 and FM 90 Plus, and the *East Central Florida Public Broadcasting Monthly* magazine, Community Communications' 80 media specialists monitor and analyze the pulse of the country's fastest-growing region, and address it in ways as unique as the corporation itself.

Membership-financed Channel 24 has the respect and admiration of hundreds of thousands of television viewers for the award-winning, provocative, and entertaining programs it broadcasts and produces. In 1980, the mission was amplified when east central Florida's first public radio station signed on. Today, FM 90 Plus rates as the number one public radio station, serving an area as large as east central Florida. Even more recently came the *Public Broadcasting Monthly* magazine, which rounds out Community Communications' total-media package.

Programs provide the most evident measurement of Community Communications' success. Highlights of Channel 24's schedule continue to shatter A.C. Nielsen viewership records, as more than 230,000 households discover the impact public television programs have on their lives. One long-running series is "Masterpiece Theatre" — a hallmark of dramatics.

Adventure for the family has made the maritime odysseys of Jacques Cousteau so popular. Intriguing expeditions by National Geographic Society's modern pioneers have been captured by cameras for public television's most highly respected specials on nature.

Those who lean toward the traditional American crafts are treated to the techniques of master craftsmen painters, woodworkers, horticulturists — even card-players — in television's most comprehensive lineup of how-to programs.

Children's lives are enriched by programs such as "Sesame Street," and adults can earn college credit at home via televised courses sanctioned by the five major community colleges in east central Florida.

Health matters to public broadcasters as much as to their audiences. Nearly every season, at least one practical series keeps viewers abreast of the latest health care advances.

Public television is also where some of the finest funny stuff can be found today. As funny, educational, or informative as many of Channel 24's programs are, very few, say the critics, can upstage a great performance. Dedicated to that premise is an ongoing series of some of the world's foremost ballets, operas, stage plays, and concerts, each featuring stars of the greatest magnitude.

Ron Cook in "Richard III," one of WMFE's many acclaimed productions.

An impressive number of Channel 24 programs originate at the Public Broadcast Center, and some are broadcast statewide or throughout the southeast, giving Channel 24 prominence far beyond Orlando.

Programs produced at Channel 24 for a local audience equip viewers with facts on which to base decisions, or with the knowledge to fulfill a life-style ambition. Recent local programming objectives are to raise the public consciousness of endangered species and the fragile Florida ecosystem, to motivate parents to fight alcohol and drug abuse among children and teenagers, and to present a forum for the community's leaders to address local concerns. The list of awards conferred upon Channel 24's hosts and producers reflects the extent to which the impact of programming is felt. That extent is far-reaching. The lengthy programming process employs public comment, member choices, viewer mail, and program availability.

FM 90 Plus is as aware of listener demands on radio as is Channel 24 of viewer demands on television. FM 90 Plus has become the badge of classical music in east central Florida. At least four major classical presentations highlight a daily schedule.

FM 90 Plus presents fine concert music by the New York Philharmonic and Boston Symphony, among others, often simulcast on Channel 24 for a stereo television effect. Contemporary radio personalities such as Garrison Keillor contribute to public radio's popularity.

Award-winning news and viewpoint programs, including "Morning Edition" and "All Things Considered," update listeners on late-breaking national and international stories. Local coverage opportunities are built into "Morning Edition," and are the sole focus of "Evening Edition." "Evening Edition" also includes informational modules on a variety of subjects, some of which are broadcast statewide.

The *Public Broadcasting Monthly* magazine, with a circulation of 30,000 area households, is particularly attractive to display advertisers. Enhancing that attractiveness are the demographic and psychographic profiles of public broadcasting members, all subscribers of the magazine, and the month-long shelf life of the magazine because of the Channel 24

and FM 90 Plus program listing sections.

Local businesses and individuals whose support represents half of the stations' operating revenues agree that investing in public broadcasting guarantees rewarding results.

Investments by members, even as little as the $24 recommended annual minimum, pay for great public broadcasting and encourage support by government agencies and foundations. Even an investment in time, such as volunteerism, has a positive effect on the bottom line.

Business and corporations take advantage of tax-deductible investment opportunities by underwriting the programs broadcast on Channel 24 and FM 90 Plus. A wide range of program underwriting assures that at least one beneficial plan fits into any advertising, marketing, or promotion budget. Relaxed underwriting guidelines, established by the Corporation for Public Broadcasting, make underwriting opportunities better than ever, enabling underwriters more time for product recognition.

Corporate members, underwriters, and members at higher levels are saluted in the *Public Broadcasting Monthly* magazine, to which they then become subscribers. Everyone, no matter what level of support, is encouraged to vote in the program selection process, and is invited to many of the stations' social events, fund-raiser previews, and parties. Trips abroad at low group rates are another membership benefit. Recent tours of Australia, London, and the Rhine have been enjoyed by hundreds of members.

Another investment opportunity is administered by the planned giving program, in which public broadcasting associates invest in the stations' endowment fund, or name the stations as a beneficiary in a will, insurance policy, annuity, trust, or pooled income fund.

Whatever the method or the amount of support, it is comforting to know how each dollar is spent. Channel 24's expense chart shows that about 60 percent goes into the programs you have come to expect of public television in east central Florida. About a quarter of that total goes into management and the general fund, and about 15 percent is earmarked for aggressive fund-raising. On the FM 90 Plus side, better than 60 percent goes for programs, about 20 percent for fund-raising, and the rest for management and the general fund.

You are invited to become a member of the public broadcasting family of east central Florida. Take your fair share of credit for the quality alternative television and radio programming available to you today and every day for as long as you wish to ensure the strength of east central Florida's most dynamic, prominent, and versatile communications treasure, all of which originates right here at the Public Broadcast Center.

One man's vision impacts quality worldwide

Philip Crosby Associates, Inc. was a natural outgrowth of Philip B. Crosby's 1979 book on quality management, *Quality Is Free.*

Quality Is Free helped to establish Crosby's reputation as a leader in the quality field, and to underscore the need for a structured method of teaching the concepts of quality management to companies interested in improving.

Having left the international corporate world of ITT, where he served for 14 years as vice president of quality worldwide, Crosby moved to Winter Park, Florida, to "play golf and do a little consulting."

It was here that Philip Crosby Associates, Inc. had its modest beginning in "World Headquarters," the den of Mr. Crosby's home, on July 1, 1979.

The occasional consulting day became a full-fledged class held in the Crummer Graduate School of Business at Rollins College. Here Crosby, supported by his family, some talented friends, and Rollins professors, conducted the first Quality College for a group of eighteen businessmen from several well-known companies.

Philip Crosby Associates, Inc. (PCA) gradually evolved from one class a month to as many as ten per week, held both in Winter Park and at various national and international off-site locations.

Today Philip Crosby Associates, Inc. is comprised of four operating divisions and employs 120 people. It is privately owned by the employees and has grown from modest first-year revenues of $150,000 to $13.2 million in 1983 — four short years later — with the projected 1984 gross of $21 million. PCA's Office of the Chairman includes Chairman and Chief Executive Officer Philip B. Crosby, President and Chief Operating Officer Jay W. Leek and Executive Vice President Larry N. McFadin.

PCA has established an international reputation as the leading quality consulting firm in the world and presently has a licensee in Tokyo and representatives in London, Puerto Rico, and Singapore. Its International Division oversees the activities of Crosby Associates International, a wholly owned subsidiary of PCA.

To date, PCA has trained over 13,000 professionals directly and touched more than 300 client companies.

In an effort to reach all the people of a company and to train all employees in the common language of quality, PCA has developed videotape and notebook systems whereby the clients teach executives and others inside their own companies. These materials have been translated into several languages, including Spanish, French, Dutch, and Mandarin.

PCA's education effort was designed to help companies recognize that management is the chief cause of their problems.

The philosophy is common sense: Quality is conformance to requirements, not goodness; the system for causing quality is prevention, not appraisal; the performance standard is Zero Defects, not "that's close enough;" and quality is measured by the Price of Nonconformance, not indexes.

In May 1984, Philip Crosby Associates signed an agreement with General Motors Corporation whereby General Motors purchased 10 percent of PCA's stock with an option to purchase an additional 10 percent in three years.

Philip Crosby Associates, Inc. has had a positive influence in the local civic environment as well as on the quality-conscious companies of the world. PCA's $4.5 million annual payroll and the $8 million it pays yearly to suppliers contributes to the economic growth of the Orlando community by supporting local businesses.

The company also commits a significant amount of its income to supporting cultural and charitable organizations, a few of which

In just five years, PCA's facilities have expanded from a den in Mr. Crosby's home to four buildings with a total of nine classrooms. The PCA Building houses the administrative offices of Philip Crosby Associates. Because of the growing demand by clients for PCA's services, a 37,000-square-foot classroom facility is currently under construction and is expected to be completed in 1985.

include the University of Central Florida, Rollins College, Winter Park Memorial Hospital, Arts United Fund, American Heart Association, American Cancer Society, Florida Symphony Orchestra, Orlando Opera Company, PBS's Channel 24, and WAJL Radio.

Crosby has stated that ". . . the purpose of business is to help people have lives. The products and services of business provide the wherewithal that implements the ideas of civilization. The salaries, benefits, challenges, and fellowship of business make possible the secular fulfillment of the individual. Because we think, work, and produce we can move forward — successful business is the transportation vehicle."

Since the Japanese are well-known for their quality products, it was a special honor for PCA to have the Japan Management Association travel to Winter Park to learn new quality management techniques. Here PCA account executive Wayne Kost gives our Japanese visitors a brief history of Winter Park.

The renaissance of downtown Orlando

Created by referendum in December 1972, the Downtown Development Board (originally known as the Orlando Central City Neighborhood Development Board) has been the agency responsible for the redevelopment of Orlando's central business district. The original five-member board was appointed by Mayor Carl Langford in early 1973, and took as its first task the development of a comprehensive master plan for the core area. Known as the Center City Plan, the Orlando City Council adopted the document later that same year as the blueprint for the future redevelopment.

Many of the projects that became realities in the mid- to- late 1970s were identified in the Center City Plan. Among those was the area identified as Government Plaza that came to include the Federal Building, the State Regional Service Center, the Orlando Centroplex, and the Vocational Technical Center. These projects totaled more than $30 million in public investment.

The most significant private development in the DDB's early years was the project that was to be known as Church Street Station. An entertainment and dining complex conceived by entrepreneur Bob Snow, this redeveloment area breathed new life into a decaying portion of the city's core. More importantly, it opened the eyes to many Orlandoans that downtown was a viable investment opportunity.

Central Florida was hit hard by the oil embargo and economic recession in 1974 and 1975. Downtown Orlando was affected more than most. Retail sales continued to drop, and previously vibrant shops became empty storefronts. Sears and Ivey's department stores closed as did Morrison's Cafeteria, Lerners, and a number of other smaller stores. Downtown had truly hit rock bottom by 1976.

Continued strong support by the city council enabled the DDB to realize one of its most cherished goals — the reconstruction and renovation of Old Muni Auditorium. In May 1978, the dedication of the Bob Carr Performing Arts Centre unveiled the "new" 2,500 seat facility that has become the community's cultural and entertainment focal point. This major investment was soon followed by the completion of Gertrude's Walk and Wall Street Plaza, the first two elements of a major commitment to enhance the pedestrian environment.

In 1981, under the auspices of the DDB, the *Core Area Growth Management Plan* was formally adopted by city council. Building on the original 1973 Center City Plan, this new document became the legal framework to renew the public and private initia-

Orange Avenue, 1973.

Church Street Station, 1978.

tives and a time frame for their implementation. Once again, the Downtown Development Board's success was reflected in the number of programs and projects that were completed under this plan.

In 1981, the old Ivey's and Dickson & Ives Department stores, long standing vacant, were restored into major office buildings. That same year, another significant milestone was passed when the Pine Street Historic District received formal designation in the Federal Registrar.

In 1982, the largest office building in central Florida was completed, the 295,000-square-foot Barnett Plaza. Soon after, the Atlantic Bank Building, Century Plaza, and Landmark Center were opened, adding almost a million square feet of new office space. Church Street Station had quadrupled in size with the completion of the Cheyenne Saloon and was attracting over a million patrons a year.

The public sector was also making major

San Juan Hotel razed in 1980.

investments in the CBD. Expo Centre's multimillion-dollar renovation into a first-class conference and exhibit facility was completed; the new $20 million library expansion was well underway as was Orange County's new $12 million Administration Building, and Orlando's first parking garage was also opened in early 1984.

Probably the DDB's most significant accomplishment of the eighties was its initiative to push for the creation of the Community Redevelopment Agency in 1982. Using the resources of tax increment financing, the CRA has already made a dramatic impact on Orlando's downtown with the completion of the six-block beautification project known as the Orange Avenue Streetscape.

The measure of the Downtown Development Board's success can be seen not only in the growth in downtown's assessed valuation — over a $280 million increase since 1973 — but also in the number of people oriented activities that have been generated and become regular calendared events for Orlandoans — Fiesta in the Park, the Christmas Parade, Picnic in the Park, Festival Fridays, and Light Up Orlando to name but a few. It has been the dedication of many people, elected officials, appointed board members, and the businesses and property owners that have ensured the success of downtown Orlando's renaissance.

The airline that grew up with Orlando

Passengers prepare to board the inaugural flight of Eastern's new jet service from Orlando to New York in 1962.

Eastern Airlines serves as the Official Airline of Walt Disney World.

The city of Orlando has been important to aviation interests since the invention of the airplane. Orlando was the location of Florida's first flying contest. In February of 1910, three aviators accepted an offer of $1,500 to anyone who could keep a plane aloft for five minutes at the Orlando Midwinter Fair. Two of the three pilots crashed, but Lincoln Beachey, in a Curtis Biplane built by the Wright Brothers, won the prize.

Eighteen years later, Pitcairn Aviation, the forerunner of Eastern, launched a small single-engine, open-cockpit plane which began carrying the mail from New Jersey to Atlanta. On December 1, 1928, the mail route was extended from Atlanta to Miami, via Jacksonville. During 1929, stops were added in Orlando, Daytona Beach, Tampa/St. Petersburg, and Macon, Georgia.

As demand for airmail service grew, so did the desire for passenger service. To accommodate this need, Pitcairn Aviation evolved into Eastern Air Transport, Inc., and on August 18, 1930, Eastern started carrying passengers between Long Island, New York, and Richmond, Virginia. The new mode of transportation was very popular, and by January, 1, 1931, Eastern's passenger service stretched southward to Florida with one trip daily to Orlando. By 1932, it was possible to fly from New York to Miami in one day, and the airline promoted this accomplishment with a radio jingle, "From Frost to Flowers in Fourteen Hours."

The airline continued to grow and prosper in spite of the Depression in the 1930s. During World War II, the company leased half of its 40-plane fleet to the armed forces. Rapid advances in commercial aviation followed the war.

Thirty-one years after Eastern began carrying passengers to Florida, the jet age commenced. The company inaugurated jet service linking Orlando to seven cities — Tampa, New York, Miami, Jacksonville, At-

lanta, Chicago, and Boston. On February 1, 1962, civic and business leaders of Orlando, then Mayor Robert Carr among them, boarded Eastern's first DC-8 jet bound for New York. This aircraft seated 117 passengers and was capable of speeds of up to 600 mph. The advent of the jet engine changed the world of commercial aviation and had a favorable impact on Florida's growing tourism industry.

A great boon for Orlando was the announcement in 1965 that Walt Disney World would be located just 20 miles southwest of downtown Orlando. As plans for the theme park progressed, a long-standing partnership between Disney and Eastern, the official airline of Walt Disney World, was formed. Each year, the two companies work together to bring millions of visitors to the many attractions of Disney World and the greater Orlando area. When the park opened its doors in October of 1971, the number of arriving and departing passengers at McCoy Airport numbered just over 1 million annually. The following year the passenger count increased 65 percent — an increase that was attributed to the opening of the park. Walt Disney's newest $800 million project, the EPCOT Center (Experimental Prototype Community of Tomorrow), opened in October 1982. This showplace of technology boosted annual Disney World attendance from 13 million to 22 million.

When the theme park opened, Eastern was by far the largest of the 4 air carriers serving Orlando. Today, more than 20 airlines serve the area, and Eastern remains the dominant carrier. Eastern has the biggest share of total air traffic in Orlando, and the largest facilities, with ten gates capable of handling eight wide-bodies jets and two smaller 727s. The airport service counter is also the largest, with 30 ticketing positions.

The Eastern-sponsored "If You Had Wings" attraction at Walt Disney World opened in June 1972 and is the park's number-one free attraction. This $10 million show located in

the Tomorrowland area of Disney World can take 3,000 visitors an hour on a roller coaster tour of many Eastern destinations ranging from the ski slopes of the West to the waters of the Caribbean.

As central Florida continued its rapid development, it became apparent that McCoy Airport was no longer large enough to handle the booming traffic volume. Construction began on a new $300 million airport facility on land adjacent the existing terminal. The new Orlando International Airport stretches across 7,000 acres of beautifully landscaped property. Eastern invested $6.5 million in this venture to pay for equipment and furniture and began conversion of its gasoline and diesel-powered ground equipment to clean and efficient electric power. A control tower housing five employees was also built to oversee the Eastern ramps. A new expanded Eastern Ionosphere Club, which incorporates the rain forest decor prominent throughout the facility, was built at the new airport to provide comfort and convenience for club members.

Orlando is at the heart of central Florida's tourist industry, where more than $1.5 billion is spent annually. When vacationers want to enjoy central Florida's many vacation spots, Eastern can bring them to Orlando from any of nineteen cities in Florida, and more than 100 other destinations in the United States, Canada, the Caribbean, and Latin America. Eastern has played a significant role in helping Disney World and other vacation spots such as Sea World, the Kennedy Space Center, and Circus World. More than 1 million passengers fly to Orlando on Eastern each year.

Eastern's commitment to Orlando, "The City Beautiful," and all of Florida has favorably influenced the growing tourist industry in the state. As Orlando and Florida continue to prosper, Eastern will stretch its wings to provide the service and convenience that have made it Orlando's number-one airline.

60 years of history in Orlando

As businesses prospered in Orlando in the mid-1920s, a strong accounting firm was needed to handle financial matters for the business community. Certified public accountants Charles C. Potter and D.J. Mason took advantage of this opportunity in 1924, establishing an accounting firm at the corner of Orange Avenue and Church Street in downtown Orlando.

When D.J. Mason died, R.C. Pribble joined Charles Potter in business. Then, after Pribble's retirement in 1939, Potter joined forces with John E. Loucks and Harry W. Bower to form Potter, Loucks & Bower.

The firm prospered, and the following future partners joined the firm: Thomas "Ed" Triplett and Angus S. Barlow in 1943; Clarence A. Peterson in 1945 and Charles M. Potter (son of Charles C. Potter) in 1946.

In 1948, the growing firm took a step that no other public accounting firm in the state of Florida had even taken: The firm built its own office building on oak-lined Main Street north of downtown Orlando.

In the mid-1950s, John Loucks left the firm — resulting in a name change to Potter, Bower & Co. — and the firm continued to maintain prominent accounts which are still clients today.

During 1960, the city connected Main Street with Magnolia Avenue, forming a thoroughfare from the downtown area to north of the city. However, much to the chagrin of Main Street residents, the name Magnolia was awarded to the entire stretch of road.

It became necessary to build a larger facility by 1965, so a two-story building was erected a few doors south, with structural capacity for a future third story.

For the next couple of years, large international accounting firms joined forces with smaller, well established ones. One of the nation's largest public-accounting firms, Ernst & Ernst, viewed Potter, Bower & Co. as the most significant firm in central Florida, and negotiated a merger. The merger took place on May 1, 1969, adding the resources that an international firm can offer clients.

Harry Bower continued as managing partner at Ernst & Ernst until his retirement in 1975. He was succeeded by Charles M. Potter. Kenneth G. Harker, who had been with Potter, Bower & Co. prior to its merger with Ernst & Ernst, became a partner in 1976.

Also in that year, Ernst & Ernst began to move some of its personnel from other offices to the Orlando office to "fine tune" its areas of expertise. It added partners Paul V. Roddy and Robert W. Meherg in 1976, and James P. Walker in 1978.

In 1979, Ernst & Ernst changed its name to Ernst & Whinney.

Charles M. Potter retired in 1980 and was succeeded as managing partner by Edward J. Manning, who moved from Ernst & Whinney's Fort Lauderdale office. In 1983, the firm added two new partners — Richard D. Hissam, who transferred to Orlando, and Kitty Wrenn, who was admitted to partnership that year.

With three partners having served as president of the Florida Institute of Certified Public Accountants (Charles C. Potter, 1934 to 1935; Harry Bower, 1953 to 1954; and Thomas Triplett, 1959 to 1960) and presently represented in leadership roles of numerous community organizations, Ernst & Whinney stands out as a leader in Orlando.

The firm has grown from 2 members in 1924, to 80 in 1984, reflecting 60 years of outstanding service to the Orlando business community.

Ernst & Winney's expansion, a completely renovated building at 332 North Magnolia.

From a bicycle-riding electrician to a fleet of trucks

Integrity, service, quality . . . these are the common threads that weave several service companies together to form Ferran Engineering Group, Inc. of Orlando. While the group had its beginnings in 1967 when Harry A. Ferran purchased Ward Air Conditioning Company, the corporate roots date back to 1913.

Johnson Electric Division. A.B. Johnson (1888–1965) founded Johnson Electric Company in 1913. He began the company's operations from his home, carrying a roll of wire over each handlebar of his bicycle, his box of hand tools on his back.

The 1921 *Orlando City Directory* lists what is probably the first Johnson Electric location — 11 Court Street. A.B. Johnson's reputation as an excellent electrician and honest businessman helped the company grow. In June 1926, Johnson hired 16-year-old Louis Christensen as stockroom boy. Young Louis worked his way up to head of the electrical contracting division. His wife Martha Christensen was also an integral part of the company between 1927 and 1981.

Johnson Electric played a significant role in electrical construction in Florida as early as 1930 with a job at the University of Florida Infirmary in Gainesville. During World War II, a large percentage of the firm's activity took place at military installations such as Orlando Air Force Base. Major jobs since 1945 include the Martin Company, Colonial Plaza Mall, Orange County Court House, Orlando City Hall, and Orlando International Airport.

When A.B. Johnson died in 1965, Louis Christensen became a partner and vice-president of the company in accordance with Johnson's will. Christensen's high-principled leadership played an important role in developing Johnson Electric into central Florida's premier firm.

In 1981, Johnson Electric was purchased by Harry A. Ferran, an Orlando native and fifth-generation Floridian. A mechanical engineering graduate of the University of Florida and the Advanced Management Program of Harvard Business School, Ferran is also a master electrician. He moved the electrical contracting services from 1155 North Orange Avenue to its present location as a division of Ferran Engineering Group, Inc., 530 Grand Street, Orlando.

Ward Air Conditioning Division. Upon moving to Winter Park in 1951, Taylor D. Ward (1898–1973) surveyed the central Florida business community and decided that an air conditioning company offered a promise of growth. He purchased H.A. Daugherty Co. on June 15, 1952. Ward Air Conditioning became a reality on July 1, 1952 at 108 West Concord Avenue.

The former director of advertising and sales promotion for Kimberly Clark Corporation, Neenah, Wisconsin, Ward used his ad-

Johnson Electric management and employees gather in front of their headquarters at 119 East Pine Street, downtown Orlando, in 1926. Founder A.B. Johnson (with straw hat) is standing third from right.

vertising talents to promote his new firm. The distinctive dark green used for Ward uniforms and trucks is still a trademark of the division.

To compensate for his lack of engineering knowledge, Ward created a corporate structure of strong department managers. During the years of his presidency (1952–1967), Ward Air Conditioning established a reputation for integrity and dependability which has remained an essential element in the firm's success today.

While the company's emphasis was on installation during Ward's leadership, it shifted to service and installation when Harry A. Ferran purchased the firm in June 1967. Ward operations moved to the Grand Street address in 1970, the current headquarters for Ferran Engineering Group, and command center for a highly automated dispatching system and the largest service truck fleet in the area.

Avery Plumbing Division; Security and Audio Division. Harry Ferran's goal is to make Ferran Engineering Group the definitive choice for service and installation in every contracting area. So in 1982, Avery Plumbing joined the group, followed by the security and audio division in 1984. This coordinated effort from each specialized division gives Ferran Engineering Group the competitive edge in bidding and follow-through on jobs that keep Orlando growing. Harry Ferran's slogan says it all: "The Best Service Companies in Orlando All Have One Name — Ferran Engineering Group."

The entrepreneurial system in action

In 1966, Tampa-born Glenn H. Martin was a high-school track coach and biology teacher in Hollywood, Florida. In his effort to supplement his teaching income, he took a summer job selling insurance and earned more that summer than he had in an entire year of teaching.

He left the school system that year and opened a one-man insurance agency in Ft. Lauderdale. His first secretary, now his wife Mimi, encouraged him in the belief that he had found his niche and should stay with it. His background in teaching and coaching were also helpful, for as a track athlete, he was familiar with the importance of goal setting, and as a former teacher, he understood motivation.

Mr. Martin felt the coaching personality would be ideally suited to the demands of the insurance profession. Coaches are competitive and used to dealing with people. With this in mind, he began recruiting representatives for his agency, launching a massive recruiting drive in south Florida in 1970, drawing mainly from the fields of academe and athletics. Many who joined him then are the key people in today's Financial Security Corporation of America.

In 1973, Martin moved his agency to Orlando, for he felt the dynamic central Florida area would be ideally suited to his young and rapidly expanding company. He located first in the Major Center with an office staff of eight, and 100 agents in the Southeast, 30 of whom were full-time. Within that three years, the agency became identified as Insurance Agency of America and had grown to become one of the largest life agencies in the country, with agents and sales representatives in ten states.

In 1976, Insurance Agency of America moved its headquarters from a 3,000-square-foot space to a 5,000 square-foot space at the American Pioneer Center in Orlando. Martin had organized a winning team, and it was off and running — fast.

The years 1978 and 1979 were milestone years. In 1978, the agency reached a phenomenal $1 million in premiums, a highly significant goal in the insurance profession, particularly for a young company. It was in 1979 that the agency moved to its own quarters, the architecturally innovative Romar Building, 15,000 square feet, adjacent to the intersection of I-4 and Colonial Drive in downtown Orlando.

The parallel between the growth of the area and the energetic young company was obvious. Business continued to prosper along with the thriving community. The agency was rapidly outgrowing the Romar space, so Martin began construction of the impressive 45,000-square-foot Financial Security Center in Maitland, which now houses the majority of the organization's diverse financial service operations, some of which still remain in the Romar Building.

By 1980, the agency had expanded well beyond doing business in a statewide or re-

Financial Security Center, 341 North Maitland Avenue, home office of Financial Security Corporation and 20th Century Life.

gional area. It now conducts operations throughout Latin America as well. It was also in 1980 that the agency mission crystallized — to effectively market superior products and services to select markets . . . through a professional organization dedicated "to the continuing development of its associates."

Since the beginning, Glenn Martin and his key people have been visionary in their concepts. As a pioneer in identifying new business horizons, Martin formed Financial Security Corporation of America. FSCA is the holding company for subsidiary organizations geared to serving every area of financial management. Insurance Agency of America still actively functions as a key component of the holding company, while the recently purchased 20th Century Life Insurance Com-

The Romar Building, 731 North Garland Avenue, was the home of Insurance Agency of America from 1979–83 and still houses FSCA subsidiaries.

pany adds to the full-service concept by functioning as the in-house carrier. Financial Security Corporation now has over 30,000 clients with more than $4 billion of in-force business.

Glenn and Mimi Martin still work as a real team, though Mimi's responsibilities have shifted to their family and local charities. The Martins have served as co-chairmen of the Cancer Crusade and hosted, at their home, the annual Trotters Ball benefiting the American Cancer Society. Mimi Martin also provides moral support and advice to the marketing force wives. The Martin's civic activities are extensive.

FSCA's next move will be to Primera, the Quality of Life Center planned by Glenn Martin. Consisting of 186 acres at the intersection of I-4 and Lake Mary Boulevard, the center core will at first consist of 150,000 square feet of futuristic office space that will be neoclassical in design and ready for occupancy in 1986.

Parks, fountains, jogging and walking paths will surround a wellness and preventive medicine center, stadium, and other facilities to be connected by tram. The accent will be on improving the quality of work and leisure life. Education in all areas will play an important part at Primera, as it has through the great years of growth of this progressive and mature financial marketing corporation.

Glenn H. Martin, CLU, ChFC, founder and board chairman, Financial Security Corporation of America.

Hard times forged its strength

The year 1933 hardly seemed the time to begin a savings and loan association. It had been only a few months since the governor of Florida declared a five-day bank holiday and President Roosevelt subsequently closed all the nation's banks in March 1933. In December, the First Federal Savings and Loan Association of Orlando was chartered. It was the first savings and loan association in the Orlando area and the 40th federally chartered in the country.

Fifty-one intrepid investors came forward with $100 each. Thus First Federal began with $5,100 and a following of 51 people who were more sanguine about the future than depressed by the Depression. First Federal opened for business on February 1, 1934, ready to serve Orlando's 27,000 residents.

The founding group of First Federal was headed by H.W. Barr, a retired manufacturer from Jamestown, New York. Barr was a business associate of celery grower and real estate man Oliver Pickney Swope, who joined First Federal on the original board of directors. Swope became president of First Federal in 1946, retiring in 1962 at age 88. Swope was the prototypical self-made man, appear-

ing at his office each morning at 6:30 when he was in his 70s.

The original board members were chiefly from the financial and business sectors. When First Federal published its first financial statement in November, assets were $275,869.58. By 1940, assets were $4 million, and $16 million by 1948. In 1953, First Federal ranked 47th in the nation in assets. Assets of $100 million were reached in 1958 and $100 million more in 1970, 1972, 1975, and 1978.

First Federal's original office was located in the Building and Loan Association Building at Pine and Court streets in Orlando. In 1959, the first additional office was opened at Dixie Village. In 1964, First Federal moved to its present location, a $2.2 million, five-story office building at 145 South Magnolia in Orlando. A merger with First Federal Savings and Loan Association of Cocoa in 1982 boosted the number of offices serving central Florida and the Space Coast to 27. Assets reached $1 billion.

The responsibilities and services of First Federal grew beyond the original savings concepts of the past decades. The familiar

passbooks were replaced in 1975 with computerized statements which set the stage for EFT (electronic funds transfer) in the future. First Federal customers in 1980 began using Tel-Act automatic bill paying and began earning interest on First Money checking accounts. Money became available around the clock in 1983 with Teller 24 automated teller machines. The First Money Market Account introduced in fiscal 1983 was the most successful savings system in the association's history.

Today, the Orlando area has a population of almost 775,000, and First Federal's original assets of $5,100 have grown to over $1 billion with nearly 160,000 investors.

First Federal Savings and Loan Association is now THE FIRST, F.A. (a federal association), reflecting the change and growth in geography and services.

THE FIRST, F.A., now has three wholly owned subsidiaries — Magnolia Service Corporation, First of Cocoa Service Corporation, and Magnolia Realty, Inc./Realtors.® Magnolia Realty, Inc., is a real estate marketing firm selling residential properties. Magnolia Service Corporation is involved in several resi-

The Orange County Building and Loan Association Building on the southwest corner of Pine and Court streets in Orlando stands today as a reminder of those early years when it served as the original office of THE FIRST.

O.P. Swope
President, 1946 to 1962

Joseph M. Croson
President, 1962 to 1976

Sherman S. Dantzler
President, 1976 to present

dential and office development projects in the area. First of Cocoa Service Corporation is involved in residential development in neighboring Brevard County.

Sherman S. Dantzler, president and chief executive officer, describes the commitment of the 450 people of THE FIRST: "We continue to give attention to moderate- and low-income housing needs as well as intercity de-velopment. Capital for lending comes from our customers' deposits, the sale of loans, borrowing, and profits. These sources of capital allow us to meet the needs of our community. This is our primary mission .... We consider this the beginning of a new era of providing full financial banking services to our customers. The directors, advisory board members, management, and staff pledge their support and commit themselves to serving the central Florida community."

The board of directors of THE FIRST, F.A., is a diverse cross-section of community leadership, including financial and business leaders, a physician, and a retired university president. The board is active, carefully viewing the monumental growth of its tri-county constituency.

THE FIRST's 450 employees take a personal interest in the citizens of the community. Although it is one of the first savings and loan associations in the country with its own computer system, THE FIRST never forgets that numbers and machines are only as good as the hearts and minds of those behind them.

THE FIRST has an old-fashioned philosophy that is timeless. J.M. Croson, president from 1962 to 1976, described what has guided THE FIRST: "A strong board of directors .... We took care to be fully insured .... Our goal was not speed of growth but strength. We took our time to build large reserves. The base of it all is friendly service. We have taught our employees that the customer is always right!"

Corporate headquarters of THE FIRST today, on the corner of Magnolia and Church streets in the heart of downtown Orlando.

Yesteryear, today . . . and for eternity!

A look back reminds us of the fortitude and courage of yesterday's strength which gives us stability and strength today. Yet each Christian generation must chart new pathways if it is to remain a vital force; if it does not, it becomes a religious relic — a mausoleum of past glories, a cemetery of memories. The ability to appreciate yesterday, enjoy today, and anticipate new challenges tomorrow gives a church balance, timeliness, and dynamic.

—Jim Henry, pastor

Perhaps no other Orlando institution better parallels the chronicle of the city's past than does First Baptist Church/Orlando, since, for the settlers of over 100 years ago, Christianity was a vibrant part of individual, family, and community life.

These early Christian settlers began meeting together in homes for services about once a month, then started to organize into churches. In 1858, a Reverend Miller from "The Lodge," now known as Apopka, came to the tiny settlement of Orlando to organize a group of twelve pioneers into a Baptist church. Just two years before, Orlando had been named the county seat of Orange County, a territory so large that it encompassed what is now four counties. But the whole county had a total population of less than a thousand.

The year 1861 was one of tragic changes, Florida seceded from the union, along with the other southern states, and the Civil War began. The little churches had to disband as the men and boys of Florida left their homes to fight in the war.

With the war's end in 1865, a new era for Central Florida was ushered in. Not only did the men come home from the war, but hundreds of others came to Florida as well. The little churches of the area began to organize again. Several of these churches decided to form an association of Baptists in Orange County. They first met in 1870. They named their association "Wekiva" after a river in the county whose Indian name means "Spring of Water."

In March of 1871, Reverend G.C. Powell from Oviedo reorganized the Baptist Church at Orlando, a village that did not reach the population of 200 for ten more years. The Bethel Baptist Church, sometimes called Missionary Baptist Church to distinguish it from

Present facility built in 1961 at 100 East Pine Street.

Architectural rendering of phase one of First Baptist's I-4 at 33rd Street campus. The first worship service is scheduled for February 1985.

the Primitive Baptists, had as its first meeting place the old frame courthouse. The Baptists took turns with other denominations meeting there.

In 1872, the church began meeting once a month in the free school building which was located where First Federal is today. There they proclaimed Jesus Christ to be the same — not only for all time but for all people — as several Negroes, both men and women, became members of the church.

In 1882, the church's first building was erected on the northwest corner of Garland and Pine streets. In 1894, the name of the church was changed from Bethel Baptist to First Baptist. In that same year, a building and lot committee was appointed. They purchased a lot on the corner of Main and Pine streets and drew up plans for a $6,000 house of worship.

The freeze of 1895 brought a blow to the entire state. Many people had put their entire life savings into the orange groves, and now they were gone. Thousands of people left the state, never to return. In just a few weeks, the population of Orlando dropped from more than 10,000 to less than 2,500.

Gradually, people started returning to Florida and in 1900 the population of Orange County was nearly as high as ten years before. In 1915, First Baptist dedicated a new sanctuary. It was filled beyond its capacity of 1,200 people as other churches joined in the service.

A period of great vision for the missionary task of the church came during the pastorate of Dr. Dean Adcock, from 1919 to 1937, and this missions' emphasis continues to be a vital part of First Baptist. Under Dr. Adcock's leadership, the Sunday School grew so large that a three-story brick annex was built on the east side of the church.

In 1938, Dr. J. Powell Tucker became pastor. Under his pastorate, the membership of the church grew from 1,796 in 1937 to 3,217 in 1955. The church continued to grow, and in 1961 a new sanctuary was completed. During this time, Dr. Henry A. Parker led the church in adopting a unified budget and completing a second educational building in addition to completing the new sanctuary.

In 1977, the new six-story Christian Life Center was dedicated. The Orlando Chamber of Commerce awarded a gold brick to the church for this improvement to the city's skyline. Pastor Jim Henry began his ministry in that same year.

The year 1981 marked another significant year in the history of First Baptist Church. Once again the church had grown beyond capacity and there was no room for expansion at the downtown site. The church voted to purchase 150 acres at I-4 and 33rd Street to build a new church complex. In only 70 days, $2.5 million was raised to purchase the land. A year later, the church began a campaign to raise $12.6 million over the following three years. In October, 1982, $13.1 million was pledged. The church will have its first service in their 6,000-seat Worship Center on Sunday, February 10, 1985.

The full-service financial institution of the future

Because of the aggressive role that the financial industry was to realize in the recent rapid growth of Orlando, it was fitting that a company such as First Fidelity would be created. First Fidelity's position as a unique financial intermediary has brought to Orlando a synergistic array of financial, risk management, and real property products and services unavailable anywhere else from a single source.

This Florida chartered stock savings and loan association was established in Winter Park in 1980 by a group of local investors organized by two Orlando law partners, Richard R. Swann and Edward E. Haddock Jr. Earlier, in 1979, Swann and Haddock had formed a group of investors who purchased American Pioneer Corporation, a holding company. The principals of the firm had envisioned the creation of a multifaceted and diversified financial institution which would serve a broad spectrum of Orlando's consumer and corporate financial needs. The purchase of the holding company was the first step in creating that entity, today's First Fidelity.

First Fidelity's present structure traces back to the founding of American Pioneer Life Insurance Company in Orlando on July 5, 1961, by Walter L. Hays, a well-known Orlandoan.

Previously, Hays had formed a number of important local firms, beginning with American Fire and Casualty Insurance Company in 1937. Over the years, he also originated American Mortgage Company of Florida, American Independent Reinsurance Company, and American Savings and Loan Association which is now owned by Coral Gables Federal. American Pioneer Life was founded to complete the "circle of service" to consumers — a concept which would be fully realized some two decades after Walter Hays' death in 1962.

The holding company, American Pioneer Corporation, was organized in 1970. A real estate development subsidiary, American Pioneer Land Company, followed two years later.

The original headquarters in downtown Orlando of American Pioneer Life Insurance Company, the predecessor to today's First Fidelity Savings and Loan Association.

The present headquarters on East Colonial Drive of First Fidelity Savings and Loan Association.

In July 1979, controlling interest in the holding company was purchased by the group of investors organized by Swann and Haddock.

Rapidly, the other elements of the planned organization began to come together. American Pioneer Title Insurance Company was formed in 1980. Later that same year, First Fidelity was established in Winter Park. The following year, 1981, saw the incorporation of American Pioneer Casualty Insurance Company.

Late in 1982, American Pioneer Corporation acquired First Fidelity in a reverse triangular acquisition. And on December 31, 1982, First Fidelity purchased First Federal Savings and Loan Association of Martin County — the leading thrift institution on Florida's Treasure Coast. This acquisition substantially increased First Fidelity's assets, marketing area, and management team.

In 1983, to complement its real estate development subsidiary, First Fidelity purchased the Savill/Sanderlin Holding Company, an Orlando-based development and construction company. Founded in 1958, this organization was the first firm to develop second-home condominium communities along Florida's east coast. The company's first such development was Holiday Cove at New Smyrna Beach, begun in the late 1960s. Later, the Sanderlin firm developed and built several condominium complexes along Florida's Atlantic Coast. Today, the company also builds high rise-apartment buildings, banks, and other commercial structures in joint venture projects throughout Florida.

Rounding out First Fidelity's broad-based financial organization in early 1984, the Company acquired the Flagship Bank of Orlando, its five branches, two branches of

the Flagship Bank of Seminole County, and one branch of Sun Bank/SW in Cape Coral, Florida.

The Orlando Bank, chartered as Citizens National Bank of Orlando in 1947, was founded by C.N. Gay, a former comptroller general of the State of Florida. In 1951, Colonial State Bank was organized as an affiliate institution. The name was changed to Colonial Bank of Orlando in 1957 and, subsequently, to Orlando Bank and Trust Company. In 1974, this entity was acquired by Flagship Banks, Inc., and became the Flagship Bank of Orlando.

The acquisition of the Flagship Bank of Orlando, long known for its aggressive commercial lending practices, gave First Fidelity experienced bank management and a base in both commercial and consumer lending, as well as trust and other fiduciary powers.

Today's First Fidelity *is* the synergistic, multifaceted, and diversified full-service financial institution which had long been envisioned. With 550 employees, 20 offices throughout central and south Florida and assets in excess of half a billion dollars, the Company has the ability to offer more financial products and services than any other entity anywhere in the Country.

First Fidelity has become singularly unique. Its goal is to provide financial services to Floridians and to Florida's business community in ways that are, themselves, unique. And though its structure is and will remain visionary and progressive, its philosophy will remain bound to the traditional values of its origins.

Orlando's football classic grew from a tangerine into an entire industry

The Tangerine Bowl was conceived in the club lounge of Orlando Elks Lodge 1079 in the spring of 1946. The members were brewing new ideas for fund raisers to help defray expenses at the Harry Anna Crippled Children's Hospital in Umatilla, Florida. The Gator Bowl in Jacksonville had been founded the year before, and the Elks saw benefits and a future in starting their own bowl.

A committee of five, later to become the Tangerine Bowl Commission, collected hundred-dollar commitments from 21 members and the game was born.

On January 1, 1947, Maryville College and Catawba College, relying heavily on World War II veterans, played the first Tangerine Bowl game before a capacity crowd of 9,000 at Orlando Municipal Stadium. The game was a success and became an annual event.

In 1951, the Tangerine Bowl found a niche as the unofficial small college championship game. Smaller schools with great records were always eager to come South in winter. The year 1958 was unusual, not only because two Tangerine Bowls were played, on January 1 and December 27, but because East Texas State won both times.

Throughout the 1950s, the Tangerine Bowl was known as "The Little Bowl with the Big Heart." Game proceeds went directly to charity, and for a time, even competing schools waived payoffs above and beyond their expenses.

In 1960, the commission rescheduled the game to avoid broadcast conflicts with larger bowls on New Year's Day. To celebrate its fifteenth anniversary that year, the Duke and Duchess of Bedford were special guest judges of the Tangerine Bowl Queen's Contest.

An organized format for competition was introduced in 1964 when the T-Bowl became the championship game of the Atlantic Coast Regional Conference.

In 1966, the bowl game was broadcast live on television for the first time by ABC network affiliates along the Atlantic Coast. Regional telecasts continued sporadically through 1972.

When attendance in 1967 hit a 20-year record low, it became apparent that a new spirit was needed to revive the bowl. A group of civic leaders led by C. Floyd Cooper, George Stuart, and Marty Greco formed the Tangerine Bowl Association. With their aid, an agreement was forged with the Southern and Mid-American conferences to send champions to Orlando.

Results were immediate. In December 1968, an overflow crowd of 16,114 in an enlarged stadium witnessed the greatest offensive scoring day in bowl history. Richmond

outlasted Ohio University, 49–42, and combined to set 20 team and individual records that have stood for over fifteen years.

In September 1972, the Tangerine Bowl Association incorporated as the Tangerine Sports Association, Inc., a nonprofit charitable organization.

In 1973, a "major" university team played

The 1980 Florida Gators keyed Orlando's first 50,000 seat sellout to put the bowl in the national limelight.

In 1955, palm trees waved between Tinker Field and the Tangerine Bowl's west stands — a time when the game was known as the "Little Bowl with the Big Heart."

in the Tangerine Bowl; curiously, it was on their home field. Florida accepted the 1973 invitation, but played the game in Gainesville since ticket demand exceeded Orlando's stadium capacity. A "major" team paid another dividend — a national television audience on the Mizlou Sports Network.

Orlando expanded the Tangerine Bowl to 51,000 seats during the 1974 and 1975 bowl years, while Miami of Ohio was routing Georgia and South Carolina amid the dust of construction.

The proof of major bowl status was confirmed in 1980 by a record sellout crowd of 52,541 at Florida's victory over Maryland.

Community support snowballed in 1982. Bahia Temple of Orlando committed to buy 7,000 tickets a year and supply manpower for all bowl events. The association, in kind, named Shriners Hospitals as the Tangerine Bowl's primary charitable beneficiary.

In 1983, the bowl changed its name to the Florida Citrus Bowl as part of a major sponsorship agreement with the Florida Department of Citrus. A long-sought major network television contract was also signed with NBC for future telecasts.

From small beginnings to the present, Orlando's bowl has thrived on community support, a hospitable reputation, and a thirst for major college football. Above all, it has been charitable to needy and disabled children.

A *major supplier of natural gas to Florida consumers*

The year was 1954. In Texas, a firm named Houston Texas Gas and Oil Corporation conceived the idea of building a pipeline from Louisiana to Florida to serve consumers in the only area in the nation then without natural gas service. About the same time, another company, Coastal Transmission Corporation, was organizing a pipeline to supply gas from South Texas to Louisiana.

These companies combined in 1957 and formed The Houston Corporation. Their two pipelines were connected at Baton Rouge, Louisiana, resulting in an interstate pipeline system that later became Florida Gas Transmission Company.

Florida's residential and commercial demands for gas, even in the winter, were not sufficient to justify a pipeline. But the company aggressively sought industrial markets and signed contracts to transport gas that would be bought by Florida Power & Light Company and Florida Power Corporation for use in generating electricity.

In June 1959, within 9 months of obtaining financing, The Houston Corporation completed construction on 1,482 miles of main transmission line and 765 miles of gathering and sales pipelines linking the Mexico-Texas border with Miami, and began delivering natural gas to Florida.

Anticipating that day, The Houston Corporation in 1958 had bought existing manufacturing and distribution systems that supplied "manufactured gas" to a number of Florida communities. These systems were converted to natural gas operations in 1959, serving customers in Jacksonville, Miami, Orlando, Lakeland, Eustis, Mt. Dora, and Umatilla with clean, economical natural gas brought into the state by the new pipeline. Service to Daytona Beach, St. Petersburg and Avon Park/ Frostproof came later.

By 1962, many changes had taken place. Portions of the company still located in Texas were moved to Florida (headquarters had been established in St. Petersburg, originally in a warehouse with rented desks); The Houston Corporation had been renamed Florida Gas Company; Houston Texas Gas and Oil Corporation had changed its name to Florida Gas Transmission Company and Coastal Transmission Corporation had been merged into it; and the pipeline had begun its first expansion program. (Additional capacity was added in other major expansions in 1966 and 1969 and in smaller expansions later.) And W.J. "Jack" Bowen, who had been Coastal Transmission's president, had been promoted to the presidency of both Florida Gas Company and Florida Gas Transmission.

In 1962, Florida Gas moved its general offices from St. Petersburg to Winter Park, occupying a previously unused building at the

Florida Gas Transmission Company constructed a twelve-mile lateral pipeline connecting its mainline with Walt Disney World when the huge vacation and recreation complex was built near Orlando. Natural gas is used in the Magic Kingdom, at EPCOT, and at Lake Buena Vista for cooking, water heating, decorative lighting, and electric power generation.

intersection of Orange Avenue and Highway 17-92. When the company built and moved into its present 7 story building in 1970, the old building — immediately adjacent — was literally sawed into 3 pieces and moved a block northeast to become an office complex.

In 1962, Florida Gas Company built a hydrocarbons extraction plant astride Florida Gas Transmission's pipeline at Brooker, Florida, near Gainesville. There, Florida Hydrocarbons Company removes hydrocarbon liquids — propane, butane, and natural gasoline — from the pipeline gas stream and markets these products over a wide area.

In 1968, Florida Gas Company's stock began trading on the New York Stock Exchange.

Florida Gas Transmission Company's headquarters are located in this 7-story office building at the intersection of Orange Avenue and Highway 17-92 in Winter Park, which was completed in mid-1970.

In August 1979, all outstanding stock was purchased by Continental Group, Inc., of Stamford, Connecticut. Following the acquisition, Florida Gas Company was renamed Continental Resources Company.

Shortly before the merger, Florida Gas Company's distribution facilities were sold to Peoples Gas System, Inc. of Tampa.

Although Continental Resources moved to Houston, Texas, in 1982, Florida Gas Transmission's headquarters and administrative offices remain in Winter Park.

Its pipeline system, now totaling approximately 4,300 miles, is the sole supplier of natural gas to peninsular Florida. Generally following the contour of the Gulf of Mexico, the system delivers to Florida daily some 725 million cubic feet of gas from producing fields in Texas, Oklahoma, Louisiana, Alabama, Mississippi, and Florida, and offshore in the Gulf of Mexico. This represents about 85 percent of all the natural gas consumed in the state.

Florida Gas Transmission also sells gas to 35 privately owned and municipal companies that distribute it to residential, commercial, and industrial customers in more than 100 Florida communities.

Under the leadership of W.J. "Red" Smith, a 26-year company veteran who became president in January 1981, Florida Gas Transmission continues to be one of the principal suppliers of basic energy to the southeastern United States.

Seventy-six years of care . . . and caring

On an October day in 1908, a small group of Seventh-day Adventists began operating a new hospital in the rural countryside outside Orlando. With faith and $9,000 (some of it raised by mortgaging their own homes), the Adventists hired two physicians and turned a wood-framed farmhouse into a 20-bed hospital.

Today that hospital — Florida Hospital — is among the South's largest, with construction underway in 1984 to bring its size to more than 1,100 beds. Its nationally recognized programs of heart care, organ transplantation, joint replacement, cancer care, and others draw more than 36,000 patients each year from throughout the United States and around the world.

But it is not buildings alone, or the excellence of its state-of-the-art equipment and technology, which have made Florida Hospital central Florida's busiest hospital.

From its earliest years, the hospital has been known for its Christian compassion for the sick — a combination of care and caring.

In its early days, that care combined rest and recuperation with a small medical and surgical program. Many patients came from the North to spend long Florida winters basking in the sun, playing croquet on the lawn, or rowing in Lake Estelle. Evenings were spent listening to health lectures or to special musical programs in the chintz-patterned parlor. Mealtimes were leisurely and gracious — white linen cloths and napkins and a fresh rose at each table.

Hydrotherapy, rest, moderate exercise, fresh air, good diet, and sunshine were major components of the medical program, along with a small surgical program.

With the beginning of the Depression in 1929, life began to change at "the San" (as the hospital was then known). Some patients paid by produce or materials, and employees received as little as 20 cents an hour, or no pay at all some weeks. Still the San survived. Patients gathered around the cool porches at night to listen to F.D.R.'s promise of a New Deal — and, gradually, prosperity returned.

The war years of the forties posed the next major challenge as construction in the nation came to a near halt. Still, new wings were added, in 1938 and 1940, and the hospital continued to grow.

At war's end, extensive rebuilding and modernization were the first order of the day, and as the soldiers returned home, boom times began. The war, however, had brought a change in medical institutions, and the nation entered the "insurance" era. Gone forever was the San's "rest cure" treatment. In its place were modern medical and surgical care.

The years since have been remarkable. The hospital has grown to more than six times its 1960 size and has been at the leading edge of new technology. Guiding the hospital through thirteen of those growth years was Don Welch (now head of the Adventists' nationwide hospital system) and his successors, Bob Scott, Mardian Blair, and Tom Werner.

Today, Florida Hospital also operates a large Altamonte Springs hospital which is seeing tremendous growth, as well as a third hospital in Apopka. Under construction are new beds, along with professional office buildings, new facilities for ambulatory care, cancer treatment, and psychiatric programs.

With all this growth, Florida Hospital today retains the same dedication to service as its founders: a commitment to the finest care available in an atmosphere of Christian caring — a commitment not just to a high quality of care, but a high quality of caring.

Florida Hospital at its opening in 1908.

Before air-conditioning, the cool porches were popular gathering places.

Hospital nurses take part in a 1930's Orlando parade.

New patient tower under construction at FH/Orlando.

Dedicated to the success of Florida's future

W*e are now in Florida to live and work. We expect to spend the balance of our days here. We have all the money necessary for any reasonable effort to help Florida grow and prosper... through helpful works, let us build up good in this state and make it a better place in which to live.*

Those were the words of Alfred I. duPont when he moved to Florida in 1926. The Florida National Bank of Jacksonville became the first unit of the Florida National group when duPont made available $15 million of his personal funds to secure its deposits, preventing its failure during the financially chaotic post-boom years in Florida.

The fourth banking organization to receive duPont's help was the Florida Bank at Orlando, which was purchased in 1930. The opening of a new bank during the times and financial conditions that existed in 1930 was indeed an unusual event. Earlier, in August 1926, the North Orlando State Bank had been established in the Fort Gatlin Hotel Building. On March 30, 1930, this bank moved to the One North Orange Avenue building, formerly occupied by the State Bank of Orlando and Trust Company, and its name was changed to the Florida Bank at Orlando. When duPont purchased the bank and moved its location, it was one of two existing banks of six that had previously operated in the Orlando area. It opened with initial deposits of $800,000. By June 1930, resources were $1,225,000. By the end of 1934, deposits had grown to $3,530,000. The trend of the economy and the growth of the Orlando area was slowly, but steadily, improving.

Alfred I. duPont, who had helped develop his family interest into one of America's greatest industrial enterprises, was now active in the development of Florida. He had a simple philosophy of life: "Be fair to everyone, do as much good as you can, be honest with yourself, which means honest with everybody ... if one would keep one's head above water, one must struggle and use such weapons as our Creator has provided."

In August 1933, Florida Bank at Orlando purchased the ten-story bank and office building it had been occupying for the previous three years for the price of $230,000. It represented the largest real estate transaction in the city since the boom years of the 1920s. By March 1945, the bank's deposits had grown to approximately $20 million.

When a National Charter was granted on February 10, 1954, the bank name changed to The Florida National Bank at Orlando. A new five-story bank building was built, and the bank moved into its present home at 801 North Orange Avenue on May 15, 1961. The bank's first branch office was opened in 1978 in the Fort Gatlin Shopping Center. Since then, four additional branch offices were built. A new data operations center that

A 1884 view of the North Orange Avenue, from atop the Florida National Bank Building.

Present location of the Florida National Bank at 801 North Orange Avenue.

serves all Florida National banks in central Florida was built in 1982. In 1983, the bank began serving Seminole County with three offices. Presently, Florida National has fifteen banking facilities in Orange and Seminole counties. All statewide Florida National banks were merged into one bank in July 1983, and Florida National Bank/Orlando was designated a metropolitan bank serving Orange, Osceola, and Seminole counties with commercial, corporate, real estate, international, and retail facilities. Throughout the state of Florida, Florida National Bank operates from 148 locations with $4.7 billion in assets.

Florida National's mission statement sums up the company's position for the future: "Florida National will be a leading financial services organization, offering superior products to our customers to increase quality assets, profit, and capital which will provide for continued growth for our people and a greater contribution to our stockholders and the communities we serve."

A generation of progress: arc lamps to primary energy supplier

Most beginnings are small. Some are memorable. Florida Power Corporation's genesis was both.

In St. Petersburg, the night of August 5, 1897 was long recalled as the time when the city's first streetlights blazed into being. Thirty 32-candlepower arc lamps (about 150 watts by today's standards) illuminated the darkening sky. The lights belonged to the fledgling St. Petersburg Electric Light & Power Company and, according to a published report in the *Sub Peninsula Sun,* "The light that the arcs now give is truly wonderful to behold."

But, when it came to streetlighting, the coastal city is considered by some Floridians to be a johnny-come-lately.

It was at the meeting of the DeLand City Council on January 5, 1888 that A.G. Kingsbury proposed that his company, the DeLand Electric Light Company, brighten the town's downtown section by installing three electric streetlights. His proposal (which was to cost the citizens of DeLand $100 a month) was for arc lights to be set at "the (Woodlawn) Boulevard railway crossing; at the corner opposite Ross' shop on New York Avenue; and at the corner of New York and Alabama Avenues." The council agreed with some evident enthusiasm and, by mid-year, the lights were in service.

Like those in St. Petersburg, they were arc lights and the subject of much comment. In keeping with their coastal counterparts, they too burned from sunset to midnight during the first few years of operation. Reaction to the lights was not one of universal praise. Wrote one unnamed chronicler, "they give a brilliant white light with a blue or purplish tinge and the effect is rather glaring and ghastly."

In St. Petersburg, the power for the streetlights came from a power plant that had been moved from its original site in Tarpon Springs, some 30 miles to the north. The imaginative name of the Tarpon Springs operation was the Polar Ice & Light Company. The

Delpico Power Plant serves the area at the turn of the century. The original building, renovated in 1950, still houses Florida Power's DeLand district storeroom, engineering, and line departments.

power source in DeLand was the electric and ice plant Kingsbury built on Rehbehn Street in 1886. The remnants of the Polar Ice Company have long since disappeared but, after extensive renovation in the 1950s, Kingsbury's original power plant still serves as a part of Florida Power's line and engineering department storeroom at the site.

Many years later, when the tiny St. Petersburg and DeLand companies had matured and eventually merged to become today's Florida Power Corporation, those early arc lights were the source of some semi-serious in-house squabbling. The discussions centered around the actual birthdate of the present corporation.

The lights shone first in DeLand, certainly. But Kingsbury's arrangement with the DeLand City Council was evidently of a personal nature. In St. Petersburg, Frank Davis was perhaps more businesslike. He applied for and received a state charter to do business. The charter is dated July 18, 1899.

Shortly after the turn of the century, the DeLand company was reorganized under the guidance of Philadelphia hatmaker John B. Stetson. It became the DeLand Power & Ice

Company (Delpico) and was given its state charter in 1908.

So, the evidence of the lights notwithstanding, the official birthdate of Florida Power is 1899, the year the St. Petersburg company was chartered.

During the first quarter of the twentieth century, small electrical power and distribution companies proliferated throughout Florida as entrepreneurs and municipalities moved headlong into the electric age. But power technology developed rapidly, and it soon became evident that one large power station could replace several smaller ones and do it economically. The day of a company serving a few hundred customers was over practically before it had begun. One after another, the small systems were bought up by organizations bent on taking advantage of the economies of scale.

It happened to the DeLand company when, in 1924, it was sold for $357,775 by the Stetson estate to New York's General Finance Corporation and, in short, became a part of General Finance's Florida subsidiary, the Florida Public Service Company.

In just nine years, Public Service acquired over $17 million worth of utility properties. The company's service area in 1933 extended some 120 miles from DeLand to Avon Park.

On the state's west coast, the same pattern prevailed as the St. Petersburg company constantly expanded its area of service.

Frank Davis' old company, incorporated with $13,000 in capital, became the St. Petersburg Lighting Company on May 26, 1915. To reflect growth, it was renamed the Pinellas Power Company on May 17, 1923. Finally, on May 15, 1927, Florida Power Corporation came into being. The company's service area ran in a broad corridor up the west coast of Florida and into Georgia. It abutted the Florida Public Service area field of operation most of the way. The merger of the two companies both from a practical and legal aspect became inevitable.

The first steps toward corporate union were taken in 1937 but it was not until January, 1944 — 56 years after A.G. Kingsbury made his proposal to the DeLand Council — that the Securities and Exchange Commission gave final approval to the merger.

Florida Power has continued to grow with the state to the point that, in 1984, the company serves almost 3 million Floridians in 32 counties. The fragile old power plants have been replaced by a combination of coal, nuclear, and oil plants capable of producing about 6 million kilowatts of power. (In 1914, Delpico's combined output totaled 375 kilowatts.) The company operates more then 20,000 miles of distribution line, employs nearly 5,000 men and women and is part of a nationwide network that enables power to be exchanged readily.

The beginnings were small; the growth has been a fascinating challenge; the future is unlimited.

DeLand, 1888, has one of the nation's earliest commercial streetlighting systems.

They changed the course of central Florida history

Florida Ranch Lands team.

Florida Ranch Lands ... the name of the company reflects its beginning in 1954 as a real estate firm formed to facilitate the sale of central Florida ranch acreage. Its founders, Craig Linton Sr. and Nelson Boice, were indeed ranchland owners themselves.

But today, that unassuming name belies the continuing impact of the brokerage firm on its community, and the fact that it engineered what has been called the single most important real estate sale in Florida history.

By 1958, the thrust of the company's efforts had shifted away from agricultural land brokerage to investment and commercial real estate, and Florida Ranch Lands had moved its offices to downtown Orlando.

Orlando, in the early 1960s, was still an easy-going, midsized Florida city, an inland commercial center surrounded for miles by citrus groves that formed the heart of the state's citrus industry. For out-of-state visitors, it was a rest stop on the way to Miami — a place somewhere west of Daytona Beach and east of Cypress Gardens.

Events in 1965 changed everything. Florida Ranch Lands, the community, and the lives of millions of Floridians for years to come would never be the same.

That year, the mysterious representative of an unnamed party appeared at Florida Ranch Lands. He was looking, he said, for about 10,000 acres of undeveloped land. The representative revealed only that he had other land searches in progress elsewhere in Florida.

Linton and Boice decided that whoever

the interested parties were, the project they were planning would benefit any area they ultimately selected. So, in addition to brokerage work, the partners set about selling central Florida itself as the best of all possible sites.

As the months passed, acquisitions for the unknown buyer quietly grew to more than 20,000 acres, eventually involving some 52 separate parcels of land. Many landholders were absentee owners, out-of-staters who had never even seen their property. The complex researching, contacting, and negotiating with so many diverse parties, while maintaining a low profile, strained Florida Ranch Lands to incredible limits.

Eventually, of course, the people at Florida Ranch Lands learned the identity of the man behind the mystery. The firm went on a footing of absolute secrecy that would have been the envy of the CIA. Any slip would have sent the price tags of remaining parcels skyrocketing and probably killed the entire project. As it was, Florida Ranch Lands managed to complete the total acquisition of some 27,400 acres for an average of $350 an acre.

In late 1965, the genial mystery buyer stepped off his plane in Orlando to make the announcement that Linton, Boice, and their staff had worked and waited months to hear. The name was Walt Disney, the announcement — Walt Disney World.

In the years that followed, Florida Ranch Lands continued to broker some of central Florida's most significant land purchases. It assembled 18,000 acres near Sanford for the

Mackle Brothers, Florida's largest land developer, and Deltona was born. In 1968, the General Acceptance Corporation appointed the firm to assemble 33,800 acres for what would become the Poinciana development. Other major clients have included Exxon, the Burroughs Corporation, and the 4,500-acre residential community of Williamsburg near Sea World.

In 1983, Florida Ranch Lands represented golfing great Arnold Palmer in his negotiations to purchase the 1,600-acre Isleworth property in Windermere, just south of Orlando, from one of Orlando's pioneer families. Located on the prestigious Butler chain of lakes, it is destined to become central Florida's most luxurious golf resort community by the mid-1980s.

Today, Florida Ranch Lands is known in the real estate industry as "the Broker's Broker," representing important land owners and dealing in transactions of $750,000 or more. Craig Linton Jr., who is preparing himself for top management in the company, said in one interview, "This is what I call a long-hand business. You've got to do everything longhanded. There are no shortcuts ... we do everything on a personalized basis."

Boice, the Lintons, and all of those at Florida Ranch Lands have used their "long-hand" style to help rewrite the story of central Florida with a flair ... and to indelibly alter the course of its history and economy in the foreseeable future.

A *history of growth, service, and innovation*

Fifty years after its founding, Freedom Savings and Loan Association continues its tradition of growth by offering innovative services to its customers. Freedom's present corporate structure was achieved through a historic merger with ComBanks in 1983. A fresh page was written in history books of financial institutions when a savings and loan association acquired a commercial bank and merged it into the existing organization. The union signaled the birth of a new era of banking power in Florida.

Freedom and ComBanks grew in many of the same ways — mergers, name changes, asset and deposit growth, new markets, diversified and innovative products, and customer service and satisfaction.

Freedom. In January 1934, 20 investors formed First Federal Savings and Loan Association of Tampa. Backed by $7,500 in subscription pledges under Charter Number 62 from the Federal Home Loan Bank Board, a business framework was established which would later mean homes, civic progress, and financial freedom for thousands of Floridians. By the end of the first year, assets totaled $96,000.

The Association's first merger, with Lafayette Federal of Tampa, came in 1940. At the end of that year, First Federal boasted assets of nearly $1.8 million. In 1951, the board voted to establish branch offices, launching a plan of growth which has taken the company across the state in recent years. By the late fifties, assets had climbed toward $80 million. In 1972, First Federal became the first Florida savings and loan to add 24-hour automated teller equipment.

Although First Federal actively competed for customers through mergers and branching, there has always been a human service side to its story. First Federal helped to build a beach pavilion in Clermont and helped to rebuild the Auburndale Library. During the early 1970s energy crisis, First Federal em-

Always a crowd pleaser, Freedom's balloon attracts passersby at a recent appearance.

ployees initiated a computerized carpooling system.

In 1974, First Federal changed its name to Freedom Federal. Freedom was more than a name; it was and is a symbol of independence and the freedom of financial security for its customers. Shortly after the name change came the familiar red double-banner logo and a new symbol of Freedom — a bright red and white hot-air balloon that remains an integral part of advertising and community relations programs sponsored by Freedom.

Freedom's hot-air balloon is a familiar sight at community events around the state.

In 1980, Freedom converted from a federally chartered mutual association to a Florida chartered capital stock association. By 1982, Freedom's $1.3 billion in assets had placed it tenth in size among Florida savings and loans.

ComBanks. Chartered in 1954, the Commercial Bank at Winter Park opened its doors for business in February 1955 as an affiliate of the Florida Bank and Trust Company. Among its founders was A.G. Bush, chairman of the Executive Committee of the 3-M Company. In 1962, E.G. Banks was elected president of ComBank/Winter Park with Bush continuing as chairman of the board. By year-end, deposits had grown to $17.5 million. In 1963, the bank received trust powers and opened a trust department by mid-year.

In 1966, on a broader front, branch banking legislation was proposed, and statewide bank holding companies were being formed. In 1967, ComBanks Corporation was organized as a one-bank holding company. During the next few years, the holding company purchased ownerships of several banks. By 1972, six banks comprised the multibank holding company.

In 1976, Marvin Warner, a Cincinnati businessman, and Hugh Culverhouse, owner of the Tampa Bay Buccaneer Football Team, completed a successful tender offer of ComBank shares. By January 1977, they owned 85 percent of ComBank stock. By 1979, Warner purchased Culverhouse's interest in the company and was serving as chairman and chief executive officer of ComBanks. Robert M. Klingler joined ComBanks as executive vice-president in 1980.

On July 6, 1981, Freedom and ComBanks jointly announced an agreement for Freedom to purchase the ComBanks commercial banking organization. The merger, consummated on March 31, 1983, added to Freedom's system a total of seventeen full-service banking locations and $425 million of assets.

Though taking separate pathways to achieve the union, Freedom and ComBanks followed the same key strategy throughout their active and innovative histories: assuring the best in customer service and customer satisfaction — new banking power at its best.

In April 1984, as a further extension of Freedom's policy to provide more services to its customers, Robert M. Klingler, newly elevated to positions as chairman of the board and chief executive officer, signaled his confidence in Freedom's long-term outlook by announcing a major joint venture with Electronic Realty Associates (ERA). The joint venture, another "first" in the financial industry, will provide real estate brokerage services in Freedom offices throughout the state.

Freedom's long-time commitment to growth, service, and innovation endures today, enabling the company to respond to the challenges in Florida's future.

A 76-year tradition of legal and community service

Seventy-six years ago LeRoy B. Giles came home from the University of Virginia law school to the small farming and citrus community of Orlando to begin the practice of law. He practiced law for several years, then with E.W. Davis, formed the firm of Davis & Giles. In 1923, Mr. Giles and J. Thomas Gurney Sr. became partners under the firm name of Giles & Gurney, which continued until 1945. After World War II, David W. Hedrick and James C. Robinson became Mr. Giles' associates. The partnership of Giles, Hedrick & Robinson was formed in 1953, and following Mr. Giles' death, was incorporated as a professional association. The members and associates of the firm presently consist of David W. Hedrick, James C. Robinson, Frederick J. Ward, William G. Mitchell, James J. Loveless Jr., Harlan Tuck, Eugene B. Cawood, John J. Reid, Carey L. Hill, Terry C. Young, Susan F. Murphy, Stephen F. Broome, Paul Newnum, and Robert Hoogland. In 1984, the firm established a branch office in Melbourne, Florida, in order to serve its clients in the Space Coast area.

The firm provides quality legal service with emphasis on all areas of civil practice, including real estate and corporate law, estate planning, taxation and probate law, administrative and governmental law, international law, and general civil litigation. It has represented Orange County, Florida, The Greater Orlando Aviation Authority, City of Orlando and other governmental bodies, utilities, transportation companies, savings and loan associations, insurance companies, real estate and development companies, and citrus interests.

Outstanding lawyers who have been associated with the firm include Supreme Court Justice Campbell B. Thornal, Circuit Judge W.A. Pattishall, County Judge John G. Baker, Circuit Judge Bernard C. Muszynski, Warren B. Parks, Edward K. Goethe, Thomas Gurney Sr., Wilson Sanders, O.B. McEwan, and Fletcher G. Rush Jr. These and others have provided leadership in the Orange County Bar Association, The Florida Bar, and the American Bar Association.

LeRoy Giles established a tradition in the firm of providing leadership in the legal, business, and community life of Orlando. He also gave everyone in the firm the feeling of belonging to a family. This continues to be an important part of its ambiance.

Following Mr. Giles' tradition, the firm's lawyers have actively participated in such community projects as the establishment and development of the University of Central Florida, the Orlando International Airport passenger terminal, the nonprofit retirement facilities of Westminster Towers and Winter Park Towers, the Central Florida Research

LeRoy B. Giles, founder, 1886–1963.

Park, Harry P. Leu Botanical Gardens, the Central Florida Civic Theatre, Loch Haven Art Center, and public broadcasting's Channel 24. Lawyers of the firm have served as officers in numerous church activities, civic organizations, scouting, and cultural and recreational organizations.

To improve the quality of legal services provided and encourage individual growth, the firm promotes and financially supports the continuing education of its non-lawyer

personnel as well as that of the attorneys.

Giles, Hedrick & Robinson, P.A., proudly reflects upon its legal and community heritage and looks forward to continuing this tradition of service in the years ahead.

"A law firm for the times"

The seed of the law firm of Gray, Harris & Robinson was planted in 1923 when G. Wayne Gray opened the doors of his law practice in "The City Beautiful." The guiding force behind the growth of the firm to its 1984 complement of 17 lawyers and 51 staff members has been a quest for excellence coupled with strong personal commitments to the civic and cultural needs of central Florida.

G. Wayne Gray began practice in Orlando after receiving his bachelor of laws from the University of Florida in 1922. A prominent lawyer and civic leader, Mr. Gray served from 1933 until 1944 as an Orlando city commissioner. He was primarily responsible for establishment of Herndon Airport, now the Orlando Executive Airport. Mr. Gray was a licensed pilot and active in aviation matters. It was through his personal friendship with the renowned Captain Eddie Rickenbacker, World War I flying ace and later president of Eastern Airlines, that Gray was able, while serving as Orlando's mayor pro-tem, to bring Eastern Airlines to Orlando. As a result, Orlando acquired its first commercial airline service. Recognized as a leading real property and probate lawyer in Orlando, Mr. Gray died in 1965.

His son, J. Charles Gray, who received his B.A. and L.L.B. degrees from the University of Florida, joined him in the practice of law in 1958. While at the University of Florida, Charles Gray served as vice-president of the student body and general chairman of homecoming and was elected to the University Hall of Fame and Florida Blue Key. After joining his father, he served as solicitor for the city of Orlando and chairman of the Florida State Turnpike Authority.

Gordon H. Harris and Richard M. Robinson, honors and high honors graduates of the University of Florida Law School and members of Florida Blue Key, joined Gray in 1970 to form what is now Gray, Harris & Robinson, P.A., a progressive, full-service law firm committed to excellence in the practice of law and providing leadership in the civic, governmental, and cultural affairs of the Orlando area.

In 1978, the firm was designated county attorney for Orange County, with Gray as lead attorney. It served in this role during the county's most explosive growth era and was instrumental in providing the legal expertise to solve critical community needs such as expanded sewer and water facilities, the Civic/Convention Center on International Drive, the County Administration Building, expanded county jail facilities, the establishment of the Orange County Library District and downtown library expansion, a new countywide fire department, regulation of adult entertainment, and improved intergovernmental coordination.

The firm partners have been active in many business, civic, and educational endeavors. James F. Page Jr. was an organizer and founding director of First State Savings &

J. Charles Gray.

Richard M. Robinson.

Loan Association, a stock savings & loan. J. Charles Gray was an organizer and founding director of Southeast National Bank of Orlando in 1969, and serves on the Regional Southeast Bank Advisory Board. Mr. Page was a leading organizer of a children's hospital for Orlando. Page and Gray were leading organizers of the Computer Science Research Institute at the University of Central Florida, and for many years Gray has served as chairman of the President's Council of Advisors at UCF. Harris served as potentate of the Bahia Shrine, president of the University of Florida Alumni Association and chairman of the Board of Trustees of Trinity Preparatory School. Firm members were also active with the Boy Scouts of America, committees of the Florida Board of Regents, ORMC Foundation, Citrus Bowl, Rotary, Orange County and Florida Bar committees, Orlando Area Chamber of Commerce and the Industrial Development Commission of Mid-Florida.

The partners of the firm are J. Charles Gray, Gordon H. Harris, Richard M. Robinson, Phillip R. Finch, Pamela O. Price, James F. Page Jr., Philip H. Trees, William A. Boyles, Thomas J. Wilkes Jr. and Thomas A. Cloud.

While active in civic, governmental and cultural affairs, the firm strengthened its legal capabilities by establishing environmental law, administrative law, and bond practices, as well as expanding its corporate, tax, probate, litigation, and real property departments to further the partners' commitment to a full-service, progressive, law firm.

Gordon Harris.

It started with one man, one mule, and one shovel

Francis Evans Hubbard of Clio, South Carolina, founded in 1920 what was to become one of the South's leading road-building firms, Hubbard Construction Company of Orlando.

In 1920, F.E. Hubbard had been married to the former Mildred Muldrow for two years and they had two children, Betty and Frank. Hubbard had a farm near Florence, South Carolina, and the Buick agency there, but he wanted other challenges. When he heard of an opportunity to get into the contracting business, he went after it.

The offer was made by the late J.D. Manly of Leesburg, whose Southern Paving Company was paving streets in Florence. With one wagon, one mule, and a shovel, Hubbard began hauling sand for the project.

He liked the work. Soon, he sold the Buick agency to devote all of his time to contracting. When Manly was awarded a paving job near Leesburg, Florida, in 1924, he offered the subcontract for clearing and grading to Hubbard, by then an independent contractor.

That led to other jobs in Florida and the creation in 1928, with two other stockholders, of the Hubbard Construction Company as a Florida corporation at Newberry, Alachua County. The authorized capital stock was $25,000. In its first year of business, the company completed work with a value of $78,920.76.

Since then, Hubbard has added other companies to its family — Orlando Paving Company, Orange Paving and Construction Company, and Contractor's Tire Company. Although different executives are in charge of the respective operations, the overall philosophy and direction was guided by the founder's son, Frank M. Hubbard, until 1984, when Selby W. Sullivan purchased all the Hubbard stock. Sullivan, former president of Florida Gas Company, has been a close associate of Frank Hubbard for many years in a

The first office of Hubbard Construction Company in Marion, South Carolina, in 1934.

The present office of Hubbard Construction Company, Orlando, was built in 1947 and is located at Silver Star Road and U.S. 441.

number of business, civic, and cultural organizations. In 1983, the revenues of Hubbard and its subsidiaries amounted to $72 million.

As the United States prepared itself for war at the close of the 1930s, Hubbard built airports throughout the Southeast, as well as other government installations, including projects for the Navy at Sanford, Florida, and Charleston, South Carolina.

The early 1950s provided a major turning point for Hubbard Construction Company, when it began working at Cape Canaveral and Patrick Air Force Base. In twelve months, the company had done more work on a single project than ever before in its history, building a total of eight launch pads for NASA at the Cape.

Over the years, Hubbard has worked on innumerable projects at Orlando Executive and Orlando International airports. Original projects were for the development of both airfields into military bases, but later projects were for the airfields' conversion and expansion into civilian airports. Hubbard did the majority of the site work for the new $400

million terminal facility at Orlando International after 1978.

Among its big projects in recent years was most of the site development at Walt Disney World, where Hubbard began work in 1967 and continued into the Disney EPCOT era of the 1980s. Hubbard and its subsidiaries have done some $80 million worth of work for Walt Disney World.

The company's largest and longest-lasting job has been the 128,000-acre Palm Coast Development of International Telephone and Telegraph in Flagler County. Hubbard has been involved at Palm Coast since 1976. By the early 1980's, Hubbard had grossed about $60 million at Palm Coast and had completed 200 miles of roads and 900,000 linear feet of sanitary sewer and water lines for the 500,000 people expected to live at Palm Coast one day.

During the 64 years of its existence, Hubbard has built thousands of projects in the Orlando area. Its mark on the community has been felt not only through the bricks and mortar, asphalt and concrete, that bear its stamp, but also by the influence of its owners, its officers, and its employees, who contribute much time and financial support to civic, charitable, educational, and religious activities of the community.

Special caring by special people

Humana Incorporated, out of Louisville, Kentucky, one of the largest hospital corporations in the world, opened Lucerne General Hospital (recently renamed Humana Hospital - Lucerne) in Orlando, Florida on July 8, 1974.

A general acute-care facility with a bed capacity of 267 beds, the hospital quickly established a reputation of personalized quality patient care and physician responsiveness.

Humana Hospital - Lucerne has led the area in many new innovative services and health-care management techniques, and although considered to be a medium-sized facility, ranks as one of the most sophisticated medical centers in central Florida with state-of-the-art equipment and technology.

Humana Hospital - Lucerne provided Orlando and the central Florida communities with the first Spinal Injury Center and is now the acute receiving center for fresh spinal injuries in central Florida and is known all over the East Coast for its expertise in spinal injury rehabilitation.

The Diabetes Care Center was also the first of its kind to open in Orlando and provides extensive inpatient and outpatient care for patients with diabetes. The Center houses a BioStator, one of three in the state of Florida, which acts as an artificial endocrine pancreas and injects insulin and/or glucose into a patient's system as required to normalize the blood sugar.

Both of the Diabetes-Spinal Centers have been named as Centers of Excellence by Humana Incorporated. In order to be designated as a Center of Excellence, a specialty unit must meet stringent criteria established by Humana, and having met this criteria, receives a grant in the amount of $100,000 from the corporation for the purpose of medical education and research.

In addition to these highly specialized centers, Humana Hospital - Lucerne houses one of the most sophisticated Cardiology and Cardiovascular Surgery floors in Orlando. During a recent $8 million renovation and expansion program, new open-heart surgery suites were added in addition to a second heart catheterization laboratory. Due to the tremendous number of cardiac patients referred to the hospital from outlying areas, Humana Hospital - Lucerne contracted with an air-ambulance service to transport both cardiac and spinal injury patients from these areas to Orlando.

Other specialty areas within the hospital include: Family Practice Floor, Internal Medicine & Oncology Floor, Gynecology Unit, ENT Unit, Neurology & Neurosurgery Unit, Retina Surgery Unit, Orthopedic Wing, General Surgery & Urology, and a 24-hour Emergency Room. In addition, for critical patients, there are two Intensive Care units, and a Coronary Care and Progressive Care Floor.

The entire hospital was refurbished in 1984, and a Special Imaging Suite was added containing a Fourth Generation Scanner, the newest CAT Scanner available, and the only Fourth Generation Scanner in central Florida.

During the past year, special emphasis has been placed on lowering hospital costs and reducing health care for patients. Humana Hospital - Lucerne has added extensive outpatient testing and outpatient surgery to its existing services.

Patient amenities include: Patient Satisfaction Guarantee Program, a patient ombudsman, gourmet meals, helicopter air-ambulance service for patients in outlying areas, townhouses and condos available for out-of-town patients and members of their families, patient education, and special patient recognition on birthdays and anniversaries.

In July of 1984, Humana Hospital - Lucerne celebrated ten years of special caring in the Orlando Community, and as part of its ten-year celebration, presented to the city of Orlando three physical fitness courses: a cardiovascular jogging course and wheelchair gamefield to be placed in Wadeview City Park and a senior-citizen walk to be placed in Al Coith Park.

Dedicated to the concept of high-quality patient care, Humana Hospital - Lucerne is proud to be part of The City Beautiful's history.

Humana Hospital-Lucerne — the newest hospital in Orlando celebrates ten years of special caring by special people (July 1984).

Growth follows a solid blueprint for progress

Downtown Orlando, with its parklike setting on Lake Eola, serves as a window to mid-Florida's burgeoning business community.

In the beginning, Orlando was a sleepy, smallish agricultural town, not concerned with industrial growth. When the boom began, the area developed into a world center for tourism as well as business. That growth was in danger of becoming disastrously haphazard. Luckily, civic leaders and prudent government officials had the foresight to establish a solid blueprint for progress that would gracefully help the region prosper in the coming decades of growth and accomplishment.

With 20,000 new residents settling in mid-Florida each year, the need for new jobs was clear, but planning and controlling growth which was running an unchecked random course was vital. Three area economic development committees were doing a moderate job of providing a master plan for growth, but the need for a cooperative, regional, professional approach to economic development to benefit *all* of mid-Florida was evident. Thus, the Industrial Development Commission of Mid-Florida was born in 1977.

The IDC is a membership-based organization with the sole purpose of soliciting, planning for, and controlling the influx of clean industry, while sustaining a high-quality lifestyle. Another major goal of the IDC is to protect the important balance between environment and progress to ensure the area remains the beautiful and bountiful place it is.

From its forerunners, including the Orlando Chamber of Commerce Committee of 200, the Orlando/Orange County Industrial Board; and the Central Florida Development Committee, the IDC took the best attributes of each and began operations. Those attributes included being primarily supported by membership funds. With a starting membership of about 125 area business people, the IDC has grown to represent virtually every facet of business and government in mid-Florida with more than 1,000 members. The Commission is a private, not-for-profit corporation that maintains a full-time professional staff reporting to a volunteer board of directors that serve on staggered terms.

The progress of the IDC has been outstanding. For many years, Florida has received the top ranking in a national study as the best business climate in the United States. Since its inception, the IDC has historically been the leader *within* the state — by a large margin — in all categories recorded, such as number of projects located, number of jobs created, square footage absorbed or under construction, and capital investment.

International attention has been focused on Orlando and mid-Florida, labeling this a "City on the Rise" and "Hot Market City," which gives the area further credibility, both as a top business center as well as a tourism capital.

Throughout the year, community tours are given by the IDC to industrial prospects visiting the area to judge firsthand mid-Florida's

A solid blueprint for progress was created with the formation of the IDC in 1977 to help mid-Florida prosper from the sleepy agricultural town it was to the vibrant business center it is today.

conduciveness to business. And great care is taken to effectively answer the flood of inquiries that are directed to the IDC.

Benchmarks in the history of the IDC include the establishment of a formal agreement with Seminole County in 1981 to provide industrial development services on a full-time basis. Seminole County now joins Orange County and the city of Orlando in supporting the IDC. Productive working relationships with several other groups have been established, with the hope that these, too, will lead to further consolidation of economic development efforts in the region.

The IDC's economic development program includes a comprehensive domestic,

as well as international, marketing program. Of note in the history of the IDC are the location of such American giants as General Electric, which established its robotics headquarters in mid-Florida; AT&T with both the Information Systems Division and Technologies operations in the area; Westinghouse, which moved its Steam Turbine-Generator Division to mid-Florida; and Martin Marietta Orlando Aerospace, which is one of the area's largest employers.

The benefits the area has to offer a burgeoning business are many. The blueprint for progress established in 1977 with the formation of the IDC is well under way, and it's working.

A retailing tradition

Ivey's of Orlando. Orange and Central avenues, 1963.

Etched glass interiors. Ivey's Colonial Plaza, Orlando, 1983.

Imported marble entrance. Ivey's Colonial Plaza, Orlando, 1983.

Ivey's Florida history began in 1944 when the J.B. Ivey Company, based in Charlotte, North Carolina, bought the Yowell-Drew stores in Orlando and Daytona Beach. The Orlando store was located in the hub of downtown, on the corner of Orange and Central avenues. It was a grand old five-story building where customers could shop for moderately priced items and visit the prayer room — an early tradition in every Ivey's store. The stores located in Orlando and Daytona Beach were operated as separate Ivey's divisions, with their own merchandising staffs.

In 1962, Ivey's built a store in downtown Jacksonville and operated it as a separate division. The responsibilities of Daytona eventually were combined with the Orlando division. Over the years, both Ivey's Orlando and Ivey's Jacksonville built branches — the Orlando division in central Florida and the Jacksonville division.

In 1962, Ivey's purchased approximately 30 acres of land adjacent to Orlando in Winter Park. This acreage became the foundation of the Winter Park Mall where Ivey's opened a branch store in 1964. In 1974, the two operating companies, Ivey's Orlando and Ivey's Jacksonville, merged into Ivey's Florida based in Winter Park. During the next six years, expansion increased throughout the state, and in October 1980, Ivey's Florida became a wholly owned subsidiary of Marshall Field and Company, Chicago. In July 1982, Marshall Field and its operating companies, including Ivey's Florida, became a wholly owned subsidiary of BATUS Inc., Louisville, Kentucky. Other operating companies of the BATUS Retailing Division include John Breuner Company, Frederick & Nelson, Gimbels East, Gimbels Pittsburgh, Gimbels Midwest, Ivey's Carolinas, Khol's Department Store, Marshall Field, Saks Fifth Avenue, The Crescent, and Thimbles Specialty Stores.

Ivey's Florida operates twelve stores in Florida, ranging in size from 12,000 square feet to 120,000 square feet — one each in Winter Park, Orlando, Merritt Island, Melbourne, Clearwater, and St. Petersburg; two in Daytona Beach; and four in Jacksonville. From its Winter Park base, Ivey's Florida operates its corporate divisions of buying, merchandising, advertising, special events, finance, credit, store planning, and human resources. Receiving, marking, and distribution are handled through Ivey's Florida Distribution Center in Commerce Park, Orlando.

Through the years, Ivey's Florida has emerged as a prominent specialty department store offering fine-quality fashion merchandise for family and home. It is dedicated to serving its customers through personalized services, high ethical standards, and community involvement.

After 40 years of retailing in Orange County, Ivey's Florida has once again opened a store in Orlando. Like the very first store, the Colonial Plaza store stands as a symbol of Ivey's growing friendship, belief, and commitment to the great cities of Orlando and Winter Park.

Service and excellence in office building development, management, and leasing

The history, growth, and success of Jaymont Realty Incorporated and its predecessor, the real estate firm of J. Rolfe Davis, have closely paralleled the history, growth, and success of Orlando, Florida.

Founded in the early 1960s by J. Rolfe Davis, former mayor of the city of Orlando and a three-term Orange County commissioner, the firm has always been located in the downtown area, first at 27 South Main Street (since renamed Magnolia Avenue) and then later at 14 West Gore Street.

J. Rolfe Davis was a full-service real estate firm, brokering homes, vacant land, citrus groves, and income producing property. However, a new Florida law established in the late 1960s, which was designed to attract regional insurance headquarters to Florida, served to thrust the Davis real estate firm into the forefront of office building, management, and leasing.

The skylines of many Florida cities began to change to accommodate these new headquarters buildings. In Orlando, the Rolfe Davis firm participated in assembling land for the southeastern regional office of CNA Insurance. Subsequently, the firm was awarded the exclusive management and leasing of CNA Tower, an 18-story, 242,000-square-foot office building that would serve as an Orlando landmark for years to come.

The Davis firm, with its new co-owner, Floyd S. Faucette, established the new company direction in office building management and leasing. Faucette, an engineering graduate and football alternate captain at Georgia Tech under Coach Bobby Dodd, quickly moved the company into the forefront of management and leasing in central Florida. In 1976, Davis retired, selling his ownership in the business to Faucette, who then consolidated and relocated the company's operations into CNA Tower.

In 1981, Jaymont Properties Incorporated, whose affiliate had acquired CNA Tower in 1979, purchased the operations of J. Rolfe Davis & Associates, Inc., and simultaneously hired Faucette to be president of the renamed Jaymont Realty Incorporated. Thus, as J. Rolfe Davis & Associates, Inc. expired, its successor, Jaymont Realty Incorporated, now stood in its place, joining hands with Jaymont Properties, a company with national ambitions.

Jaymont Properties is headquartered in Chicago, across the street from The First National Bank of Chicago, which has played a pivotal role in the establishment and growth of Jaymont. It was through First Chicago that the Abdul Lateef Jameel family of Jedda, Saudi Arabia, met Lewis H. Harmon, then a senior vice-president with the bank. When the wealthy merchant family decided to establish a U.S. portfolio of prestigious properties in high-growth urban markets, they hired Lew Harmon to accomplish these goals.

Beginning in 1978 as the company's sole employee, Harmon guided Jaymont's growth to include over 60 employees managing, leasing, and developing an ever-growing portfolio that includes 8.5 million square feet of properties either finished or in planning.

Barnett Plaza represented Jaymont's first Orlando development. Early planning indicated the building might take the shape of a tower atop a parking garage; however, Lew Harmon had recalled the enjoyment experienced by Chicago's urban workers when First Chicago included a large plaza adjacent to its headquarters building. As a result of his first-hand observations of a large urban plaza where city workers could enjoy public entertainment or simply visit with one's friends, Harmon made sure that Orlandoans might also have a place to gather. The plaza, a half-acre surface featuring a canopy of trees and a three-plumed fountain, has been described as the focal point of the city's new growth management plan. Barnett Plaza adjoining CNA Tower is part of Jaymont's Orlando management portfolio of 620,000 square feet.

Jaymont's commitment to Orlando's downtown renaissance continues. In 1984, construction began on a 20-story office tower wrapped in granite and glass that will overlook Lake Eola from the corner or Orange and Washington.

A tradition of high-rise management, leasing, development, and brokerage — coupled with faith in the growth of Orlando that was begun with J. Rolfe Davis in the sixties and furthered by Floyd Faucette in the seventies — is continued by Lew Harmon and Jaymont in the eighties.

Barnett Plaza and CNA Tower — the heart of Orlando's financial district.

Serving America's banks with excellence and creativity

Ask any banker for the name of an outstanding financial software firm and you are likely to hear the name of a Kirchman subsidiary. Why? It is because these five companies are the undisputed champions of the national banking software industry, each serving a different level of banking and all contributing to the growth of The Kirchman Corporation, one of Orlando's largest and most successful young business organizations.

Since 1969, The Kirchman Corporation has matched central Florida's remarkable development step for step. And, like the city of Orlando, it has been virtually unaffected by the economic hardships that have touched many industries throughout our nation. Through its success, the Kirchman Corporation has created tremendous career opportunities for area residents, and by maintaining its constant commitment to serve the ever-changing needs of America's banking industry, it has contributed a great deal to our nation's financial stability.

The Kirchman story began in the late sixties when Kenneth P. Kirchman, a creative young entrepreneur, recognized the banking industry's trend toward technological independence. Banks had begun writing their own individual software programs, but the time, talent, and expense required made the process generally impractical. Kirchman determined that with the right combination of financial and technical expertise, he could develop and market innovative, standardized application software systems that would revolutionize the industry.

A native Floridian, Ken Kirchman anticipated central Florida's potential and chose Orlando as the home for his new enterprise. And, in April of 1969, with a staff of four, he created the software system that launched Florida Software Services, Inc. Today, Florida Software Services' systems can be found in over 5,000 of America's banking institutions, including more than half of the country's top 300 multibillion dollar banks.

In the early seventies, Ken Kirchman saw that there were many banks that needed sophisticated data processing but were just not equipped to handle large, in-bank systems and staffs. Diversification of Florida Software Services was the most obvious option, but Kirchman's strong industry sense led him to another conclusion, and the foundation for his corporate philosophy. Rather than dilute the strengths of one company, new companies would be created to meet specific objectives, with their functions well-defined within a particular phase of the industry. In that way, each company could continue to operate on a concentration of its expertise.

So it was that a newly formed entity, The Kirchman Corporation, initiated a multi-million-dollar research and development program aimed at isolating the particular needs of the banking industry. One by one, new Kirchman companies were born.

The Kirchman Corporation's International Headquarters, a 63,000 square-foot facility, is the home base for all Kirchman companies.

In 1976, Infoserve, Inc., was introduced to accommodate banks that wanted superior processing from an outside data servicer. Soon after, the corporation established Omni Resources, Inc., and the first in-bank data processing system developed exclusively for the small independent bank.

In 1984, The Kirchman Corporation unveiled two more companies: Kencom, Inc., suppliers of a sophisticated, all-in-one system created to serve America's mid-range banks; and Link X, Inc., a personal computer software company with unique management analysis concepts for the progressive banker.

Today, the five Orlando-based Kirchman companies generate combined annual sales of over $40 million, employ between 400 and 500 people, and occupy several working facilities in the central Florida area. Besides their International Headquarters in Orlando, there is The Banking College in Orlando, which annually involves thousands of bankers in continuing education seminars; and the Corporate Research and Development Institute, which formulates information technology for the advancement of innovative banking software systems. There is also a special facility in Los Angeles to serve the needs of West Coast bankers.

The Kirchman Corporation is also responsible for one of America's most prestigious bankers' organizations, FURST (Financial Users Researching Systems Together). Each year, thousands of bankers converge on Orlando for the annual FURST conference, where they exchange ideas, share experiences, and prepare for the future challenges of their industry. In addition, they hear from some of the brightest and most powerful personalities in America, including such notables as Walter Cronkite, Gerald Ford, Neil Arm-

Kenneth P. Kirchman introduces President Gerald R. Ford at the Kirchman Corporation's annual bankers' conference, FURST (Financial Users Researching Systems Together). President Ford was the event's keynote speaker in 1982.

strong, Art Buchwald, and Alvin Toffler.

The Kirchman Corporation has become an integral part of Orlando. It takes great pride in the city of its birth, and a Florida orange, the corporate symbol, is proudly worn on the lapel of every Kirchman employee. Since 1969, The Kirchman Corporation has been committed to serving the needs of its community. As new companies, services and systems are created, The Kirchman Corporation will continue to represent Orlando's growing reputation as a vibrant and economically powerful city — the software capital of America's banking industry.

Innovative solutions to business opportunities

The Landmarks Group has long and accomplished history of excellence in commercial real estate development throughout the Southeast. However, it is best known as a company with a vision of the future.

Landmark Center, located at 315 East Robinson Street in downtown Orlando, typifies the company's development theme in office environments throughout the Sunbelt.

The Landmarks Group, a sixteen-year-old Atlanta-based office developer, has fashioned a new development style which anticipates the demands of the future and seeks to meet them in an unprecedented fashion.

Open since October 1983, Landmark Center embodies The Landmarks Group's "New Era" concept. The complex is designed to function as an exceptionally efficient and economical business facility in an aesthetically compatible setting. Landmark Center overlooks beautiful Lake Eola. The building's innovative configuration offers panoramic views of either the lake or the building's full-height atrium.

The atrium serves as a dramatic focal point for the building. Rising six stories from a lushly-landscaped central lobby to a sky-lighted ceiling, the atrium adds dimensions of spaciousness and beauty to the building. The skylight sends sunlight streaming onto lush, tropical foliage and a free-form water pond with gently flowing waterfalls. Multi-colored, soft sculpture butterflies are suspended from the skylight and add impressive beauty to the interior. A balcony at each level on the upper five floors provides a view of the atrium, the city, and the lake and its park. The building's interior offices also enjoy a glass-partitioned view of the atrium.

The atrium captures the entire indoor/outdoor concept of the building design, making extensive use of natural surroundings. Florida's year-round natural beauty is actually brought into the office environment, enhancing its functionality as both a showcase and work place. It is a well established fact that the office environment has a significant impact on job productivity and satisfaction. In essence, aside from its aesthetic appeal, Landmark Center Orlando offers a workplace which offers unsurpassed functionality in the present with a keen eye to the future.

A conducive work environment that also encompasses and has the capabilities to support modern technology embodies the "high-tech-soft-touch" development philosophy at The Landmarks Group. State-of-the-art features surround a landscaped world of art, gardens, ponds, and flowers — adding warmth to a highly practical facility, thus providing the "soft touch."

Landmark Center also features impressive architecture characterized by high-technology finishes and colors, expansive windows, and the atrium. Rich, blue, reflective glass

Landmark Center shares the spotlight with Orlando's great downtown landmark — Lake Eola.

framed in a blue gridwork sheaths the reinforced concrete structure. A variety of high-tech features include accommodations for teleconferencing, satellite earth station facilities, automation and telecommunications capabilities, and the most innovative building and tenant security features presently available. Building safety is supplemented by a mid-rise, ladder-reachable design with such notable lineaments as electronic security controls, surveillance cameras, smoke detectors, smoke-proof wiring, and sprinkler systems.

The building also incorporates a number of energy-efficient features uncommon in many structures making such extensive use of glass. The atrium's skylight significantly reduces lighting loads on interior offices, and the utilization of reflective glass panels provides shading on critical exposure areas. These building characteristics not only provide comfortable, effective climate control, but save energy and cut operating costs.

Skillfully blending this "high-tech-soft-touch" philosophy into a structure that also provides a unique environment for social interaction was a challenge. The Landmarks Group met that challenge with a building that offers reduced noise, improved visibility, ample parking, and a relaxing yet stimulating atmosphere. This atmosphere provides a sense of community for tenants and visitors alike.

Landmark Center exemplifies the spirit of the future without sacrificing The Landmarks Group's commitment to the present. Orlando is a growing, thriving city, and The Landmarks Group is proud to have a part in

Landmark Center's atrium brings the beauty of Orlando indoors.

the city's development. Phase II, identical and adjacent to the first building, will be completed by summer 1985.

Looking ahead, one can only wonder what fresh, new challenges are in store for Orlando. With an eye to the future, The Landmarks Group is prepared to face these challenges with imagination, ingenuity, and a commitment to excellence.

Transmitting The City Beautiful to prosperity

From the day the Lee family arrived in Orlando in 1882, their philosophy of building a better and more beautiful city has prevailed in one endeavor after another. Following his father's example of hard work and perseverance, Thomas G. Lee and his wife Elizabeth built T.G. Lee Dairy of Orlando into a business that, on its 50th anniversary in 1975, was furnishing employment for some 400 people and generating better than $30 million in revenue annually.

The family dairy has undergone many changes since 1925, and today Orlando is witnessing the emergence of yet another Lee legacy — the LeeVista Center. Located north of Orlando International Airport on a 2,000-acre tract of land that once served as grazing pasture for 1,400 dairy cows, LeeVista Center is being developed as central Florida's most complete and comprehensive community for business and industry. Master planning was begun in 1979 by Mr. and Mrs. Lee's son Richard, who remains deeply involved in the family business.

The late Charles Lee came to Orange County from Louisville, in 1882, with a load of sheep which he sold in Sanford. Then, he established a hardware business at the corner of Central and Orange avenues. Next, he went into citrus while keeping cows in the fenced-in groves. The business suffered through freezes and lost money eight years running.

Thomas Gilbert Lee was born in 1894, the year the big freeze ravished the Florida citrus business. At the age of 16, he enrolled in a two-year business course at Rollins College and went on to study agriculture for two more years at the University of Florida. When World War I erupted, he enlisted in the Signal Corps, later transferring to the Army Air Service. After the armistice was signed, T.G. Lee spent three years working in the Texas oil fields.

In 1925, his father gave him 20 acres of land, the family cow, co-signed his note for another cow and a calf at the Old Church Street Bank, and the T.G. Lee Dairy was born. Despite losing most of his herd to sickness in 1930 and the Depression, the business began to show signs of his future empire in the early 1930s.

When it became obvious that the grazing fields on Colonial Drive and Bumby Avenue

T.G. Lee's grazing fields — 1954. The 2,000 acre tract of land near the airport, now LeeVista Center, will eventually encompass an 18-hole golf course, 3,000 multi-family residences, hotels, restaurants, a shopping center, and executive offices.

T. G. Lee, shown in 1925, with the cow and calf that started him on the road to success.

would not be adequate as the dairy expanded, T.G. Lee began buying the land that now constitutes LeeVista Center. Between 1938 and 1954 he purchased the 2,000-acre tract in 20 different parcels and moved the herd there in the mid-fifties.

Although the Lees were approached several times over the course of the years by de-

velopers looking to purchase the LeeVista tract, they held on to the land. They felt their involvement in the growth of central Florida for more than half a century gave them insight into what type of business/industry community is needed in Orlando that others might not have. Joint ventures with outside developers will ensure a high degree of involvement by the Lee family as LeeVista Center continues to unfold.

After visiting most of the top-quality business parks in the country, Richard Lee determined that an "open space" concept of planning with highly restrictive design standards would prevail. Serving as permanent buffers, wide boulevards, extensive landscaping, berming, and lakes will all protect the beauty and future value of the land for those who build there.

Five years of careful planning finally paid off for Richard Lee and his staff of four when LeeVista's first tenant, the Orlando Airport Marriott Hotel, opened its doors on December 15, 1983. Within 15 years, LeeVista Center will encompass an 18-hole golf course, up to 3,000 multi-family residences, and a mixed use business park containing hotels, restaurants, a shopping center, executive offices, distribution and R&D centers, light industry, and a 25-acre recreation park owned by the city.

The total development cost for LeeVista Center is expected to be $600 million (1983 dollars), making it Orlando's largest project to date. At build-out it will support close to 16,000 permanent on-site employees with an annual payroll of $260 million and generate $26 million a year in tax revenues.

LeeVista Center will carry on the tradition established more than half a century ago as the Lee family continues their involvement in the progress and prosperity of The City Beautiful.

Serving Florida industry since 1900

On December 28, 1899, two events helped mold the future of Harry P. Leu, Inc. On that date the employees of Cain O'Berry Boiler Works, forerunner of Harry P. Leu, Inc., received their first wages. Also on that date, Paul J. Stine was born. Stine later purchased the company from Harry P. Leu and was the catalyst for its success from the 1930s through the 1970s.

The Cain O'Berry Boiler Company was incorporated in 1904, with J.W. Cain at the helm. That year, Harry P. Leu also joined the young company as a jack-of-all-trades, including timekeeper, shipping clerk, and salesman. Leu learned his job quickly, while the company's reputation soared. It manufactured efficient boilers for sawmills, citrus packing houses, phosphate mines, and locomotives.

During the early part of the century, boilers were the major form of energy for businesses eking out an existence in the backwoods and hammocks of Florida. As the demand for boilers increased, the company added a fabrication shop to its existing facility — a small tin-roofed office. The shop contained an overhead shaft drive powered by some of the first electric motors installed in Florida. The office and shop stand today as reminders of the roots from which Harry P. Leu, Inc., grew.

Seizing the opportunity to acquire company stock, Leu bought out O'Berry in 1914 when the latter moved west to mine gold. Two years later, Leu became president and began to change the company emphasis from manufacturing boilers to providing mill supplies. Diversification paid off, and by 1922 a large warehouse was added on the corner of Livingston and Garland, housing myriad supplies for the expanding citrus industry.

After a quarter-century of operation, Cain O'Berry Boiler Company officially became

The Harry P. Leu truck fleet, 1949.

Boiler crew, 1907. The company manufactured boilers for sawmills, citrus packing houses, phosphate mines, and locomotives.

Harry P. Leu, Inc., when Leu secured controlling interest in the company. For the next eight years, Leu manuevered the company through the Great Depression, inducing growth under adverse conditions. Then, as always, Leu was active in the promotion of his community and was instrumental in improving the highway system of central Florida.

In 1934, Paul Stine was hired as a salesman for the Leu firm. With his foresight and acumen for the industrial-supply business, he guided the company to establish a broader line of industrial supplies. His expertise allowed him to advance quickly, and by 1939 he was sales manager. In 1940, Stine pur-

chased the company from Leu. Stine's leadership catapulted Harry P. Leu, Inc. through World War II and beyond.

Stine recognized that company expansion was directly related to the growth of Florida. Consequently, the same tenacity he applied in guiding the company was directed to the industrial and business development of Orlando and the state of Florida. He served as president of three industrial development groups, predecessors of the Industrial Development Commission of mid-Florida.

Under Stine's stewardship, Harry P. Leu, Inc. took advantage of many opportunities and added sophisticated product lines and business techniques to its operation. The first major opportunity came in 1947 when orange juice was concentrated. Because of the firm's experience and knowledge, it became a prime supplier of mechanical power-transmission supplies. The space age blast-off in the mid-1950s brought more challenges to the company, prompting Harry P. Leu, Inc., to establish branch operations in Miami and Tampa.

Continued industrial growth in the mid-1970s stimulated the company to search for new management and marketing programs. In order to maintain its place as a leading industrial supplier in Florida, Harry P. Leu, Inc., instituted advanced computerized techniques in inventory management, marketing, and forecasting. As a new marketing concept, the company established Total Lower Cost (TLC), a system contract tailor-made to suit individual customer needs through prompt and efficient service.

Today, the dependability established by Paul Stine continues under the direction of his two sons, Joseph P. Stine and Jon C. Stine, and the flair for innovation and service has never been greater.

Our approach has been to think locally and finance globally

M.G. Lewis & Co., Inc. was founded in October, 1977 by James L. Lentz, who remains the president of the firm. Mr. Lentz came to Florida after working and progressing in a number of investment banking firms on Wall Street.

The business was initially established as a regional investment banking firm to provide only underwriting and financial advisory services to the issuers of tax-exempt securities. The firm's home office remains located in Winter Park, Florida, where it is centrally positioned within Florida's "fertile crescent," the corridor between Daytona Beach and Tampa along the Interstate 4 highway system.

Since 1970, central Florida has experienced significant growth in terms of both residential population and business activity. When he founded the firm, Mr. Lentz had the concept in mind that a quality Florida-based investment banking firm could knowledgeably serve the governments and agencies within the state who were attempting to deal with the demands that growth was placing upon them. These demands manifest themselves as a need to finance and expand the capital infrastructure systems of those jurisdictions.

Initially, M.G. Lewis & Co., Inc. began with only two employees, but has grown steadily, and today some 22 individuals comprise the staff.

Since its inception, the firm has seen a number of significant expansions of both a geographical and functional nature. In 1978, the sales and marketing department was added in order to allow the firm to more adequately access the tax-exempt capital markets for the benefit of its issuer-clients as well as to provide services to a wide range of institutional and retail investors. A year later, the sales and marketing department was further expanded with the addition of a trading desk. The trading function began to allow the firm to buy and sell tax-exempt securities for its own benefit.

The first geographical expansion took place in 1980 when Mr. Lentz opened a "public finance" office in Pompano Beach, Florida. The purpose of this expansion was to establish a presence in the rapid growth area of south Florida.

One of the major corporate milestones for M.G. Lewis & Co., Inc. involved the initiation of an annual conference in the central Florida area with the purpose of aggressively educating and informing tax-exempt investors of the advantages of Florida bonds and Florida issuers. The conference, styled "Florida Forecast," has been bringing institutional investors, national underwriters, governmental issuers, and regional dignitaries together for a two- or three-day period in a secluded setting in order to foster understanding and awareness about the capital markets and Florida's economy.

The Orlando Regional Medical Center expansion, a 1983 financing.

The Orange County Administration Building, a 1982 financing.

The year of 1982 saw the firm break through the $1 billion mark for cumulative participation in public financings. Additionally, the firm continued to geographically expand with a "public finance" office being opened in Daytona Beach, Florida.

Since then, the firm's growth has taken a rapid jump in all aspects. Another branch office was opened in 1983 in Tallahassee, Florida, the firm's cumulative participation in public financings reached the $3 billion plateau in the spring of 1984, and a subsidiary corporation named M.G. Lewis Economet-

rics, Inc. was also formed. This sister corporation's president is Dr. Henry Fishkind, who is widely known and revered throughout Florida for his knowledge of its economy and future potential. M.G. Lewis Econometrics, Inc. will not only support the investment banking organization, but also represents the first of a number of planned functional diversifications for Mr. Lentz and the M.G. Lewis group.

High-technology development: state-of-the-art laser systems

Orlando born and bred, International Laser Systems (ILS) has had a vibrant past and is expecting to experience an equally dynamic future.

Founded in 1968 as a research and development firm, ILS had grown during its formidable years under the guidance of company president and founder, William Schwartz. The year 1977 brought a change to the young company as the first major production program was awarded. This was a new area of emphasis, since it called for a shift from a research and development posture to a more capital-intensive manufacturing thrust. The need for capitalization prompted ILS to seek alternative methods of funding. This was accomplished through the sale of controlling interest to the Martin-Marietta Company, thus providing the necessary capital to establish ILS as a viable production entity. The final change came in May 1983 as ILS became the subject of acquisition by Litton Industries as a complement to Litton's high technology emphasis.

International Laser Systems is presently a division of Litton's Electronic Warfare Systems Group and has received a high degree of moral and financial support from Litton to continue research, development, and manufacturing of laser systems for both military and commercial applications. The company has established itself as a major U.S. manufacturer of military lasers and has supplied the laser designators for virtually all U.S. Air Force and Army aircraft which utilize laser designator pods.

Growth has been dynamic since 1977, expanding to include gallium-arsenide laser systems for weapons simulation/training and a wide variety of rugged Nd:YAG laser systems for field, laboratory, military, medical, and industrial applications.

The transition from a relatively small, upstart firm to its present position as a major supplier of aircraft laser systems is primarily due to the determined, hard-working members of the Litton ILS family. Research and development continues at a rapid pace, supported by highly capable and professional engineering and business development teams. These efforts are supported by an operations group which transforms, designs, and plans into finished products.

The vibrant growth and development of ILS has resulted in an expansion to six buildings located in the Fairvilla area of Orlando, with a total square footage of 110,000. However, this was not enough to meet the needs of the business.

August 1984 marked the next step in the growth of Litton ILS, a new facility designed to meet the demands of a high-technology

A Target Acquisition Designation Sight laser rangefinder is being produced for Martin-Marietta to be utilized on the U.S. Army Apache helicopter.

environment. Litton architects designed the contemporary structure with the ability to expand and modify the square footage as required. All personnel work together under one roof, eliminating the intrinsic problems inherent in a multi-building concept. The site, located with the assistance of the Industrial Development Commission of Mid-Florida, is situated on U.S. Highway 441 north of Lockhart and encompasses a 25-acre parcel of land. The multi-million dollar building includes 140,000 square feet of interior space, and exemplifies the Litton concept of, and commitment to, high-technology development.

Litton people are special people and believe in supporting the communities in which they live and work. Finding Litton employees involved with the United Way, Ki-

The Aquila, a remotely piloted vehicle produced for the U.S. Army by Lockheed, contains an ILS laser transmitter which illuminates targets for laser-guided weapons. The payload system containing the laser is produced by Westinghouse for day utilization and by Ford Aerospace for night activity.

wanis, Central Florida Blood Services, or most other charitable and professional organizations is not out of the ordinary. Representatives support the Additions Program through the Orange County Public School System and the Dividends Program through the Seminole County Public School System by conducting seminars and presentations in laser-technology principles, whetting the appetites of young students to high-technology concepts. Company representatives serve on the faculties of and conduct seminars for area colleges in the fields of laser and electronics technology, business, management, and economics.

The dynamism of Litton Industries and the leadership of Division President Willard P. Wicks has put International Laser Systems into a position of leadership in the development, design, and manufacture of laser designators, weapons training simulation, and high-technology research. The future looks bright as successful research results in more adaptable lasers to meet the needs of a greater number of people and organizations in the military, training, and commercial fields.

Growing with Orlando

The Lowndes, Drosdick, Doster & Kantor, P.A. handsome French colonial office complex on Lake Eola overlooks downtown Orlando.

Though the law firm of Lowndes, Drosdick, Doster & Kantor, P.A. has not been part of all of Orlando's modern history, it has been part of a very dynamic portion of it. Formed in the latter part of 1968 when the Disney World construction had stimulated one of Orlando's famous real estate booms, the firm has grown over the ensuing fifteen years along with Orlando, and in much the same exciting manner.

At the beginning, the firm consisted of eight people, four lawyers, and four lay persons. Today, the firm has 30 lawyers and 50 lay persons. The firm has grown with the area and, in many respects, is a microcosm of Orlando.

As with many of the people of Orlando, the members of the firm have come from many different parts of the country to seek their fortunes in central Florida. The lawyers are from fourteen different states and from 32 different colleges and law schools. None are Orlando natives, very few are Florida natives, but all are proud citizens of Orlando and feel extremely fortunate to be able to practice their profession in such a wonderful community.

Moreover, as in the case of Orlando, the business of the law firm has always been very closely related to the real estate and

construction industries. These industries have been intimately associated with the rapid growth of Orlando.

The firm was founded by John Lowndes, Fred Piersol, Ernie Drosdick, and Bill Baker, who had all been practicing law in Orlando for several years with Robert T. Anderson and James K. Rush. Today, only John Lowndes remains with the firm. Ernie Drosdick died in 1982, and Piersol and Baker are practicing law in the area with other firms. Bill Doster joined the firm a few months after it was founded. Hal Kantor came with the firm upon his graduation from the University of Florida Law School in 1972. Since that time, many lawyers have joined the firm and a few have left. Most have been with the firm since their graduation from law school.

The firm has specialized in real estate, taxation, and commercial litigation, and it has been professionally involved with many of the major real estate projects and businesses in the central Florida area. Members of the firm have served, and continue to serve, in many important professional and civic positions.

Originally, the law firm was quartered in the First Federal Building on Church Street. It bought the office space, furniture, and library of long-time Orlando lawyer, "Funie" Steed, from his widow, shortly after Steed's death. The firm began its business in these offices on January 2, 1969, and on that day

welcomed to its office, among other friends and well-wishers, its oldest and most important client, Lester N. Mandell of The Greater Construction Corporation.

After practicing ten years on Church Street, the firm built its own building on Lake Eola, on land purchased on Eola Drive in 1973 from another long-time Orlando lawyer, Troy Musselwhite Sr. The land had been in Musselwhite's family since the late 1800s.

In 1980, the firm's new, French colonial building on the east side of Lake Eola won the "Gold Brick" beautification award from the city of Orlando. However, the firm quickly outgrew its new building and, in 1983, purchased the old Sky Line Apartments, originally built in 1939. The firm remodeled these apartments into office space with a French colonial style facade and joined them to the original firm building.

Today, Lowndes, Drosdick, Doster & Kantor, P.A. occupies its handsome French colonial office complex on Lake Eola overlooking downtown Orlando and counts the many blessings it has received from being a part of the vital, growing, beautiful Orlando community. It looks forward to the next fifteen years, indeed the next century, with great excitement and high expectations.

Serving a growing Orlando for over 65 years

When the United States entered World War I, so did attorney Raymer F. Maguire, a 1915 graduate of the University of Florida Law School. Upon returning from the service in 1919, Maguire and Wilber Tilden formed the Orlando law firm of Tilden & Maguire.

Tilden & Maguire, operating from its offices on Central Boulevard, began to enjoy a steady flow of business as the firm's reputation for quality legal work became known in the Orlando area. Consequently, Harry Voorhis was invited to join the firm in 1920. One year later, Tilden, though only 35, retired from the practice of law, and the name of the firm became Maguire & Voorhis.

Maguire & Voorhis continued to grow in both reputation and in work load, and in September of 1923, two energetic brothers, Maxwell and J.R. Wells, were hired as legal secretaries to assist in handling the firm's work load. Both brothers subsequently became lawyers, and in 1925, Maxwell Wells was invited to become a partner in the firm. After a short stay in Miami as an attorney, J.R. Wells rejoined Maguire & Voorhis as a partner in 1929.

As Orlando and the nation recovered from the Great Depression, Maguire & Voorhis saw its practice increase and diversify. In recognition of the contributions to the firm in 1939, the name was changed to Maguire, Voorhis & Wells — the name it retains today.

As Maguire, Voorhis & Wells entered the 1940s, it was able to look back on a history of steady growth, and the founding partners were able to look forward to a new generation of lawyers in their firm as their sons passed the Bar and joined them in practice. Raymer F. Maguire Jr. (now the firms senior partner) joined the firm in 1948 after serving in World War II, and Joel R. Wells Jr. (now president of Sun Banks, Inc.) joined the firm in 1951. With the help provided by its founders' sons, Maguire, Voorhis & Wells was on its way to becoming one of the preeminent law firms in Florida, just as Orlando was on

Clockwise from above, Raymer F. Maguire, Harry M. Voorhis, Maxwell W. Wells, and J.R. Wells.

its way to becoming a major metropolis.

In 1954, Maguire, Voorhis & Wells moved to new offices at 135 Wall Street to make room for the larger staff necessary to handle its increased clientele. New partners, associates, paralegals, and staff were added, and the firm departmentalized its services to include real estate law; corporate, banking and securities law; litigation; and tax, estate planning and probate law.

In 1960, John F. Kennedy was elected president and challenged the Soviet Union to a race to the moon. With Cape Canaveral only an hour away, Orlando boomed, and so did Maguire, Voorhis & Wells. Although Raymer Maguire Sr. died at the very beginning of this boom, the firm continued to prosper.

In 1970, the firm incorporated as a professional association, Maguire, Voorhis & Wells, P.A. Several additions were made to its offices

at 135 Wall Street, but the facilities were simply too small for the firm's expanding needs. In 1980, 61 years after the firm was founded, Maguire, Voorhis & Wells, P.A. acquired the historic Dickson-Ives Building at the corner of Orange Avenue and Central Boulevard in downtown Orlando — a structure that had housed a department store from 1923 until 1965. Renovation of the building was completed in 1981, providing 50,000 square feet of office space conveniently located in Orlando's busiest sector. The new building, which was renamed "Two South Orange Plaza," won the firm several awards for preserving a historical site while providing modern office space.

Today, Maguire, Voorhis & Wells, P.A. consists of 38 active attorneys, including 21 stockholder-members and 17 associates, together with the staff and facilities necessary to provide a full range of legal services to the firm's clients.

Maguire, Voorhis & Wells, P.A., like Orlando, has grown through good times and bad. And like Orlando, it has endured and is well prepared for a future as prosperous as its past. Its history of success has resulted from the firm's strict adherence to the cardinal principle established by its founders — providing quality legal representation for its clients.

The Dickson-Ives Building, circa 1920.

The Dickson-Ives Building, now Two South Orange Plaza, was restored to serve as Maguire, Voorhis & Wells' offices in 1981.

For 25 years, a major resource serving America's armed forces

A quarter-century ago, the governor of Florida stood presiding over a ribbon-cutting ceremony, saying, "I declare this plant formally dedicated to the service of America."

Today, this dedication remains inscribed on a plaque alongside the main entrance to Martin Marietta Orlando Aerospace. The years have covered the plaque with a gentle patina. The words, however, echo loud and clear in the daily work of an industrial operation that also is a major resource for the nation's armed services.

Actually, the Orlando operation was off and running well ahead of its ceremonial opening in late 1957. Two major missile systems — Bullpup and Lacrosse — were in production after transfer from the parent Baltimore plant. The Army's Missile Master air-defense command-and-control system, deployed across the country in the early 1960s, was under development.

The pattern was set. Twenty-five years of hard work, growth, and change produced a roll call of contracts won, programs performed or in progress, challenges overcome, missions accomplished, for the Department of Defense.

For a visitor with some recall of recent history, a tour through Orlando's laboratories and manufacturing areas, test facilities, and offices brings to mind a phrase from an earlier era — "arsenal of democracy." At workplaces like Orlando Aerospace, the nation's commitment, resolve, and resources are translated into the sophisticated weaponry essential to national strength and international security in the modern world.

Orlando Aerospace has concentrated its efforts on the development and production of high-technology weapon systems and associated equipment. Some of these systems have already passed into history — Bullpup and Lacrosse, mentioned earlier, Matador and Mace, and Sprint. Another, Pershing, with one

Governor of Florida, Leroy Collins, cut the ribbon opening the new Orlando plant in December 1957. Others participating were Linton Allen (at left), local banker who led the land-acquisition effort, Martin president George Bunker, and Orlando vice-president and general manager Edward Uhl.

foot in history and the other in the future, has stood with NATO deterrent forces for two decades. Improved over the years with advancing technology, it is expected to continue this vital role past the end of this century.

Patriot, on the drawing boards and in development since 1966, has become a viable air-defense system capable of protecting United States and allied ground forces from any aircraft now in being or contemplated.

A pioneer in the development and application of lasers and other advanced electro-optical equipment, Orlando Aerospace nursed this new technology through research and development into working systems that guide smart artillery projectiles and missiles and help crews of attack aircraft find their targets in daylight or darkness and bad weather.

The Pershing missile, begun at Orlando Aerospace in 1958, was put on public display for the first time in February 1963 at the centennial celebration of General of the Armies John J. Pershing. This defensive system has been a significant element in NATO deterrent forces since 1964.

Orlando Aerospace traces its heritage back 75 years to 1909 when Glenn L. Martin built and flew his first airplane in Anaheim, California. The company he founded was responsible for many significant achievements in aeronautics — the first multi-passenger aircraft, the ocean-spanning Clippers, the huge Martin Mars, the bomber that General Billy Mitchell used to demonstrate the potency of air power. During World War II, Martin Company built thousands of warplanes — like the B-26 and B-29 bombers and Navy patrol aircraft — and later, the B-57 and commercial airliners.

Martin Company turned to the new technology of missiles and, again a pioneer, built the Viking that orbited America's first satellite, Vanguard, in 1958. The Martin Titan launched American astronauts into space in the Gemini spacecraft with a perfect score, laying the groundwork for Apollo, Skylab, and the Space Shuttle.

In 1961, Martin Company merged with American Marietta to become Martin Marietta, a diversified corporation with major operations in aggregates, cement, and chemicals, as well as aerospace, and later, aluminum and data processing.

Today, Orlando Aerospace is one of the top industrial employers in Florida. Employment is over 9,000, with a heavy percentage of degreed personnel and an annual payroll of more than $250 million.

In 1983, employee and corporate contributions to United Way amounted to more than $700,000, bringing total contributions since 1956 to over $6 million. In addition, the corporation and individual employees provide significant support for community educational and cultural institutions and activities.

With its sister operations in Orlando — Martin Marietta Data Systems and Orlando Central Park — Orlando Aerospace is proud to be a part of this central Florida community.

Mills & Nebraska — the best known address in town

Central Florida Lumber began in 1932 when the directors of Kissam Builders Supply saw a need for a lumberyard in Orlando. Kissam's, one of Orlando's oldest concrete and building materials dealers, started business in 1922. Kissam's had participated in the boom of the twenties, watched as several lumber companies failed during the Depression, and felt these failures made a lumberyard necessary to round out its participation in local building needs and growth. The Kissam's directors owned a piece of property at the corner of North Mills and Nebraska Avenue which they felt would be a good location for the new venture. All that was needed was an outstanding local lumberman to operate the new company. Such a man was Alan Kissam's friend, Francis Igou of Kissimmee, owner and operator of the Kissimmee Lumber & Supply Company, who at that time was trustee for the liquidation of a large lumber company in Orlando. They joined forces and in June 1933, Central Florida Lumber Company was incorporated with nine stockholders — the six Kissam directors holding 75 percent of the new venture, and the three new lumber company officers, Francis Igou, his wife Pauline, and Elbert Ivey.

In 1933, Mills Street ended at Nebraska Avenue. While the land and buildings were prepared, Igou ran small ads in the newspaper that referred to the company's "Mills & Nebraska" location and posted "This is not Mills & Nebraska" signs all over town. Just prior to opening, a large sign was erected at the entrance to the lumber yard that read "This IS Mills & Nebraska." And so Central Florida Lumber opened with one employee, in addition to Igou and Ivey, and three vehicles, a 1928 Pontiac Sedan, a 1925 White Truck, and a Model-T pickup. The first six months were very slow. However, the Depression provoked government projects, and a hurricane swept through Orlando blowing the roofs off of a great many buildings, greatly improving business!

The company's first expansion was a mill-working facility to produce windows, door frames, and finish lumber to specifications. Success came quickly, and the small millwork shed was replaced with a two-story concrete block structure. By 1937, the extension of Mills Street north through Winter Park was underway, and Alan Kissam suggested remodeling "to an extent that would be in keeping with the new road."

In 1941, the delivery fleet had increased to five trucks, but World War II's material freezes and restrictions on residential construction threatened the young lumberyard. Then the company received a contract from Correct Craft of Pinecastle to build wooden hulls for landing craft. The mill ran three shifts a day with peak employment of 33. After the war, central Florida began its long-term building boom and Francis Igou's son Phillip returned from flying B-29s to join the company.

Mills & Nebraska as it looked in 1952 with original lumber sheds in the rear and Kissam block plant on the right.

The fifties was a decade of change and growth. In 1957, Francis Igou passed away and was succeeded by his son Phillip as president. Francis Igou had opened the doors of Mills & Nebraska and successfully nurtured it for almost 25 years. He was active in the Florida Lumber and Building Material Dealers Association, serving as their president from 1951–53. In 1966, the Francis J. Igou Lumberman of the Year Award was established to recognize people who exemplified Igou's service to the community and the association.

With the new president came other board changes. Pauline Igou became secretary, and Kenneth Hill of Kissam's, became vice-president. At the same time, Roy Pulsifer, one of the original stockholders from Kissam's, gave his stock to his sons John and Tom. In 1959, John became a member of the board of directors and Tom became secretary following Pauline Igou's death in 1969. At the close of the sixties, Kissam Builders Supply was sold, and John and Tom Pulsifer acquired the Mills & Nebraska stock previously held by the Kissam directors. This brought the original nine stockholders down to four — Mrs. Allen (Doris) Kissam, wife of one of the original founders, plus Phil Igou and John and Tom Pulsifer, all second-generation stockholders.

Throughout its over 50 years of history, Central Florida Lumber has been at the forefront of progress in Orlando. Under Phil Igou's innovative leadership, Mills & Nebraska continued to prepare for the coming years of growth. In 1957, it became the first Orlando lumberyard to manufacture its own roof trusses. A modern home-center store was completed in 1960, and a central Florida landmark appeared in the form of "The World's Largest Board." M & N Door & Trim started manufacturing prehung doors in 1972, then U-Cart concrete, concrete blocks, aggregates and brick were added, followed in 1975 by hollow metal doors and frames and, most recently, window products. During the last three years the Hollow Metal Door Division received the Outstanding Sales Achievement Award from Ceco Corporation for sales volume in America. Also during this time the minority stockholders, Doris Kissam and Phil Igou, sold their stock back to the corporation, and John and Tom Pulsifer assumed more active roles in the Mills & Nebraska companies.

From the original three employees and annual sales of $100,000 in 1939, Central Florida Lumber today employs 155 people and has projected sales of $19 million. The original one and a half acres occupied by the company has grown to seventeen.

Throughout all of this growth, innovation, and change, Central Florida Lumber has remained not only family owned but also has had a family approach. Eighteen employees have been with the companies for more than 10 years. In several instances, second-generation employees work along with second-generation ownership. The dedication of all its people over the last 50 years to high standards of quality and customer service has truly made Mills & Nebraska "The Best Known Address in town."

Vision and engineering created a special place for business and nature to work together at Orlando Central Park

When visitors to Orlando Central Park drive along its wide streets and see the Orlando offices of nationally known firms like the *Wall Street Journal* or the Chrysler Corporation or Red Lobster, there's little chance they could imagine the way that same property looked in the early 1960s. Yet, like most of the rural land along US Highway 441 just south of youthful Orlando, then it was pasture and early Florida homestead — palmettos, wiregrass, and lakes with natural stocks of large-mouth bass and bluegills.

And yet, while most people would agree today that it took vision and energy and a great deal of development know-how to create one of the country's largest and most successful industrial, office, and distribution complexes out of that pastureland, few could realize how much innovation and effort it did take.

For Orlando Central Park is still growing and still leading the way in business developments. With only about one-half of its 4,200 acres developed, Orlando Central Park's management continues to create a park-like environment suited to central Florida's special ecological conditions, while providing the kind of roads and access and utilities that a broad mixture of businesses require.

Initial planning for the park began in early 1963 on land owned by The Martin Company, a predecessor company to the Martin Marietta Corporation. A separate corporation jointly owned by The Martin Company and Brooks, Harvey & Company of New York was created to develop and manage the park. It was under the enlightened and steadfast direction of Ralph F. Breum that the basic concept, planning, and construction progressed until his retirement in 1975.

It was a pioneering period, with wide streets opening the way for construction adjacent to US 441, the main highway leading into Orlando from the north and south. A major hotel, the Gold Key Inn, was built there, which featured the Piccadilly Restaurant and Pub — popular then and now as one of the finest restaurants in the area, and the Executives Club, the finest business club to be built outside of the central business district and designed to be an amenity to businesses locating in the park.

From that early nucleus of buildings and businesses, Orlando Central Park's history parallels Orlando's — tremendous growth, but controlled growth, for the plan was always to keep or improve the existing natural values while accommodating the demand for active companies. In its first 20 years, more than 150 buildings were built, more than 30 miles of streets were paved and curbed, and over 10,000 people come to work in the Park every day in offices, warehouses, factories, laboratories, and stores. New structures are

In early 1963, Orlando Central Park was just beginning to take shape. Left to right is US-441, 17, and 92 with the new Orlando Central Parkway pointing to the west and Lake Ellenor. The same view today would show Walt Disney World on the horizon.

completed in the Park on the average of one every 47 days; there are 5 or 6 under construction at all times.

Many famous names began to appear on the Park's roster — names like the Chrysler Corporation, CNA Insurance, DeSoto Corporation, Sonotrol, Southland Corporation, Super Foods, and many others. Red Lobster Inns, which began operations from a 1,500-square-foot headquarters in the Park, began its phenomenal growth to over 137,000 square feet of office space spread over seven buildings.

Meanwhile, the Park's rail service and its closeness to both the new Orlando International Airport and to the main highways leading out to the major cities of Florida made it a natural choice for a distribution center. And, as the number of advanced technological firms began to fill the needs of Florida's growing aerospace and electronic industries, many of them found the Park's central location and business environment to be ideal for their technical, professional, and executive work forces.

The Park's full potential, envisioned by Ralph Breum in 1963, is now being fulfilled by a professional development and marketing staff under James B. Brown, who became

president in 1975. Brown, who shared the responsibilities of planning and management with Breum from the very first, is directing a continuing program of carefully controlled growth throughout a full spectrum of development for retail, office, distribution, R&D, assembly, and manufacturing operations.

Recently, the area's growth in the tourism industry permitted Orlando Central Park, Inc. to allocate a portion of its land to the development of one of the first totally planned tourist/commercial properties, and Plaza International was developed along the Park's western boundary with Interstate Highway 4. This development, which is the site of Orange County's Convention/Civic Center and a number of major hotels and tourist facilities, has become a highly successful model of restricted commercial development. When fully developed, millions of visitors a year will visit Plaza International.

Orlando Central Park and Plaza International continue to attract the attention of planners and developers the world over who wish to see the ongoing process of providing development opportunities for companies in distribution, manufacturing, professional services, retail and hospitality, and entertainment. And even though it is more and more difficult to imagine the way Orlando Central Park looked in 1963, it is even more obvious that its progress is the consequence of vision and commitment to responsible development.

Over 40 years of patient care by caring people

Orlando General Hospital was founded in 1941 as a 15-bed facility by a small group of osteopathic physicians. The original hospital, known as Orlando Osteopathic Hospital, was located in a residential area on Hillcrest Street in Orlando. By 1957, the original 15-bed hospital had expanded to 28 beds.

During 1960, the name was changed to Orlando General Hospital. In 1961, the decision was made to relocate to Lake Underhill Drive. The result was a modern 48-bed facility. The hospital expanded again in 1971, adding an additional 53 beds and bringing the hospital to 101 patient beds.

Orlando General Hospital's current expansion program began in 1982 and was completed in the spring of 1984. Seventy beds and three floors were added to the facility, bringing its current completion to 171 beds.

Today, Orlando General Hospital is a 171-bed not-for-profit institution which last year served more than 5,300 inpatients. As a full-service general hospital, Orlando General offers surgical and maternity services, internal medicine, pediatrics, orthopedics, radiology, intensive and coronary care, progressive care, laboratory, uro-dynamics, respiratory and physical therapy, vascular laboratory, and CT scanner.

The hospital operates a 24-hour Emer-

Orlando General Hospital in 1984; a 171-bed, full service, osteopathic institution.

gency Room and Trauma Center which, during 1983, received 12,000 visits.

In an effort to meet the medical needs of its patient community, where hospitalization is not necessarily required, Orlando General Hospital has developed a rapidly expanding Outpatient/Ambulatory Services Department. Many tests and procedures can now be done on an outpatient or on a short-term stay basis. The purpose of ambulatory or one-day surgery is to have the surgery performed as specified by the patient's doctor in a safe surrounding and return the patient to as near a normal state as possible.

Orlando General Hospital welcomes 500 newborns each year and offers family-centered maternity services. This includes birthing rooms with total stay; labor, delivery and postpartum facilities; a birthing chair; prepared childbirth classes; in-room sibling visitation; maternity workout, and postnatal recovery programs.

As an osteopathic institution, Orlando General Hospital's active medical staff are doctors of osteopathy (D.O.) as opposed to medical doctors (M.D.). Osteopathic medicine is concerned with the prevention, diagnosis, and treatment of human illness, disease, and injury. Founded in the late 1800s by Andrew Taylor Still, M.D., the osteopathic philosophy incorporates certain principles

partially utilized by the allopathic (M.D.) and holistic schools of medicine. "Osteo" means bone and "pathos" means to suffer. Dr. Still wanted emphasize the major role that the musculo-skeletal system plays in the health of an individual. The musculo-skeletal system includes all the bones, joints, muscles, tendons, and ligaments of the human body — approximately 60 percent of the total body makeup.

D.O.s are not chiropractors. Neither are they bone specialists or physical therapists. Only D.O.s and M.D.s are qualified to be licensed as physicians in all 50 states and to practice all branches of medicine and surgery.

Orlando General Hospital operates its own in-house Home Health Care Agency. The hospital is adding a 26-bed Alcohol and Substance Abuse Program to its present facility at 7727 Lake Underhill Drive in east Orange County.

Last year, the hospital had over 5,300 inpatients and over 12,000 visits to the Emergency Room. The hospital is accredited by the American Osteopathic Association and the Joint Commission on Accreditations of Hospitals.

A tradition of health care excellence through caring

The story of Orlando Regional Medical Center is actually the story of two hospitals, Orange Memorial and Holiday. It recounts a long tradition of farsighted leadership and progressive changes to meet the challenge of providing the best, most sophisticated health care available to the people who live in central Florida.

For over 50 years ORMC has been a leader in medical care for the six-county region it serves. It has grown steadily to become a 1,035-bed tertiary medical center capable of treating the most severe medical problems in patients of all ages. The state verified ORMC as a Level I trauma center for emergency care, and it has the physicians and facilities to provide specialty care in every area of medicine. The expansive medical center houses the most up-to-date diagnostic and treatment facilities. More than 70 resident physicians are training in a comprehensive medical education program.

Through the years, caring has been the foundation for all the programs at ORMC. The medical center's number-one priority has always been to demonstrate a caring attitude toward each patient who walks through its doors. The staff believes that new facilities and technological advances cannot replace the importance of personalized, quality care to patients, their families, and friends.

ORMC grew to its present status from a simple beginning on undeveloped lowlands on the outskirts of Orlando. Orange General, renamed Orange Memorial in 1946 in tribute to the soldiers who served in World War II, was first proposed in 1916 by a concerned group of community leaders, physicians, and the hospital commission of the Orlando Board of Trade, who gathered at People's Bank in the heart of downtown Orlando. The group felt there was a tremendous need for a general hospital to serve the area, which even then showed a great promise for growth.

The tradition of concerned citizens backing the hospital and taking a committed interest in the community's health care has continued since the early days.

The original site of Orange Memorial was on a tract of land south of the city limits. Orlando's population in 1916 was almost 10,000, and a city was beginning to grow in the midst of orange trees and freshwater lakes. A two-lane brick road, winding its way around Lake Lucerne, was the only thoroughfare leading to the hospital.

The original 50-bed hospital was a $100,000 investment at the time of construction. Building progress was hampered by a severe frost and torrential rains and a railroad strike in 1918, which brought delivery of equipment and supplies to a standstill.

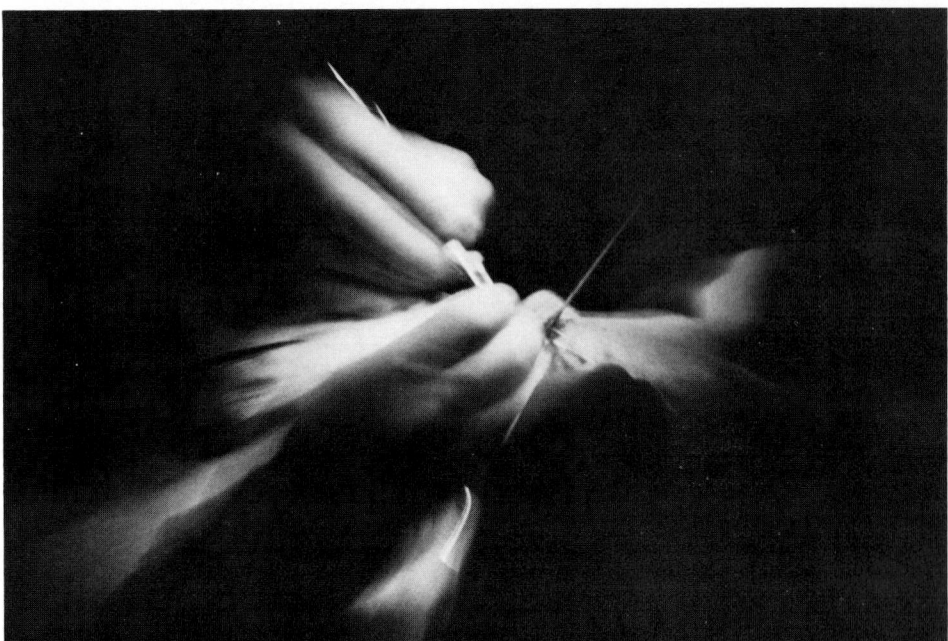

ORMC is one of the leading medical centers in the Southeast.

The original Orange General Hospital.

When Orange Memorial was officially dedicated on July 4, 1918, the ceremony was the highlight of the young city's Independence Day festivities. It was the beginning of an era of health care excellence for Orlando.

As Orlando grew, so did Orange Memorial Hospital. Spurts of growth continued from 1929 to 1977 with eight major expansion projects that increased the hospital's size from 50 to 775 beds. Beginning in 1929 with the addition of a 50-bed east wing, building continued through the sixties with construction of an intensive care unit, coronary care unit, mental health center, and a medical/surgical unit. In 1976, ground was broken for a 40,000-square-foot outpatient emergency department and radiation oncology center to provide the finest and most effective cancer treatment known.

Through the years, as Orange Memorial grew to meet the health care needs of Orlando, so did its counterpart, Holiday Hospital.

Holiday Hospital was chartered by the state of Florida in 1950. The name "Holiday" had a long association with health care in Orlando. Since 1939, the two-story Holiday

House, located east of Orange Memorial, had been a treatment site for children with rheumatic heart disease.

Construction proceeded rapidly on the new 114-bed hospital, designed to meet the needs of both acutely ill patients and those with less serious problems. In 1965, construction began on a seven-story patient care tower in the center of Holiday Hospital that brought the total number of beds to 243.

In 1977, the Orange Memorial and Holiday hospitals consolidated to form Orlando Regional Medical Center. Increased efficiency and cost savings by eliminating duplication of services and equipment were primary reasons for the joining of the two hospitals. Most importantly, combining the specialties of the two hospitals improved the overall quality of patient care.

ORMC became one of the largest private, not-for-profit, full service health care facilities in the Southeast. ORMC's financial structure is one in which all profits or excess revenues are reinvested back into the medical center for renovations and new equipment, personnel, and new facilities.

With the opening of Walt Disney World in Orlando, new growth in the southwest part of the city was inevitable. Orange Memorial Hospital opened a small hospital division, Orange Vista, on a site near the attractions to meet the medical needs of tourists and visitors.

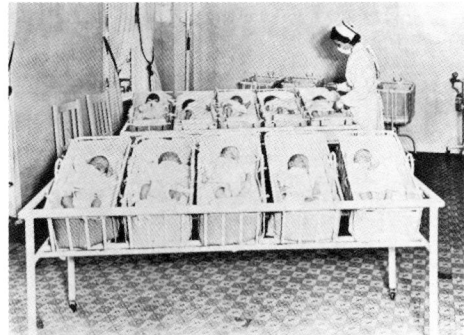
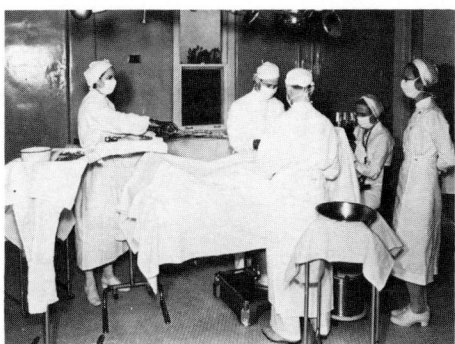

The nursery and operating room as they were in the early years of the hospital.

As ORMC entered the eighties, the greatest strides in the growth of the facilities and advances in care occurred. Greater flexibility to supply quality health care in the most effective manner prompted ORMC to reorganize its structure in early 1983 into four separate corporations.

The four components of the new health care system are Orlando Health Network Inc., a not-for-profit holding company that serves as a parent to three subsidiaries that include Orlando Regional Medical Center; the ORMC Foundation, a philanthropic organization involved in development and fundraising; and Healthnet Services Inc., a for-profit corporation that will engage in health and non-health activities.

ORMC is one of ten regional neonatal intensive care units providing lifesaving care to premature and critically ill newborns.

The ORMC downtown campus, consisting of the original Orange and Holiday divisions, now has over 3,000 employees and 525 physicians on staff.

In addition to all its patient services, ORMC is a fully accredited teaching hospital and offers residency training programs in surgery, orthopedics, pathology, internal medicine, obstetrics and gynecology, and pediatrics.

ORMC is a fully equipped and staffed trauma center for 6 counties. It has a brain injury rehabilitation center for stroke victims and patients with other brain injuries, a comprehensive cancer diagnosis and treatment program, and a radiation oncology center where over 100 cancer patients a day receive the most sophisticated radiation therapy treatments.

The regional perinatal intensive care center is one of 10 in the state providing skilled care to high-risk mothers and newborns. A 35-bed neonatal intensive care unit is equipped for premature and critically ill newborns. A special child life education program helps children and their families through the sometimes frightening events associated with hospitalization and serious illness.

ORMC has a regional center for burn treatment and a poison prevention center with a 24-hour hotline. An endocrine unit treats individuals with diabetes, and a complete patient education program is organized to accompany it. A six-bed renal dialysis unit provides acute dialysis care. A broad range of areas is covered by the medical center's outpatient clinics for treatment of problems such as spina bifida or cystic fibrosis.

With ORMC's position established as a leading provider of the most comprehensive medical care available in central Florida, the medical center has begun looking toward the future and planning ways of expanding.

As the southwest portion of Orlando continues to develop, ORMC has a 150-bed medical/surgical hospital under construction to meet the health care needs of this rapidly growing section. Planned for completion in 1985, the Sand Lake Campus hospital will offer a full complement of services, ancillary care, and the same quality already established by ORMC at its existing hospitals.

In the tradition of community support for ORMC, a capital fundraising campaign is underway for a children's hospital and perinatal center adjacent to the downtown Holiday division. The added hospital pavilion would centralize existing children's services and programs for high-risk mothers and babies, house the neonatal and pediatric intensive care units, and be the site for all the outpatient services pertaining to children.

Through the years, ORMC has taken steps to plan for the future and secure a strong position to meet the needs and challenges of the rapidly growing central Florida region. With a strong commitment to excellence in care, ORMC will continue to provide the finest, most sophisticated medical treatment to meet the changing health care needs of area residents.

From provincial beginnings to world-class stature

The end of World War II brought tourists pouring into Florida to bask in the sun and live it up after years of austerity. Tourist guides sprang up around the state, simple little booklets with tips on where to dine and look at alligators. Orlando's guide, founded in 1946 by Hugh Waters, was entitled *The Orlando Attraction.*

Circulation through the roadside motor courts that catered to Orlando's handful of winter visitors was little more than 1,000 copies an issue. Early editions carried 16 pages, a figure that slowly grew over the years to 30 or 40. In 1949, you could mail an *Attraction* home for 3 cents.

In the late 1950s, Hugh Waters sold the business to Lawrence Towe, a former newspaper broker from Michigan.

Edward L. and Artice Prizer purchased the magazine, now known as *The Orlando-Winter Park Attraction,* on February 10, 1962. Prizer had been an editor and general supervisor with the Associated Press in New York, a position he left to move to Orlando.

Like many another small business in this pre-Disney era in Orlando, publishing *The Attraction* was a hand-to-mouth existence. Prizer sold the advertising, wrote the few editorial items, and supervised production at Kirstein's, the local jobshop that printed the magazine.

Artice Prizer handled the mailing department, prepared the coming events, and put together the dummy of each issue. A secretary came in once a month to do the books and get out statements. A high-school boy delivered the weekly issues each weekend.

Walt Disney's momentous announcement of Walt Disney World in November 1965 galvanized Orlando's little guide magazine into action. The concept was broadened to include information for families moving to Orlando and investors coming into the area.

As the Disney land boom mounted, advertising volume of the magazine soared. Realtors, developers, apartment complexes, condominiums filled the ad pages.

The once-tiny booklet had now swelled to almost 100 pages. Editorial content had been expanded to cover a far wider span of subjects — particularly those relating to growth and development of the area. The magazine now had a full-time managing editor, Joan Puett, and assistant, Fran West, and it commanded growing recognition within the community.

It was time to take the next giant step forward. This came in the fall of 1969 as construction was moving ahead on Walt Disney World. Now using the name *Orlando-land Attraction Magazine,* the publication aban-

Edward L. Prizer, editor and publisher, compares a current issue of Orlando Magazine *with one of the earliest magazines from the 1940s, a pamphlet originally entitled* The Orlando Attraction. *Offices of the magazine, background, were moved to this building in Winter Park in 1970.*

doned the small guide format and went to full magazine size, printed on a full-color web press at the *Daytona Beach News Journal.*

It became the role of *Orlando-land* to chronicle the early days of the Disney era and the rapid changes sweeping through the grovelands and pine woods of central Florida. The editorial pages became an unfolding saga of the emergence of a small town with a whimsical name into the ranks of world-class cities.

In a region where newcomers were beginning to dominate the local scene, a magazine specializing in area information was essential. *Orlando-land Magazine* (having dropped the word "Attraction" entirely) added more members to a staff supervised by Carole DePinto as managing editor. Specialists wrote on subjects from interior decoration to land and water management.

The boom took the magazine to 160 pages, and then the severe recession of the mid-1970s brought another era of austerity. Dur-

ing a long, slow effort to recoup lost ground, the scope of the magazine was broadened even further — into such fields as architecture, engineering, and medical care.

The name was finally shortened to *Orlando Magazine* in 1981. Now the Orlando publication had reached the top ten in ad volume among city magazines of America. The staff numbered some 30 full-time, part-time and free-lance men and women. National advertising appeared regularly in issues carrying 180 to 212 pages monthly.

In two decades, page space had grown 900 percent, cirulation 1,400 percent and gross revenues 4,600 percent. Like Orlando, the *Orlando Magazine,* from small provincial beginnings, had grown into an institution of world-class dimensions and stature.

We make your life easier

The Palmer Electric story began in 1939, when founder Howard Palmer and a partner joined together and formed an electrical contracting and service company known as Cook Electric. The business was started in a small garage behind a residence at 842 Orlando Avenue in Winter Park, but soon moved to a store front at 348 Park Avenue and expanded to include retail paint sales. Fate was good to the firm, and by the end of 1940 it had grown to include five journeyman electricians with five helpers. Among their jobs were the Student Union Building, the Shell Museum and French House at Rollins College, the Monocoupe Airplane and Engine Factory at Orlando Airport, and the remodeling of the Alabama Hotel.

Wartime interrupted, and in 1942 Howard Palmer sold his interests in Cook Electric and moved to Lynn, Massachusetts to take a steam turbine engineering position with General Electric, doing design and test work for the U.S. Navy wartime effort. In 1950, he returned to Orlando and purchased Simonet Electric at 316 West Colonial Drive. The name was changed to Palmer Electric and incorporated in March 1951.

By 1955, the business included a retail store selling lighting fixtures, home appliances, and air conditioners. A warehouse with a small set of offices had been opened on Jackson Avenue in Winter Park. The electrical contracting and service business had grown to a fleet of nineteen vehicles and 39 electricians.

Colonial Drive became a main traffic artery and rendered the original facility impractical for the needs of the business. In 1959, the facility was closed and the entire operation moved to the location on Jackson in Winter Park. By 1959, the employee roll had grown to 75.

During the 1960s, Palmer Electric continued to expand operations. Much of this growth can be attributed to the many jobs performed at Cape Canaveral for the space program and electrical construction jobs for the Martin Company and other defense related agencies.

Other notable projects included Orange Memorial Hospital, Holiday Hospital, and Winter Park Memorial Hospital. These major jobs together with numerous schools in both Orange and Seminole counties, shopping centers, office buildings, and a growing residential marketplace helped Palmer Electric prosper. In 1969, and early 1970, the facilities were expanded in Winter Park to include a two-story showroom for the lighting fixture and appliance Divisions, and three warehouses were added to meet the needs of the growing electrical construction divisions.

The recession of the early seventies and

Group photo of employees and fleet on Colonial Drive in 1955.

the resulting slowdown in construction hurt Palmer Electric as it did many businesses, but diversification of products sold and services offered coupled with employee attitude saw the company through those hard times. The later seventies saw growth and new marketplaces. Facilities were added and electrical-related work was performed throughout the state. What had evolved was a firm comprised of several different businesses or divisions all working together under one name.

The early eighties found Palmer Electric stronger in the electrical industry in Florida. The company had grown to over 400 employees with a fleet of 160 vehicles. Each of the divisions with their respective specialities continued to grow within their marketplace. Commercial and industrial wiring, residential wiring, commercial wiring service, lighting fixture sales, home appliance sales, commercial lighting and signs, residential wiring service, electronics service, and finally, light commercial wiring have become the many different fields of Palmer Electric's involvement. Through these divisions, most types of electrical construction or repair, regardless of size, can be performed. The diversification into sales of lighting fixtures, major home appliances, and electronics message centers expanded the impact made on the electrical industry in central Florida.

Major accomplishments in the early eighties were numerous and included such jobs as the *Sentinel Star*'s new press facility, TV station WCPX, and the roadway lighting for Disney's Epcot interchange. Thousands of new residents had their homes wired and the

Winter Park office and warehouse complex shortly after completion in 1955.

lighting fixtures and appliances installed by Palmer Electric. Many other central Floridians called for the repair of everything from their electrical service to their television sets.

Palmer Electric is proud of its accomplishments, and through the pride of the many professionals in this totally employee-owned company, it will continue to make your life easier for many years to come.

Responding to the complexities of growth with diversified expertise

Like the city that brought its founders together, the law firm of Peirsol, Boroughs, Grimm, Bennett & Griffin, Professional Association, has earned a reputation greater than its years. Drawn to Orlando in the 1960s and early 1970s by the area's apparent growth potential, accompanying opportunities for professional advancement, and intelligent local government, the firm's four founding members took positions with established practices and went on to develop specialized practices of their own: Frederick W. Peirsol in federal taxation and estate planning; P. Thomas Boroughs in real estate; William A. Grimm in corporate and securities laws; and R. Lee Bennett in commercial law and litigation.

Before the spark that was Disney ignited to produce an unprecedented influx of new industry, the principal lawyer activities in Orlando were real estate and litigation. Of necessity, this began to change as the business community became increasingly sophisticated and complex. Seeing the need for a firm capable of serving fully the multifaceted legal and business needs of existing companies and new industries entering central Florida, Peirsol joined with his three colleagues to form Peirsol, Boroughs, Grimm & Bennett, P.A., in October 1979. Because it was clear to them that downtown Orlando would one day be the financial heartbeat of central Florida, they established their offices in the Southeast Bank Building.

The original concept behind the firm's formation was threefold. First, it would be a well-rounded firm with strong department heads in every area of practice. Second, each partner's prior experience in one or more other fields would make him a "business generalist" as well as a legal specialist — an important prerequisite for a counselor. Finally, the firm would pursue a path of controlled growth to reach its goals — not growth for its own sake.

This formula for success provided a solid foundation for the future. As the community has grown, the firm has increased in both size and standing. With the expansion and diversification of its clientele, the firm's trial practice burgeoned. In early 1983, Jacqueline R. Griffin, a trial lawyer with several years experience in civil litigation, joined the firm to head its litigation department. Later that year, two additional lawyers became members of the firm — Thomas F. Kerney, who has a master of laws degree in taxation, and John R. Simpson Jr., who has practiced real estate law for several years. The firm currently has 14 lawyers and 21 non-lawyer personnel, including three paralegals. To keep pace with this growth, the office is being expanded for the fifth time. After current expansion and renovation plans are completed, the firm will occupy over 10,000 square feet of space — nearly four times what it started with in 1979.

The firm's tax practice, headed by Fred

From left to right — William A. Grimm, P. Thomas Boroughs, Jacqueline R. Griffin, Frederick W. Peirsol, and R. Lee Bennett, reviewing the plans for a major office expansion and renovation.

Peirsol with the assistance of partner Tom Kerney, is comprehensive, embracing all aspects of federal and state taxation with a heavy emphasis on estate planning, employee benefit planning, taxation of real estate transactions, syndication related tax matters, and corporate and partnership taxation.

The firm's real property practice is handled by department head Tommy Boroughs and partner John Simpson, with assistance from other attorneys specializing in real estate taxation and syndication. With this team approach, the department handles a broad range of real estate transactions, including site acquisition, construction, condominium development, investments in real estate, landlord/tenant matters, contract negotiation and preparation, land use regulation, tax-free exchanges, and commercial and residential closings.

The securities practice of the firm is noted throughout central Florida for its ability to provide clients full service legal work in connection with public offerings and private placements, particularly on behalf of technologically innovative companies. This practice has developed out of Bill Grimm's prior training as a mechanical engineer, experience as the controller of a publicly held company, and a member of the corporate finance department of a regional investment banking firm. With a master of business administration degree as well, he is a member of the board of directors of several high-technology companies, including two publicly held companies.

The growth of Orlando's business activities and the diversification of the transactions encountered by the firm's clients in the early 1980s created a need within the firm for additional commercial law expertise. Thus, a new department was formed in early 1983 to

deal with commercial transactional law, international law, and general business law. Lee Bennett, who heads this department, currently serves as a director of a publicly held computer software company and represents a number of high-technology firms, many of whom are exporting their products and expertise to Europe and the Far East.

Many firm members hold positions of leadership in the American, Florida, and Orange County bar associations and civic organizations. Fred Peirsol has served as president and is currently an active member of the board of trustees of the Southern Federal Tax Institute. He has also served on the board of directors and as vice-president of the Florida Symphony Society. Current chairman of the Attorneys' Review Committee of the Land Development Code for the city of Orlando, Tommy Boroughs has served two terms as chairman of the Real Property Section of the Orange County Bar Association. He also served several years as a member of the executive council of the Real Property Law Section of the Florida Bar and as chairman of the Federal Regulation of Land Use Committee of the Florida Bar. Additionally, he is a member of the Development Review Committee of the Downtown Development Board.

Lee Bennett is presently a director of the Mid-Florida Council for International Visitors, a member of the Orlando Leadership Council and the World Trade Center in Orlando, and is active in the Orlando area United Way. Bill Grimm is a regular speaker at business seminars regarding raising venture capital and was appointed by the Florida Secretary of Commerce as a leader of the Technical Entrepreneurship Task Force. Jackie Griffin is an active member of the Fidelity and Surety Committee of the American Bar Association.

Growth, achievement, and progress through the free enterprise system

The Dr. Phillips companies were started by Dr. P. Phillips, who was born on January 27, 1874 in the state of Tennessee. He was a practicing physician in Tennessee but devoted his time in Florida to agricultural pursuits.

He settled in Florida in 1897 when he bought pastureland in Osceola County and a grove on the south edge of Big Sand Lake in southwest Orange County. He initially started in the cattle business but discontinued that to involve himself totally in the citrus industry. He moved to Orlando in 1905.

For many years, he was considered the world's largest individual grower of citrus, and in the southwest part of Orange County — called Dr. Phillips, Florida — he owned the world's largest tangerine grove. In 1928, the Dr. Phillips Organization produced the first acceptable type of canned orange juice through a patented process called "flash pasteurization." The Dr. Phillips canned citrus product was the first to achieve the seal of acceptance of the American Medical Association.

The Dr. Phillips Companies owned and operated a fresh fruit-packing house in Fairvilla, a canning plant in Orlando at Princeton and Orange avenues and, in the Dr. Phillips Florida area, a packing house and fertilizer plant that were at that time the most modern in the industry.

In the 1930s, a post office was established in the Dr. Phillips, Florida area, and in the late forties the idea of a community at Dr.

Airplane view of the World's Largest Packing House at Dr. Phillips, Florida.

Dr. P. Phillips.

Phillips was started. Since the citrus business was highly seasonal, Dr. Phillips used his labor force to begin building and leasing commercial and industrial buildings on other properties that he had acquired as he wanted to provide continuous employment for his people.

In 1954, all of the Dr. Phillips citrus holdings were sold to a subsidiary of the Minute Maid corporation called Granada Groves. In selling the grove operations and the grove real estate, Dr. Phillips retained all raw land

that was not planted into groves. It is on this land that he continued the operation of building and leasing commercial and industrial buildings which then became the major activity of the surviving corporation.

One of that company's prime objectives is still to provide employment to people within the central Florida area. Although a relatively small organization administratively, the company now leases in excess of 175 buildings and has under lease more than a million and a half square feet of building area.

The development of the lands controlled in the community of Dr. Phillips, Florida, in southwest Orange County, became the primary objective of Dr. Phillips' son Howard. A complete master plan of that area was finished in 1969. It was the first of this nature in Orange County and covered about eighteen square miles of land and water. This area now includes the nationally known golf course community of Bay Hill, along with numerous other prime developments which reflect what good and timely planning can accomplish.

After Howard Phillips' death, Dr. Phillips, Inc. became wholly owned by a charitable support organization which had been provided in his will. This organization, now known as the Howard Phillips Fund, uses the profits received from Dr. Phillips, Inc. for the benefit of education and charity.

It was Mr. Phillips' desire that the profits that were earned in the community of Dr. Phillips, and in the central Florida area in which it operates, be returned to the community through the support of those efforts.

Red Lobster, a seafood success story

It's quite a "lobster tale" — the story of how Bill Darden's desire to develop a seafood restaurant with quality food and service at moderate prices resulted in the nation's largest seafood dinner house restaurant company . . . Red Lobster Inns of America.

The Red Lobster concept can be traced to 1963 when Darden, already an experienced restaurateur, bought an Orlando, Florida, restaurant called Gary's Duck Inn. The restaurant grew in size and reputation quickly, and Darden had an idea.

Wouldn't Americans love a seafood restaurant that served quality food at a good value with quick and efficient service? Darden gambled that they would, but he hedged his bet by placing his first Red Lobster restaurant in the small Florida town of Lakeland, an area which at the time lacked an outstanding seafood restaurant.

Darden was hoping to build a customer base slowly so that his restaurant staff could learn from on-the-job training. But so many seafood lovers swamped that first Red Lobster on the second day of business that Darden and several of the restaurant's investors had to work in the kitchen just to get the food out.

Business hasn't slowed down much since.

Today, there are more than 370 Red Lobster restaurants in 36 states. Outside of the Untied States, Red Lobster operates in Japan and Canada.

There is good reason why Red Lobster has come so far, so fast. For example, there's the quality. Red Lobster has established one of the most elaborate quality control programs of any restaurant company in the nation.

Suppliers are required to meet strict standards in the harvesting and processing of their catch, and product samples are carefully evaluated for proper weight, size, flavor, texture, and aroma.

Courteous, efficient service has also been a focal point of the Red Lobster concept. From management personnel to kitchen workers, employees at Red Lobster benefit from the most thorough and professional training program in the food service industry. Evidence of the success of the program is the upward mobility of many Red Lobster employees to supervisory capacities.

Red Lobster menus have long been a source of excitement and value for customers, reflecting a variety of items and price

Beginning in 1968 as a single seafood restaurant in Lakeland, Florida, Red Lobster Inns of America has become the largest seafood dinner house restaurant operation in the United States today.

Red Lobster moved to a new look in mid-1984 — a look designed to generate broader consumer appeal for a greater variety of eating and drinking occasions.

points. Beginning with the introduction of new seafood discoveries previously unknown to most seafood lovers — such as popcorn shrimp and langostinos — to more recent additions like seafood pasta, there is always something new at Red Lobster. Steak, chicken, and seafood-steak combination platters are also offered, as well as daily fresh fish features, tasty appetizers, and dessert items. Red Lobster's charcoal mesquite grill preparation enhances the flavor of seafood as well as chicken and steak entrees.

To meet changing consumer tastes, Red Lobster launched a $104 million nationwide repositioning program mid-1984 to

create a more fun, relaxed, casual ambiance for guests. The repositioning program featured nautical decor, mesquite charcoal grills, and oyster bars, where guests could relax over appetizers and cocktails while observing skilled employees shucking oysters and clams.

Despite ongoing changes to remain responsive to trends in the industry, Red Lobster is committed to its original concept of quality, value, and service.

Accent on excellence provides basis for company success and growth

Thomas W. Ruff had but one goal when he opened his new office furniture business in Columbus, Ohio, in 1936 — to be the BEST in his dealings with customers, suppliers, and employees. This simple but demanding goal continues to be the basis of the Thomas W. Ruff and Company philosophy and has propelled the business into one of the nation's largest and most respected office and commercial furniture dealerships.

Ruff drew on his business experiences as an office equipment buyer for Railway Power and Light, and then as sales manager for an office furniture manufacturer, in emphasizing the value of service to the customer and how important employee attitudes are in providing that service. Not once during the hard years to follow did he lose this accent on excellence.

World War II eliminated new sales, but contact with the customers was maintained, and Ruff continued in business by personally servicing and maintaining his customers' furniture and equipment. After the war, new showrooms and offices were opened, and the business prospered until the Korean War again curtailed shipments. Although sales were made by allocation, Ruff was able to stay in business and even expanded his staff to eight.

When Tom Ruff died in 1953, one of his employees, Jack Gorman, was appointed manager. Gorman later purchased the company from the Ruff family and continued to build and maintain the original goal of excel-

Thomas W. Ruff and Company, Orlando. The company now has three locations and is one of the nation's largest and most respected office and commercial furniture dealerships.

lence learned from Tom Ruff. He quickly brought an era of innovation and pioneer spirit to the company and to the office furniture industry.

The two decades following Gorman's ascension to the leadership of the company saw Ruff and Company continue to develop. Total in-house services were established in 1957 — Interior Design, Carpet, Drapery, Delivery, and Installation departments. This proved to be a giant step as expertise was gained in each of these disciplines.

A banner year for Ruff employees was 1965, as the company established an employee pension plan trust and a profit sharing trust (later converted to an employee stock ownership plan).

As the company continued to grow, Jack Gorman recognized the need to establish an additional showroom facility in the Southeast to better serve the national accounts generated over the years. Orlando, Florida, was recognized as the most dynamic area in the Southeast at the time, and in 1974 Thomas W. Ruff and Company of Florida was incorporated and a showroom established in Maitland, just ten minutes from downtown Orlando. Under the leadership of John Chambliss, president, Ruff of Florida — from a modest beginning of just five employees —

quickly became a major factor in Orlando and in Florida office furnishings circles.

The Florida company followed the same concept of customer service and employee awareness established by Tom Ruff. It now has 50 employees in Orlando and 30 in Miami, Ruff's newest facility, opened in 1981.

From its three locations, Thomas W. Ruff and Company serves customers in the Middle Atlantic, Southeast and Midwest states. Sales of $40 million are projected for 1984, and all 180 employees in the three locations are involved in extensive programs preparing for new growth in the office furniture industry. Rapidly changing office environments dictated by efficiency, energy, electronic data processing, and space utilization offer Thomas W. Ruff and Company a challenging future.

Active involvement in civic and service organizations continues a tradition begun by Tom Ruff. A foundation established in his memory supports charitable and educational groups in Columbus, Orlando, and Miami. Numerous civic and national awards, including Geyer awards for design and installation, emphasize the success that resulted from one man's initial commitment. As the Thomas W. Ruff and Company celebrates its tenth anniversary in Florida and approaches its golden anniversary in Ohio, the goal of the founder remains consistent — to be the very best.

Sentinel growth parallels Orlando's growth

Today's modern *Orlando Sentinel* is a far cry from the *Orange County Reporter* of 1876, which marked the beginning of Orange County journalism.

The *Reporter,* a tiny weekly newspaper, was lovingly published by Rufus Russell, editor, on a hand-operated 2-page press in a 1-story wooden building in downtown Orlando. The press itself had been brought by boat to Sanford (then called Mellonville) and by ox-cart to Orlando, a frontier town of 200. Two men printed 200 papers — an hour-long process by hand — after pouring melted molasses and glue into a well-greased iron mold to form a roller with printed impressions on it.

The first issue of the *Reporter* hit the streets on June 6, 1876. Its name was destined to appear in the masthead of newspapers published in Orlando for the next 70 years.

After two rapid changes of ownership, the *Reporter* was purchased in 1880 by Mahlon Gore, an experienced newspaperman. He came from Sioux City, Iowa, and reportedly had some problems finding Orlando. Gore arrived at Sanford by boat and then took an Indian trail to Orlando — on foot.

According to Gore's nephew, E.H. Gore, Mahlon Gore walked for two days. He finally asked a cowboy for directions. "You damned fool," the cowboy is reported to have said, "you're in Orlando now."

In 1903, Orlando acquired its first daily, *The Evening Star.* Two years later, the *Orange County Reporter* was upgraded to a daily, giving Orlando two evening dailies and no morning paper. That situation was rectified in 1913, when Josiah Ferris, who had financial interests in the *Star* and the *Reporter,* established the *Orlando Morning Sentinel,* a resurrection of an earlier newspaper, the *South Florida Sentinel.* Ferris was progressive, installing telegraph service in 1912 and joining the International News Service in 1913. A year later, he sold the *Morning Sentinel* to Walter Essington and William Glenn.

In 1916, R.B. and J.C. Brossier, twins from Miami, purchased control of the Reporter-Star Publishing Company, adding a Sunday issue in 1925 to provide seven-day-a-week coverage. In addition to using ten Linotype machines, the *Reporter-Star* also added a new press and installed Orlando's first Associated Press wires.

In 1931, Texas publisher Charles E. Marsh, head of General Newspapers Inc. and owner of the *Reporter-Star* since 1925, bought the *Orlando Morning Sentinel,* forming a company known as Orlando Daily Newspapers

1884: The Orange County Reporter *moved to the north side of lot where Angebilt Hotel opened in 1923.*

Inc. Marsh sent Martin Andersen, who later became the newspapers' owner and publisher, to Orlando as a troubleshooter. Andersen had served as managing editor of an Austin, Texas, paper owned by Marsh.

"When I arrived in 1931," Andersen recalls, "the paper had been the victim of the Depression through no fault of its own." Andersen later wrote, "The property seemed to owe everybody, locally and around the country, but one by one we managed to straighten out the debts and dodge the sheriff's padlock. . . .

"Somewhere along in 1932, when Roosevelt closed the banks, we, along with the banks, ran out of money so we printed our own. We paid 80 percent of everybody's wages in *Sentinel-Star* scrip, which was accepted at grocery and other stores, and nobody put us in jail for printing counterfeit money.

"Merchants took the scrip and paid their advertising bills and circulated it around town. *Sentinel-Star* money was in common use."

A year later, Andersen founded Goodfellows Inc., a charity which provided food and, later, clothing for needy Orlandoans during the Depression. It was the forerunner of Sentinel Communications Charities Inc., which now provides hundreds of thousands of dollars annually to local charities and nonprofit organizations on behalf of Sentinel Communications Company.

In 1937, Andersen negotiated a deal with Marsh to purchase the newspapers on credit. The purchase was finalized in 1945 when Andersen swapped his interest in the *Macon* (Georgia) *Telegraph* and signed a long-term note. A year later, the papers were renamed *Orlando Morning Sentinel* and *Orlando Star.*

The papers' first construction came in 1946 when Andersen built a warehouse on

1950: Sentinel Star offices were on the site later occupied by Sun Bank.

North Orange Avenue, current site of the newspaper. The presses were moved, but the rest of the operation remained in the Fraternal Building on South Orange Avenue, the McElroy Building, and the Ohse Building at Boone Street and Slouch Alley, where it had been through the late 1930s and 1940s. Mats used for making press plates were carried from one site to another by a courier — on a motorbike.

By 1949, new presses were rolling, financed in part by Andersen's sale of his orange groves. Then, in 1950, it was announced that Orlando Daily Newspapers Inc. would build a $300,000 plant at the North Orange Avenue location. It opened August 12, 1951, and continued growth led to a $1 million, 2-story addition in 1961.

1980: When the satellite dish was installed at Sentinel's present location, it was one of first three in Florida.

Andersen's influence extended far beyond the newspaper. In 1958, he was named one of Florida's six most influential men by *Florida Trend* magazine. His efforts were instrumental in making Orlando the hub of the state's road network. Later, Walt Disney and others considered Orlando's easy access from all parts of the state when selecting a Florida location.

Andersen's interest in the road system began soon after his arrival in Orlando. He quickly perceived that tourist dollars were needed to help Orlando recover from the Depression. However, tourism required roads. He joined a group of volunteers who traveled around the state to attend "road lettings," part of Florida's unique system of allocating roads at that time. The object was to corner state highway commissioners and sell them on running their roads through Orlando. Other cities were doing the same thing.

The first success came when State Road 50 was being built from West Coast to East Coast. The placement of State Road 520 (the Bithlo cutoff) and Interstate 4 and the widening of bridges to Cape Kennedy (now Cape Canaveral) all were influenced by Andersen. In 1967, a road named in his honor, the Martin Andersen Beeline Expressway, was opened between Orlando and the Cape.

Andersen's political influence was heightened in the 1960s when Lyndon B. Johnson, a friend and fellow Marsh protégé, became president. It was in 1965, a year after Andersen helped organize a warm campaign welcome for Johnson in Orlando, that the Naval Training Center came to the city. Andersen's efforts also aided in the establishment of Florida Technological University (now the University of Central Florida) near Orlando. In 1966, he received a John Young Award as one of Florida's most influential men. In 1977, he was named to the Mid-Florida Business Hall of Fame, in recognition of his efforts on behalf of Orlando.

Shortly after Andersen's 1965 sale of the newspapers to the present owner (Tribune Company, Chicago), reporter Emily Bavar got her biggest scoop. She wrote that Walt Disney World was the "mystery industry" which had caused speculation in central Florida for months. In 1966, Andersen retired and William G. Conomos was appointed editor and publisher. Disney's 1971 opening was a fur-

ther catalyst, spurring the growth of the city and of the newspapers as well.

When Andersen gained full control of the papers, circulation was about 10,000 and he was earning $40 a week plus expenses. In 1958, combined circulation of the newspapers, then called the *Orlando Sentinel* and *Evening Star,* had reached 100,000. That was 15,000 more than the population in the city at that time. In 1984, Sunday circulation exceeded 300,000 for the first time.

Technology, advancing at an ever-increasing pace in the 1970s, helped meet the needs of the growing newspapers, which consolidated into the all-day *Sentinel Star* in 1973. In 1978, a year after Charles T. Brumback became president and chief executive officer, computerized typesetters were installed, eliminating the newspaper's noisy, slow Linotype machines. By 1979, the newsroom had made the transition to computer terminals at a cost of more than $1 million. In 1980, a satellite dish was installed at the paper to receive Associated Press news transmissions.

In 1981, Harold R. Lifvendahl became president and publisher, replacing Brumback, who was selected by Tribune Company to head the *Chicago Tribune.* Soon after, the *Sentinel's* new $38.8 million production center opened, leading the way to a complete transition to offset printing, 18 years after the first offset press and first computer to aid in typesetting had been purchased. A modern *Sentinel* press can produce 1,000 newspapers in less than a minute.

To serve a continually growing and more sophisticated readership, bureau offices were added and staffs enlarged. Today, nearly 50 years after Andersen opened the first bureau in Leesburg in 1935, the *Sentinel* has eighteen bureaus, including Miami, Tahallassee, Atlanta, and Washington, D.C. The breadth and depth of the newspaper's coverage has been expanded and the business diversified. In 1982, the newspaper's name was changed to *The Orlando Sentinel,* to build better identification with the central Florida market. The same year, the company became Sentinel Communications Company, reflecting its diversified activities — direct mail, commercial printing and cable information services. And, in 1983, Tribune Company became publicly held.

Just as Orlando has grown from a small town to the world's number-one tourist destination, the *Sentinel* has developed from a tiny weekly to Florida's fastest-growing newspaper. Oriented to the future, the *Sentinel* still remembers its past. An exhibit of the newspaper's former hot-type equipment, donated to the Orange County Historical Museum in 1983, reminds visitors of the passing of an era in newspaper technology. In much the same way, the azaleas and tabebuia that Andersen once offered as seedlings during newspaper promotions have also grown and now beautify Orlando, acting as a reminder of the newspaper's ties to the community it serves.

A *unique synthesis of marine education, research, and entertainment*

It seemed an improbable ambition when in 1971 San Diego-based Sea World announced it would build a marine life park in Orlando — miles from an ocean. But the challenge of re-creating seawater had been met several years earlier when Sea World opened its Cleveland zoological complex.

By the time Sea World of Florida opened on December 15, 1973, separate seawater systems for mammals and fishes were in place. A decade later, both have been expanded to compensate for splash, evaporation, and new habitats.

Habitat design always has been a high priority, says George Becker, Sea World president. "From the $5 million Shark Encounter we opened in 1979 to the $15 million killer whale performing and research complex opened in 1984, we try always to push back the frontiers of this particular display art. The new whale complex, in addition to being the largest of its kind in the world, in time will allow us to apply the knowledge we've accrued in our dolphin breeding program to killer whales," he says.

Results of much research are shared with marine science centers worldwide. Sea World's participation in the Southeast Stranding Network, for example, has helped establish what the scientific community calls

baseline data on aquatic mammals, amphibians, and birds. Network members rescue and, when possible, rehabilitate beached or injured animals. Such efforts are made possible by comparing analyses of ailing animals to those of healthy animals in the Sea World collections.

Sea World's long-term goal of housing the human species was met in 1984 when the Wyndham Hotel at Sea World was opened. It complements the dining, shipping, and entertainment complex called Florida Festival, which opened in 1979. Florida Festival was the first of a number of satellites planned for adjacent acreage.

Sea World also hosts some 60,000 students

annually in its unique education program, Exploration Breach. From kindergarten through college, scholars attend classes on topics as varied as the marine food chain and underwater acoustics.

The educational emphasis is pervasive in Sea World's shows, which entertain while enlightening, and often are based on staff research. Shows change about every second year, reflecting the growing sophistication of audience and staff. As attendance has grown from 1.7 million to 3 million annually, so have guest expectations. It is the continuing demand for high quality, educational entertainment which Sea World addresses as it plans for the future.

This 1974 aerial photo shows a young Sea World as it looked at 125 acres. The park opened in December of 1973 with the Whale and Dolphin and Seal and Otter stadiums, Fountain Fantasy

Theatre, World of the Sea Aquarium, Tide Pool Exhibit, Dolphin and Seal Feeder exhibits, and Japanese and Hawaiian villages.

A worthy rescue mission: Sea World Animal Care specialists lower Moby, a West Indian manatee who had been rehabilitated at the Orlando marine life park, back into home waters in the Caloosahatchee River.

NOSE TO NOSE. Dolly, an Atlantic bottlenose dolphin, rubs noses with her old friend, Sea World animal behavior supervisor Thad Lacinak. A favorite of Sea World audiences since 1971, Dolly can be seen several times daily in "The Shamu Experience" whale and dolphin show, along with killer whale friends Shamu and Namu and dolphin co-stars Cindy and Sandy.

FLORIDA FESTIVAL. Sea World's novel $7 million dining, entertainment, and shopping emporium contains slices of Floridiana under a sweeping Teflon-coated Fiberglass roof. The indoor tropical marketplace features visiting artisans, continu-

ous entertainment, Florida foods and beverages, and shopping pavilions in a climate-controlled environment. The Festival, located across from the theme park, is open daily. Free shuttle service is available to and from the park until closing.

Sheraton-Twin Towers reach unprecedented heights

After ten glorious banner years of American productivity in the sixties, it appeared that the seventies would bring unparalleled prosperity. Then the bottom fell out. Instead, the seventies brought oil embargoes, gas lines, double-digit inflation, Watergate, and a recession.

In central Florida, Walt Disney World was doing magic for the local economy — transforming Orlando, a sleepy centennial town, into the number-one tourist destination in the world — practically overnight. The race to build enough rooms to accommodate the deluge of tourists, coupled with the nation's economic woes, eventually resulted in a serious glut in hotel rooms.

One ingenious hotel builder, Charles M. "Skip" Brennan, saw the changing economic tide and the inevitable surplus of roadside motel rooms and in 1971 began to build a super-convention-type hotel complex. The same entrepreneur, who at the age of 31, had already established and operated nine Sheraton Motor Inns in the Southeast, founded Institutional Development Corporation (INNDEVCO) to build and manage the Sheraton-Twin Towers Hotel and Convention Center. His brilliant economic forecasting, marketing, and financial planning braced the hotel for the economic hard times which followed. The determined, enterprising owner piloted his 750-room hotel through a financial storm, undaunted by the threat of recession and virtual bankruptcy.

"American ingenuity works best when it is tested by problems, as history proves," financial expert Austin Kiplinger once said.

Today, Brennan can be spotted on the property, overseeing the operations of the two gleaming Sheraton-Twin Towers through day-to-day operations. Last year alone, the Towers grossed in excess of $15 million. Brennan credits financial reorganization and new management policies with saving the Towers.

Towering above Florida's crossroads — the intersection of Interstate 4 and the Sunshine State Parkway — the eighteen-story complex has become a familiar central-Florida landmark. Convention home to hundreds of state and regional associations and major corporations, Orlando's Sheraton-Twin Towers is one of the largest convention centers in central Florida. With more than 73,000 square feet of meeting and exhibit space, the Towers can provide banquet service for 2,000 people; over 2,500 more can be seated in the Exhibit Hall. As a result of hosting such corporate giants as Exxon, Ford Motors, Kraft, Hertz, and National Car Rental, some national

Sheraton-Twin Towers Hotel, Orlando, Florida.

conventions are already booked into the next century.

Besides the success of the convention center, the Towers is ranked among the finest resort hotels in the Southeast, with rooms and amenities to suit business and pleasure travelers alike. Guests have a choice of spacious rooms, suites, and top-floor penthouse suites. Each fully appointed penthouse features two bedrooms, three baths, bar stereo, and two color televisions. For small groups, the latest in convenience are the four seventeen-floor executive suites. These exquisite suites are designed to entertain up to 40 people, with complete wet bar, full bath, and adjoining bedrooms on each side.

On the lobby level are a host of specialty shops — drug store, shirt shop, liquor store, and boutiques. A full-menu restaurant, elegant dining room, and lounge with piano bar serve appetizing entrees and delicious cocktails in a southern-garden atmosphere. For encores, a second lounge features entertainment after hours.

Recreational activities include golf at three nearby country clubs, each featuring eighteen-hole championship courses and lighted tennis courts. A snack bar, poolside cocktail

service, saunas, and chaise lounges complement the casual pace around the heated swimming pool.

One well-known trademark of the Towers is its fleet of thirteen motor coaches. The fleet doubles as a separate tour-business company for Brennan, and as a free shuttle service for guests heading to Walt Disney World, Epcot Center, and other area attractions, all less than fifteen minutes away. Brennan adapted the same principle to the hotel's laundry facilities, providing commercial laundry service to the hotel and outside companies.

What is perhaps most intriguing about the Towers is the reputation it has as the unofficial White House guest hotel of almost every presidential candidate since the Carter/Ford campaign in 1976. The hotel's professional security team has worked closely with White House Secret-Service agents and, during President Reagan's latest stay, the team received White House security pins for their efforts.

What sets this fine hotel apart is the special touch added by a dedicated staff of well-trained hospitality professionals with one thing in mind — pamper the guest.

If ever a hotel reached unprecedented heights in the hospitality industry in such a short period — against such great odds — certainly the Sheraton-Twin Towers is that hotel.

Family flavor: key ingredient to restaurant's success

In the beginning was the White Turkey.

Well, actually, it all began long before that, long before 1948 when Champ Williams opened the White Turkey, his first restaurant, at 1911 North Mills Avenue in Orlando.

Let's look back to the early years of the century to the town of Black Rock, a milk-run stop in Arkansas. Here, as in most small towns of that day, the main eatery was located in the hotel near the railroad station. In Black Rock, the Southern Hotel was owned and operated by Williams' grandmother, who catered to traveling salesmen, renting them rooms and furnishing them with meals for a fixed price.

On weekends, however, a big gap was left in the dining room when the salesmen returned to their homes. Thus it was on Saturdays and on Sundays after church, that townspeople and families from the nearby farms and hamlets came in to dine.

Williams was a boy then, but he remembered those times indelibly. Little did he realize as he watched his grandmother prepare the food that these were the flavors, that this was the family atmosphere he would one day bank on to launch his own commercial dining room in Florida.

In 1948 there were fewer than a half-dozen full-service restaurants in the immediate Orlando area when the White Turkey first opened its doors. It employed 35 men and women, had a seating capacity of 210, plus drive-in service, and stayed open from 11 a.m. to 2 a.m., closing only on Mondays. Turkey, chicken, fish, and ham were top-of-the-menu items.

The move that shaped the future for the Williams family was in 1952 to Herndon Airport

The White Turkey — Champ Williams' first restaurant.

(now Orlando Executive Airport) and the first Skyline Restaurant. Because the small airport handled only two commercial flights daily, it became vital to develop restaurant trade from within the community.

The Skyline's business developed beyond the family's most elaborate dreams, and the White Turkey property was leased to outside interests.

Between 1952 and 1963 — when increases in commercial flights dictated relocation of the airport to the southern skirt of Orlando at McCoy Air Force Base — the Sky-

McCoy Civilian Airport.

line had become one of the town's most popular restaurants. Reservations were a necessity as people came to marvel at and dine on the elegant and unlimited buffet offerings, the homemade recipes, and gracious southern hospitality. Nearly every Orlando family had someone who attended a wedding reception, high school prom dinner, or birthday at the Skyline.

In 1963, the second Skyline Restaurant opened at McCoy Airport. The Williamses ran both establishments with equal success until 1952, when the lease at Herndon expired. Instead of renewing the Williams' lease, the city of Orlando decided to put it up for bids. Rather than get involved in such bidding, Champ Williams decided to close the restaurant there and sold his equipment. For the first time in 20 years, Herndon Airport was without a restaurant.

Now, however, the Williams family could concentrate all its efforts on the Skyline at McCoy. It should be noted that the original decision to open a restaurant at McCoy represented an enormous investment and gamble on Orlando's future, because at the time there wasn't even a rumor that Walt Disney World would soon cast its mammoth, lucrative shadow across central Florida and the state.

As Orlando flourished, so did the Skyline Restaurant. But the biggest move and gamble was yet to come.

In September 1981, after nine months and close to $6 million, Champ's Plaza was un-

Orlando International Airport's opening ceremonies, September 1981.

veiled in the brand new Orlando International Airport. The unique complex consists of 21 specialty themed restaurants and lounges, each with an individual flavor, decor, and menu. This unexpected "non-airport approach" won a 1982 National Interior Design Award and continues to attract the local and flying public. At the center of this innovative complex, the original family recipes and one-to-one attention of the Skyline Restaurant are still served up in unlimited portions.

And so, as Orlando has grown and come to offer the best of big city sophistication and small town warmth, so has the Skyline Restaurant and Champ's Plaza.

Paving Orlando's future — without hesitation

From almost any vantage point, the fifteen-story, Southeast Bank tower appears to be the hub of Orlando. This is as it was intended when negotiations for its establishment got underway in 1969. And, so it is today, supported by a dozen more offices locally. Statewide, Southeast Bank represents over $9.0 billion in assets, as reported June 30, 1984.

In 1969, Orlando was on the brink of evolving from a quiet city into the primary destination for world travelers, international developers, and corporations on the move. A major enterprise, with a mouse as its logo, was coming to town. Orlando was not to be the same again.

It was in early 1969 when J. Charles Gray, a practicing Orlando attorney in the Gray, Harris and Robinson firm, and chairman of the Florida Turnpike Authority, was contacted by John Roberts, then vice-president of marketing for The First National Bank of Miami, an affiliate of Southeast Banking Corporation, and asked about putting the wheels into motion for bringing a Southeast Bank to Orlando. Three other community leaders also were contacted — John Quinn of Quinn Realty and Investment; J. Willard Peebles, a Wildwood business owner; and William D. Bishop Sr., owner of Bishop Office Furniture. After careful research and negotiations, approval was given for a Southeast bank to be established.

Gray notes, "We were asked to review the area for the best possible bank site. We narrowed it to four considerations — the former Orange Buick site at the corner of Orange and Robinson, the old Sears Building on Orange Avenue, the former San Juan Hotel site, and a site near the shores of Lake Eola at the corner of Rosalind and Pine. Everyone preferred the Rosalind and Pine site."

Surveys were made by a leading national firm, which reported that the Rosalind and Pine site was the poorest choice. Charles Gray reported the findings to Hood Basset, Southeast Banking Corporation's chairman of the board, but requested approval to begin negotiations for the Lake Eola site anyway. Approval was given.

A sampling of the velvet-gloves handling given this project was when banking officials negotiated with the Sorosis Club for an additional parcel of land adjacent to the original site. This parcel was the site of the group's specially constructed meeting facility, a building made possible by the mayor of an earlier administration. First attempts to acquire the property met strong opposition. Eventually, however, an amicable solution was reached. The terms: Southeast had to find a location close to Lake Eola and construct a new facility.

Southeast purchased property on Livings-

Located at 201 East Pine Street, downtown Orlando, the Southeast Bank Building reflects the progressive growth abundant in the City Beautiful.

ton Street and retained Allen Trovilion, a commercial contractor, to build the new clubhouse. Today, Sorosis groups still operate from this facility.

Of all the stories to come out of the quest to put Southeast in the skyline here, the transporting of the bank's temporary building from a New Jersey manufacturer was the real cliff-hanger.

Gray explains, "It was 'T minus 10 and counting' for our July 27, 1970 opening. The only problem: We didn't have a building. It had been held up in Georgia due to being too wide a load. I contacted the Florida Highway Patrol who contacted Georgia's highway patrol for help. The last module arrived on Monday morning, and our opening was held at 1:00 p.m. that same day."

Today, fourteen years later, Southeast encompasses the following banking centers: Apopka, Bay Hill, Casselton, East Orange, Forest City, Maitland, Orlando Downtown,

Parkway, Presidents Drive, Sanford, Sweetwater, and Winter Park.

Testimony to the bank's community concern is its major underwriting support given to such projects as the Greater Orlando Aviation Authority for the Orlando International Airport and the Orange County Civic Center.

Southeast Bank provides major funding to such groups as the Florida Hospital, United Way, University of Central Florida, Rollins College, Valencia Community College, the Orlando Science Center, Loch Haven Art Center, The Florida Symphony, and the Atlantic Center for the Arts.

Robert E. White Sr., vice-president and Region IV executive for Southeast Bank emphasizes, "We have clearly demonstrated our commitment to this area and have frequently paved the way where others were hesitant to venture."

Serving the Orlando area for more than 80 years

In 1896, the Orlando Telephone Company, owned and operated by John Lennon, was established. It changed hands several times and was ultimately purchased by the W.H. Reynolds family on March 10, 1908.

Southern Bell came to Orlando in 1903, but provided strictly long-distance service. The office was located in the Rock Building at 7 North Orange Avenue. Miss Belle Limerick and Miss Bonnie Patrick served as the day operator and night operator, respectively.

In 1916, Southern Bell purchased the Orlando Telephone Company from the Reynolds family for $90,000. At that time, there were 895 phones in service. R.R. Reynolds, the son of W.H. Reynolds, was appointed wire chief, a position he held until his retirement in 1946.

By 1924, Southern Bell had begun to outgrow its office and equipment space. By 1926, a modern three-story building was erected on the corner of Main Street (now Magnolia Avenue) and Wall Street. New switching equipment was installed that allowed the customers to dial local calls using four digits without operator assistance. Among the men who worked for Western

The first Enhanced "911" system in the United States was established in Orange County in October 1980.

Electric installing this equipment was film star Buddy Ebsen.

During World War II, the Bell System was heavily devoted to the war effort. Long distance service was at capacity and new telephones were extremely difficult to obtain. However, between 1940 and 1945, Orlando

still managed to gain almost 4,500 new telephone customers for a total of 14,000.

By 1960, Orlando's population had jumped over 400 percent; it was now the fifth fastest growing metropolitan area in the nation. That same year, Orlando had 75,000 telephones, and Southern Bell moved to new administrative facilities at Sun Bank's present location at 200 South Orange Avenue.

During the next two decades, Southern Bell brought several technological advancements to Orlando. In 1962, Direct Distance Dialing was made available. Electronic switching was introduced in 1971 and provided custom-calling services such as three-way calling, call forwarding, call waiting, and speed calling. Telephone operators began using computerized switchboards in 1972.

In 1980, Southern Bell employees moved from Sun Bank to their new five-story administration building at 500 North Orange Avenue, reaffirming the company's continued commitment to the economic health and development of downtown Orlando. That same year, the first Enhanced "911" system in the nation was installed by Southern Bell in Orange County. This system has saved numerous lives and continues to be the state-of-the-art for emergency systems.

On January 1, 1984, the Bell System was broken up, and AT&T was required to divest itself of Southern Bell. Providing almost 200,000 lines to customers in Orlando, Southern Bell became a subsidiary of a new holding company, BellSouth.

Throughout Southern Bell's history in Orlando, the company has been very supportive of the community. Employees at all levels have participated as volunteers in various projects such as United Way, Junior Achievement, chambers of commerce, civic and cultural groups.

Southern Bell has over $71 million in capital investment in the Orlando area and pays annual taxes and fees in excess of $7.6 million. This includes new technology such as fiber optics and a new electronic service called "Touchstar."

Telecommunications technology has entered the Information Age with unlimited possibilities on the horizon. Southern Bell plans to play a major role in providing this new technology to its customers.

In 1926, customers began to dial their own local calls. The directory at left gives dialing instructions with alphabetical listings on the right. The switching equipment was in the building now located at Magnolia Avenue and Wall Street.

Build your community and you build your bank

It would be difficult to find an institution which has been more intimately involved in the growth of central Florida than Sun Bank, N.A. (National Association).

Founded in the midst of the Great Depression as The First National Bank at Orlando, it grew to become the lead bank of Sun Banks, Inc., second-largest bank-holding company in Florida.

When the bank opened its doors on February 14, 1934, it had 15 employees and assets of $240,000. Fifty years later, Sun Bank, N.A. employed more than 1,600 people at 55 offices in Orange, Seminole, Osceola, Brevard and Lake counties, with assets in excess of $2.3 billion.

Despite its size, Sun Bank has remained a hometown bank with hometown concerns,

The original First National Bank at Orlando Building was a downtown landmark for decades.

Main office of Sun Bank, N.A., Orlando, Florida.

dedicated to the philosophy of one of its founders, Linton E. Allen: "Build your community and you build your bank." Sun bankers have taken leadership roles, with little or no public perception of those roles, in furthering efforts that have nourished the dynamic growth of central Florida.

In 1964, Linton Allen and the Bank's president at that time, William H. Dial, organized a group of citizens who put up $10,000 apiece to secure the property on which the University of Central Florida is now situated.

The following year, Dial worked with an intermediary representing an anonymous buyer to facilitate the purchase of 27,000 acres of land southwest of Orlando. He did not know the identity of the buyer but was told that the purchase would significantly alter the destiny of Orlando. And that it did! The purchaser was Walt Disney, who was looking for a site on which to build Walt Disney World.

Dial was also instrumental in relocating the paths of Interstate 4 and the Florida Turnpike closer to Orlando than was called for in the original plans. Without the change, Disney might have selected another site for the most popular tourist attraction in the world.

In 1956, Allen put up $2,500 of his own money for a 15-day option on more than

This billboard near the old main airport east of Orlando welcomed visitors while advertising the bank.

6,000 acres of land south of Orlando. Having met with the principals of the Glenn L. Martin Company, he was positive that they would select that site for the new aerospace plant they were proposing to build. Allen was right, and Martin Marietta Aerospace became one of the state's largest employers.

More recently, when the $300 million Orlando International Airport construction was halted by a lawsuit in May 1980, bonds could not be issued due to the litigation. Under the direction of Buell G. Duncan Jr., bank chairman, Sun Bank organized a consortium of banks that put together a $57 million interim financing package to assure the project's completion.

Sun Bank, N.A.'s continuing commitment to central Florida was graphically demonstrated by the decision in 1983 to construct a multi-use complex in the heart of downtown Orlando to house the headquarters of Sun Banks, Inc. and Sun Bank, N.A., as well as provide a first-class businessmen's hotel, restaurants, shops, and a parking garage.

During a 1984 press conference announcing Lincoln Property Company of Dallas, Texas, as the developer of the multimillion-dollar project, Orlando Mayor Bill Frederick recognized the importance of Sun Bank Center to the area. "Sun Bank Center is the most substantial single development in the history of the city, and without a doubt will enhance in magnificent style the character of the entire downtown area," he said. "This project is a dramatic show of confidence by Sun Bank in the future of Orlando and symbolically underscores the rapidly advancing opportunities for all the people of central Florida."

Sun Bank's contributions, old and new, large and small, have succeeded in building a better, brighter central Florida community. And the community has responded by making Sun Bank central Florida's leading financial institution, just as Linton Allen foresaw so many years ago.

A law firm of Orlando's past, designed for its future

Over the last seven decades, Swann & Haddock has provided quality legal representation to an ever-changing Orlando. But from the first day Pervie P. Swann hung his shingle in 1924, the one thing that has not changed is the firm's continuous and overriding commitment to excellence. That commitment, and the vision of a dynamic law firm shared by son Richard Swann and Edward E. Haddock Jr., has made Swann and Haddock one of Orlando's largest firms, with expertise to meet all the new, diverse, and complex legal needs of this emerging metropolitan area.

Pervie Swann traveled throughout the South as he pursued his professional baseball career, but chose to practice law in Orlando because of its friendly and industrious people. He started downtown at 116½ South Orange Avenue and later moved his office to 17 South Magnolia. In his 54 years of practice, Pervie Swann served the needs of an agricultural town, drafting everything from abstracts to wills and providing the type of sound advice that made his clients think of him as the consummate counsellor at law.

In 1963, Richard Swann returned to his native Orlando after graduating from Duke University Law School and became the junior member of Swann & Swann. Although Orlando was still primarily an agricultural

The site of Swann & Swann and Swann & Haddock at 17 South Magnolia.

The lobby of Swann & Haddock's new offices on the eleventh floor of the First Bankers Building.

town, Richard Swann saw then the vast potential here for commercial and residential development. Ed Haddock shared that vision of Orlando's future, and moved here after graduating from the University of Virginia Law School in 1972. Since 1974, when Mr. Haddock joined the firm, these two men have carefully designed the firm to meet the city's growing needs and opportunities. They perceived an expanding demand for counsel that would provide legal expertise to support Orlando's emerging commercial base, and recognized the importance of the firm's dedication and loyalty to the welfare of the city.

With this commitment to legal excellence and to Orlando's future, the firm has grown to its current size of 22 lawyers. The offices were moved from 17 South Magnolia to the American Pioneer Center in 1979, and in 1983 moved again to its present location downtown in the First Bankers Building. A Tallahassee office has been opened for support on matters of statewide importance. The firm is actively engaged in all phases of law practice, with expertise in specialized areas such as commercial litigation, banking and insurance law, mortgage financing, government bonding, real estate development, tax planning, representation of governmental bodies, insurance litigation, administrative liquidation litigation, labor law and environmental law.

The attorneys at Swann & Haddock have also contributed directly to the city's commercial growth. Richard Swann and Ed Haddock are the primary founders of First Fidelity Savings & Loan Association, one of the fastest growing and most profitable savings and loan associations in Florida. Chartered here in 1980, the financial institution now has 20 offices in central and southern

Florida, and assets in excess of one-half billion dollars. First Fidelity, merged in 1984 with the Flagship Bank of Orlando, also owns two other Orlando-based holding companies, American Pioneer Corporation and the W.M. Sanderlin Corporation, engaged in insurance underwriting and residential construction, respectively.

Two of the city's most significant developments are among the many exciting projects sponsored by Swann & Haddock clients and counseled by the firm. Swann & Haddock represents MCA, Inc., the parent corporation of Universal Studios. The firm is providing counsel to Universal in developing a tour theme park and a state-of-the-art film production complex in the southwestern part of the city, similar to that in California. The firm also represents the Pillar-Bryton Company, the owner and developer of the duPont Centre, a $400 million campus of office buildings, high fashion retail stores, luxury hotel, and international trademart that will dramatically reshape the skyline and the very character of downtown Orlando.

Like the city it serves, Swann & Haddock takes great pride in its past and present achievements. As it looks ahead, the firm will continue to commit itself to anticipate and fulfill the future needs of the city with the same dedication to excellence that has characterized the first seven decades.

A community commitment of people helping people

In November 1938, Robert S. Carr was reviewing his notes for a meeting with representatives of ten civic clubs to discuss a mounting problem. He looked across his business calendar and added up the long list of local charities that had solicited his Central Title and Trust business for contributions during the past year.

There had to be a better way, and Robert S. Carr had it. That day, Carr proposed that local businesses help charities organize a single all-inclusive drive for funds, to be held once a year. Together with 10 other businessmen, Carr incorporated a charter to form the Community Chest of Orlando. In February 1939, the first drive was held with Tom Gurney, a successful local attorney, as the first general campaign chairman. The 10-day drive for $34,100 used more than 400 volunteers and exceeded the goal by $6,055.

But organizing local charities into a combined campaign was not an easy task. Several agencies which had been receiving substantial national and community support decided not to join the Community Chest, thinking they would not receive as much from a combined campaign. Also, the Community Chest covered only the Orlando area, so other "Chest" drives were being held in the nearby cities of Winter Garden and Winter Park.

Although the number of solicitations had been greatly reduced, businesses in Orange County were still subjected to multiple charity drives for the next fourteen years.

In May 1955, Charles O. Andrews, a prominent attorney, supplied the impetus to once again organize a united campaign. At a meeting at the chamber of commerce, he gathered with 50 civic leaders and businessmen with a proposal to form a United Appeal which would include the nineteen agencies of the Community Chest and eleven additional agencies. Because of the amount of support generated from this meeting, an action committee was formed and the United Appeal was born.

To secure the endorsement of local businesses, Martin Andersen, owner and publisher of the *Orlando Sentinel Star,* donated a page of the newspaper for local businesses to sign a pledge that they would support only

Mrs. Sue Bussells Rosenfelt, representing the United Appeal, cuts the ribbon to the Salvation Army Welfare Center. Watching, left to right, are Joseph Arra, Mrs. Commissioner W. Dray, Don Mott, Arthur White, Commissioner Dray.

the newly formed United Appeal at their work place.

That first United Appeal campaign, under the chairmanship of F.B. Surguine Jr., a former county commissioner, raised $303,736.

During the next few years, while the United Appeal's influence grew, volunteer leadership felt that in order to realize full potential of the fledgling organization, experi-

enced professional leadership was needed. So in 1958, the executive committee hired its first executive director, Egbert W. Neidig. By 1962, Winter Garden and Winter Park had joined the Orlando United Appeal, marking the first countywide fundraising effort. By 1969, Osceola and Seminole counties, while still autonomous organizations, joined with Orange County in a cooperative effort for the first tri-county campaign. United Appeal's growth continued through the early and mid-1970s moving from the $1 million mark raised in 1968 to over $2 million by 1974. In 1976, local volunteer leadership changed the corporate name to United Way, following a trend of local organizations to adopt a uniform identity in order to benefit from national promotional materials such as the National Football League's public service announcements.

In 1977, the United Way formed the division of Central Florida Capital Funds Committee, which conducts capital funds drives every three years for area human services and cultural agencies.

By 1983, the United Way had climbed over the $5 million mark, providing funds for more than 70 agencies and services in the tri-county area. The commitment of community leaders to understand and be responsive to the needs and wishes of the central Florida area provided the grass roots effort to begin the United Way. Now, faced with a dynamic, rapidly growing community, that commitment of community leaders carries on and is reflected through the successes of United Way campaigns.

Newly elected executive committee at the 1975 Annual Meeting and Awards Banquet.

Pictured: (Left to right) David W. Hedrick, Charles T. Brumback, John W. Rourk, Jr., Kenneth D. Kienth, Buell G. Duncan Jr., Craig Spearman, James H. Fenner, Grover K. Gregory Jr.

Stable and profitable since 1925

The Piney Woods section of south Georgia didn't offer much to a man wanting to build a business. The year 1925, just ahead of the Depression of the thirties, was a "boom" year in Florida. Alvin James ("A.J." to family and friends) looked to the South for a renewed and better life for his wife and four children. In that year, armed with a Ford truck and $300, he headed for central Florida to start the business he knew best. A.J. was a lumberman.

Once settled, the serious business of selling began. The site of the main yard was chosen at 210 West Gore Street. A small building served as office and store for several years. Limited funds proved to be a blessing in disguise. The "boom" busted. Lumber and building materials dealers with large inventories who bought at prices far greater than those of the post-boom era were trapped. Accounts receivables suddenly became accounts uncollectibles. Land values caved in. A.J., selling mainly for cash and from a limited inventory, felt fewer ill effects as the economy declined. Highly priced inventories held by competitors gave him the opportunity to move into a front-runner position among the local yards.

Thomas Lumber Company moved into new quarters. Thomas' largest order to date, 1.5 million feet of lumber, was sold to the Cross State Canal in 1935 — the price: $12,000. Stocks were greatly expanded and diversified to a full range of lumber and building materials. With two additional youngsters in the fold, the years of expansion now began. In 1931, a lumber yard was opened in Winter Park. The year 1939 saw the purchase of an additional business to the west, the Winter Garden Lumber Company.

With the establishment of the Army Air Force Training School and its vast array of requirements, businesses in the area were active. Hundreds of barracks requiring thousands of doors, windows, and moldings gave an opportunity to expand from a small to a large millwork shop. The company was awarded the Army "E" for Excellence for timely and quality production.

The war years were busy for this solely owned business. As the war ended, there came thoughts of sons and a son-in-law in the service who would soon join the business. Marriage brought a new son-in-law and a coming of age for another son. In 1949, each company was incorporated. Several property holding companies were formed.

A.J. didn't confine his interests to business. He believed that taking from the community created an obligation to return a generous portion in time, talent, and substance. This he did readily. As an active Mason and Shriner, he was a prime mover in the building and establishment of the Bahia Shrine Temple. He was an active Kiwanian and member of the founding board of United Cerebral Palsy and other organizations beneficial to the community. Following his philosophy, family members have served as officers and directors in hospital work, bank boards, professional organizations, city-owned commissions and boards, the Orlando Utilities Commission and have served regularly in fundraising activities. Kiwanis and Rotary Club activities for community betterment are also included in long-term affiliations.

In 1967, A.J. Thomas died. A new slate of officers and directors now operated the company. The new chairman of the board, Valdeen Thomas, was also elected president of the Winter Park operation. Sam Wilkins was made president of the Orlando yard and Max Millitzer headed the Winter Garden store and yard as its president.

Feeling a need for more buying power, Thomas became affiliated with Cotter and Company and the True Value label in 1966. Later, an additional door to buying was opened with the Lumbermens Merchandising Corporation. With this great buying power, competition with the largest chains was now possible.

Conservatism, excellent employees, quality materials, and competitive pricing have brought this company through the trials of seriously falling and rising economies. Orientation toward commercial builders, quality home builders, institutional buyers, and homeowners, have made the Thomas Lumber Company both stable and profitable since 1925.

A.J. Thomas, founder of the Thomas Lumber Company. He remembered to share with those in need.

Entertaining a big group in the 1930s for a company barbeque was no problem.

Pioneering television in the dynamic Orlando/central Florida market

For more than 30 years, WCPX-TV (originally WDBO-TV), Channel 6, Orlando, has been the pioneer in the development of television broadcasting service to the dynamic and fast-growing Orlando/central Florida market.

WDBO-TV, Orlando — central Florida's first television station — began telecasting on July 1, 1954. For nearly two years, it was the only television station in central Florida. The station was constructed by Orlando Broadcasting Company, Inc., which also owned and operated Orlando's first AM and FM radio stations — WDBO (AM), a pioneer Florida station on air in 1924 and first licensed to Rollins College in Winter Park, and WDBO-FM, operational in 1949.

Studio and technical facilities were housed in a pre-fabricated steel building located on North Texas Avenue at what was then Orlando's western city limit. The program schedule in the early days totaled approximately 56 hours weekly with the majority of time devoted to nighttime offerings of CBS, WDBO-TV's primary network affiliation, and select programs from the NBC, ABC, and DuMont television networks, with which the station had secondary affiliation agreements. The program schedule jumped to 103 hours weekly in 1955 and to what was considered an almost normal broadcast day the following year.

Attracted by the potential growth of the Orlando/central Florida market, suitors interested in buying the Orlando Broadcasting Company stations began knocking on the door within two years of WDBO-TV's debut. One was Cherry Broadcasting Company, a New England broadcasting group, which succeeded in the acquisition of WDBO-TV and WDBO AM/FM and became the operating licensee in May 1957.

Orlando still was essentially a one-station television market at the time of ownership transfer. The best of CBS, NBC, and ABC programs continued to be seen on Channel 6. The stars came to central Florida via WDBO-TV — Jack Benny, Ed Sullivan, Lucille Ball, Burns and Allen, Jackie Gleason, Arthur Godfrey, Red Skelton, Lawrence Welk, Garry Moore. Top-rated programs also debuted, such as "GE Theatre," "Our Miss Brooks," "What's My Line?," "Wednesday Night Fights," "House Party," "Person to Person," "Captain Kangaroo," as well as several daytime series still on the air, including "As the World Turns," "The Guiding Light," "The Price is Right." The local news presentation

WCPX-TV Broadcast House.

was a quarter-hour at 6 p.m. and 11 p.m. The network evening national news slot, also a quarter-hour, went to ABC's John Daly, while CBS's Walter Cronkite then anchored a ten-minute midday news strip. Among locally originated program highlights were "Central Florida Showcase," an award-winning panel discussion series; "Adventures with Uncle Walt," "Cartoon Carnival," and "Romper Room," all kiddie favorites; area musical groups performing under the titles "The Five Owls" and "The Rebels."

In February 1958, a little over three-and-one-half years after WDBO-TV made its appearance, Orlando/central Florida became a fully competitive television market with three commercial stations, each having a primary network affiliation. But competition did not lessen WDBO-TV's pioneering spirit, as WDBO-TV continued to introduce television "firsts" along with improved techniques and performance, including: 1960 — installation of film processing and video tape recording equipment; 1961 — expansion of nightly newscasts simultaneous with charter participation in a new CBS Television Network news recording service; 1965 — conversion to color film, tape, and slide facilities; 1967

Newswatch Helicopter.

Original WDBO-TV studios which later became WCPX-TV.

Studio A Control Room and Audio Booth, showing some of the state-of-the-art equipment.

— maximizing to a full-color capability with installation of color studio cameras and associated equipment; 1969 — commencement of telecasting from the tallest structure in Florida via an antenna facility 1,549 feet above mean sea level — a facility marked by the first installation of an advanced antenna design which, along with the increased antenna height, upped WDBO-TV's coverage by 25 percent.

During these developments, WDBO-TV again passed to new ownership. The second transfer came in August 1963 when the Outlet Company, New England retail and broadcasting firm based in Providence, Rhode Island, became the licensee of WDBO-TV and WDBO AM/FM. The Orlando stations were Outlet's first major broadcasting acquisition — the forerunner in an expansion program that later saw Outlet's station list grow to five VHF television stations and, at one time, as many as seven AM and FM radio stations.

From the commencement of operations and for many years thereafter, one of WDBO-TV's most distinguished public affairs program series was "Central Florida Showcase." This award-winning, weekend evening half-hour panel program, involving local civic organizations in discussions with newsmaking guests, frequently made the program ratings top 20. Also heralded was "It's the Law," pre-sented in cooperation with several area law enforcement agencies and winner of Florida Bar's Sixth Annual Media Award; "Channel 6 Reports," in-depth coverage of major area news happenings; and several series dealing with local and area issues — "30 Minutes," "Black Awareness," and "Spectrum."

Despite pioneering and progress, WDBO-TV was not immune to misfortune. In June 1973, the so-called "tall tower" antenna facility, then serving several area television and FM radio stations, collapsed as an antenna was being installed for another television station. But WDBO-TV immediately switched operations to its auxiliary transmitter and antenna — the original facility located at the North Texas Avenue studio site — and continued to serve the public. Transmission from the "tall tower" site resumed in November 1975.

In July 1981, it appeared that WDBO-TV and other Outlet Company broadcast stations would be involved in a merger agreement between Outlet and Columbia Pictures Industries, Inc. This pointed to the need for divestiture of WDBO AM/FM, since existing Federal Communications Commission rules no longer permitted the transfer of both television and radio stations to a new licensee in the same market. In anticipation of the sale of WDBO AM/FM, and because basic call letters remain with the radio stations in the event of divestiture, Outlet received FCC approval to change its Orlando television station call letters from WDBO-TV to WCPX-TV, an identification suggesting the Columbia Pictures corporate name. In June 1982, after almost 28 years, WDBO-TV became WCPX-TV.

Outlet's merger with Columbia Pictures did not materialize. But early in 1983, Rockefeller Center, Inc. (RCI), a privately held company owned by the Rockefeller family and founded by John D. Rockefeller Jr., offered to purchase WCPX-TV and the other Outlet stations. The FCC approved the application for sale and transfer, and RCI acquired Outlet's five television stations and five radio stations at the end of January 1984.

As negotiations between Outlet and RCI progressed, so did construction of WCPX-TV's $9 million state-of-the-art Broadcast House fronting on Orlando's John Young Parkway near its U.S. 441 intersection. Work on the ultramodern studio-office facility of approximately 50,000 square feet (almost five times larger than the North Texas Avenue building which housed the station for almost 30 years) began in January 1983 and was completed about a year later. Operations from Broadcast House began at the end of February 1984 with formal dedication on April 6.

April 1984 also was a month of relabeling for RCI and Outlet. Rockefeller Center, Inc., known by that title for more than half a century, became The Rockefeller Group, and Outlet Company, so-identified for almost a full century, became Outlet Communications, Inc., one of The Rockefeller Group's six real estate, broadcasting, and entertainment subsidiary companies.

WCPX-TV, now WDBO-TV, pioneered television for over 30 years in what is now the nation's 30th largest television market; developed a program service from 56 hours to a current schedule exceeding 160 hours weekly; gathered a staff of 155 professional employees, compared with 30 in 1954; constructed a state-of-the-art Broadcast House five times larger than the station's original studio/office facility.

More development and innovation are ahead as WCPX-TV continues to respond to the growing interests and needs of the dynamic Orlando/central Florida market — a vast community WCPX-TV and The Rockefeller Group are proud to serve.

Setting a tradition of excellence

Rarely, in all history, has a community seen change at the pace of central Florida. Few of its institutions have fielded rapid differences so well as the area's leading communications outlet — WFTV.

In the early 1950s, when the original applications for Orlando's Channel 9 were filed, the applicants prepared to serve a potential audience of 100,000 residents. Now, the number of viewers tops 2 million — an incredible 20-fold increase, not including the 25 million visitors to central Florida this year.

When operations began in February 1958, agriculture essentially formed the sole economic base of the Channel 9 community. Today, rockets, transistors, tourist attractions, and high finance match citrus products and cattle in local importance.

If the rate of change continued for central Florida and other metropolitan areas into the middle of the next century, the 50-television market served by WFTV would be one of the nation's largest. The momentum will likely continue, at least until the market becomes one of the top 20 in the United States. If history fortells the future, WFTV will grow at least as abundantly in service to its viewers.

From the earliest days, Channel 9, known as WLOF-TV for its first five years, has worked to maintain and often improve the style of life in central Florida. Most obvious through the station's programming, efforts have often extended well beyond broadcast word and picture.

From the year the station first signed-on in 1958, management has continued a commitment to local children's shows. Channel 9 won its first of many nationally-important prizes, the prestigious Thomas Alva Edison Foundation Award for service to youth in 1962.

Though the concept now borders on the archaic, the positive values stressed by clowns and puppets of "Popeye's Playhouse" and "Bobo's Big Top" hopefully helped shape the behavior codes of many current central Florida adults. "Major Mecury" introduced youngsters to the wonders of science and high-technology, now so much a part of the local economy.

In more recent years, central Florida youngsters have produced and starred in Channel 9 production of "Kidworld" segments and "On the Go." Now the station is beginning distribution of its children's offerings to other markets.

In 1964, the station's commitment to broadcasting in the public interest was confirmed by receipt of the Alfred I. duPont national citation for that year. Won due to the young station's editorial and documentary efforts, it has been matched by similar plaudits dozens of times since.

The "Skywitness" helicopter enables WFTV to cover fast-breaking news stories from anywhere in central Florida.

One effort of particular note took place in the early 1980s. Florida was facing a crisis in that fresh-water supplies were being used at a rate faster than nature's replacement. WFTV undertook a major effort to forestall emergency. Through a long-continuing series of editorials, graphically illustrated, and a major documentary that took Channel 9 crews thousands of miles, the station informed that public of the problem. Station researchers discovered the specific technical methods of assuring adequate fresh water for later generations in this state. WFTV representatives briefed the governor and the cabinet. Two legislative committees made station visits for detailed seminars. Other media cooperated in the effort.

Now new laws safeguarding water supplies are on the books; innovative procedures to conserve the resource are going into place. Most importantly, attitudes of the public and the lawmakers toward conservation of Florida's environment argur well for continued, appropriate attention to necessary gifts of nature.

WFTV has led its industry and community in other ways. Concerned that the mix of occupations left to little chance of advancement, the station produced an important motion picture for the Industrial Development Commission of Mid-Florida. Officials credit the film with a major role in attracting new high-technology industry to the area. Twice since the original, the station has participated in similar efforts with salutory results.

Concerned with health of its viewers,

Channel 9's first effort was the live, in-studio production of "With These Hands." In the form of a drama, the series provided essential information concerning health topics. Recently, WFTV began the health fair concept in its market, providing free annual health screenings to thousands. Blood Brother Day is another open-ended station effort at assuring adequate fresh blood supplies in central Florida.

As concerned with the cultural health of central Florida, WFTV has long-participated in aiding the maturation of area arts activities. For many years, the station has conducted an annual television auction to help fund the development of music, dance, theater, and the graphic arts in its community. Years ago, the station spearheaded an effort that allowed continued life for the area's most notable community theater. For three years, the station produced programs displaying the attractions and benefits of Orlando's major art gallery and museum. A recent major documentary honestly positioned central Florida's cultural makeup with that of other metropolitan areas.

The station was the first to broadcast color in the early days, the first to provide 24-hour service, the first to air reports live from a hot-air balloon and then a ship at sea. The station is seen in more homes than any other in central Florida and is surpassed by none in the industry in its research and marketing capabilities. Superlatives, though, are most

The station's "Instant Eye" mobile news trucks provide live coverage of local news events.

WFTV offers the latest in production equipment to create local programming and commercial announcements.

appropriate in addressing the WFTV news operation.

With central Florida's largest and most-experienced broadcast news staff, WFTV's "Eyewitness News" has brought maturity to information programming in the market. When channel 9 began its effort to upgrade television news in central Florida, the market quickly saw a revolution that beneficially influenced every local news operation.

"Eyewitness News" aired the first news summaries at other than traditional times. Now the station maintains a news staff around the clock and broadcasts reports at regular intervals throughout the day and night.

WFTV introduced live reports from the scene of the news. Use of live reports from its "Instant Eye" vans and helicopters is now commonplace. The station was first with "Eyewitness News" satellite reports by its own staff from other countries. No station travels further to track the stories of local importance.

Regular local news broadcasts by WFTV now occupy over 20 hours per week, giving time for some features other than hard, fast-breaking reports. Finance, performing arts, consumer topics, and other such regular features have become among the most popular programming on Channel 9.

Weather coverage in an area visited by tornadoes, and violent thunderstorms is particularly vital to central Florida residents and visitors alike. First with radar, direct satellite signals, a lightning detector, Accu-Weather, a weather alert system, and other tools, the "Eyewitness" weather staff is first choice when weather threatens.

Sports coverage, too, is the winner at WFTV. With the largest sports staff and the most advanced tools, "Eyewitness Sports" leads the market in its category.

But clearly the most pertinent reason for "Eyewitness News" dominance in central Florida is the in-depth, informed reporting of local events. The only real difficulty experienced by the station's news operation is the frequent loss of reporters to larger markets and the networks. All too often, the staff of WFTV is viewed as network quality. Fortunately, the station's excellence in broadcast journalism continues to attract a staff with ever-increasing skills.

In 1984, the station was sold to SFN Companies, Inc., a major publisher with intentions to become an equal leader in the broadcast industry. With the acquisition of WFTV, the corporation now has a model to follow in building a broadcast group of worldwide respect.

WESH-TV firsts have paced area growth

Keeping pace with central Florida's growth has been both challenge and opportunity for WESH-TV during its nearly three decades of service to the region.

WESH-TV was founded by broadcast pioneer W. Wright Esch, from whose name its call letters came. Just six weeks before he signed the station on the air at 4 p.m. on Monday, July 11, 1956, with an invitation to viewers to make suggestions for programming, Esch sold the station to Florida publisher and civic leader John H. Perry.

Perry moved quickly to expand the station's service to central Florida, and only a little over a year from its sign-on, on November 5, 1957, the WESH-TV signal began transmission from a 1,000-foot tower located near the St. Johns River in Orange City. Simultaneously, WESH became the central Florida affiliate of the NBC Television Network. In 1960, the station activated the studio from which its Orlando operations have since been based, at the corner of Nicolet and Minnesota avenues. It became then the first station in the central Florida area to emphasize service to the then slowly growing region with broadcast facilities in both Orlando and Daytona Beach. In later years, this first was supplemented with the first on-the-scene coverage of the Space Coast area of Brevard County and the first fully staffed bureau to cover the Ocala-Gainesville-Leesburg area.

On May 1, 1966, the Federal Communications Commission approved the sale of WESH-TV to a subsidiary of Cowles Communications, Inc., now Cowles Broadcasting, Inc., the publishing organization that had given America *Look, Family Circle,* and other well-known magazines and had publishing and broadcast activities throughout the country.

In April 1969, the nature of tourism worldwide was changed with the announcement that Walt Disney World would be built near Orlando. WESH-TV was the first television station to show central Florida the dream Walt Disney envisioned, using a hastily arranged prime-time hour to air a film the Disney studio had prepared. It gave the first hint of the impact that the creation of the Magic Kingdom would have on central Florida.

Keeping pace with the growth of central Florida has been a race throughout WESH-TV's history, and the coming of Disney accelerated the pace. A concern that growth be carefully planned caused WESH to become one of the first stations in the nation to regularly telecast editorials on matters of local interest. A concern that Florida's changeable weather not catch either newcomers or old-timers unawares led to the first area utilization of official U.S. Weather Service radar on the air and the first computerized weather graphics used in the region.

Under the leadership of John M. Haberlan, its general manager from 1968 to 1984, WESH-TV recognized that involvement with

WESH-Television Winter Park Studio in 1966.

its viewers was a key to success in its fast-growing coverage area. Thus, WESH became the first station to bring "mini-cams" and mobile microwave transmitters to central Florida, letting its reporters be "live on the scene" from breaking news stories and important events. Under this same impetus, WESH-TV was first to use a helicopter for news coverage, with its 'Sky Eye 2' aerial unit. Most recently, WESH introduced formal investigative reporting to the Orlando area with 'Unit 2,' a full-time team dedicated to probing behind the headlines.

In 1980, WESH asserted technological leadership in central Florida television as it inaugurated a powerful new transmitter at Orange City powering the first circularly polarized, state-of-the-art picture from the top of the tallest transmitter tower operated by any Florida television station. Late in 1983, this signal was supplemented when WESH

placed on the air a translator station at the south end of the Space Coast in Brevard County to improve reception for residents there.

WESH-TV personnel are and have been involved with civic activities in Daytona Beach, Orlando, the Space Coast, and Marion County where the station maintains facilities and works to assist worthwhile projects throughout the coverage area. John E. Evans, who succeeded John M. Haberlan as general manager on May 7, 1984, serves on the board of the Daytona Beach Community Foundation and on the steering committee of Project 2000, a long-range planning approach to Orlando's future.

WESH-TV is looking forward to its future with confidence, and as long as its focus is on those it serves, that future will be bright.

Building on a tradition of service to clients since 1931

In the fall of 1959, when the largest law firms in Winter Park boasted no more than three members, the present firm of Winderweedle, Haines, Ward and Woodman was formed.

The five founding members of the firm included W.E. "Red" Winderweedle and Webber B. Haines, each of whom had practiced law separately in Orlando and Winter Park since graduation from the University of Florida Law School in 1931. Two other founding members were Harold A. Ward, III, a Winter Park native who graduated from the University of Chicago Law School and served as a law clerk to U.S. Supreme Justice Hugo L. Black, and John Dem. Haines, also a lifelong resident of Winter Park and a graduate of Stetson University School of Law.

The law firm's growth over the ensuing 25 years has been essentially from within, by the addition of associates, their subsequent elevation to membership status, and the expansion of the firm's offices and facilities to support that growth. By 1984, there were thirteen attorneys, maintaining a general civil practice in all state and federal courts, with particular emphasis on corporation and real property law, probate and estate planning law, and tax law.

The firm's present offices on the sixth floor of the Winter Park Office of Barnett Bank of Central Florida are coincidentally on the same site which the firm occupied in a small two-story building at its founding. When the Bank acquired that property for eventual construction of its new banking facility, the firm occupied office space for sev-

Front door of the Law Firm's Office, Park Avenue, 1969.

Park Avenue, Winter Park, 1969. "The Villager" tram is in the foreground and the Law Firm Office Building is in the background.

eral years in the Winter Park Federal Savings and Loan Association Building just a block away. Growth of the Savings and Loan Association and of the law firm necessitated a return to larger offices in the new bank building in 1974. Further growth of the firm and the expanding demands of its clients dictated opening of an Orlando office in the Barnett Plaza Building in 1983.

The history of a law firm is necessarily intertwined with the history of its client base. Major institutional clients of the law firm from its beginning have been financial institutions, local businesses, and nonprofit organizations. Members of the firm have been instrumental in the formation of several of those clients, and retain a close relationship with them.

Because Winter Park has retained its unique residential character in the midst of extensive growth in the surrounding greater Orlando area, individuals have always been a substantial part of the client mix. Members of the firm have written and lectured in the field of tax and estate planning and administration, and the law firm is among the area leaders in these fields. The increasing volume and complexity of the practice of real estate law caused the firm to pioneer the development of automated systems for the handling of real estate transactions. In-house computer hardware and systems provide real es-

tate closing documents as well as trust and fiduciary accounting reports and services.

A major impact of the law firm in the community is through the active involvement of its members in community organizations. In addition to local civic clubs, cultural organizations, and business councils, members of the firm serve on the boards of several private foundations and on the board of Rollins College. The firm continues its longtime representation of the city of Winter Park and of the Winter Park Memorial Hospital. Members of the firm have also demonstrated their commitment to their profession by active membership and service in local and statewide bar association and bar-related organizations and activities.

While rapid growth of a business or professional organization is relatively easy to achieve in an area such as east central Florida, Winderweedle, Haines, Ward and Woodman has consistently maintained a philosophy of steady expansion to meet the needs of its clients, with emphasis on timely delivery of quality professional services. Members of the firm are dedicated to the maintenance of this philosophy as the firm enters its second-quarter century.

Eighty years of dedication to a dream

A city's character, like that of a child's, is formed in its earliest years. What is now the city of Winter Park started in 1863, when David Mizell planted his citrus grove and built his residence on the property bounded by Lake Mizell, Lake Berry, and Lake Virginia. Its character started that same year, when Mrs. Mizell planted a sycamore switch to beautify her yard. That switch is now a magnificent, big old tree.

In 1880, the South Florida Railroad opened up the Winter Park region to travelers; it built its depot — the first building in town — in 1882. In 1881, the town of Winter Park was started with a population of 12 families. It soon became a trading center and shipping point for fruit growers.

In 1883, President Arthur came through on the railroad and said, "Winter Park is a charming village, the prettiest town of all." In 1887, the town was incorporated with a population of 500. Time passed, and by 1904, the city of Winter Park and that sycamore tree were growing up together. The city's horizon included Rollins College, the Seminole Hotel, winter residents, a few commercial buildings, wooden sidewalks, clay streets, and pine, palm, and oak trees.

Charles Hosmer Morse, a Chicago industrialist, had been coming to Winter Park for winter vacations and he became interested in the potential and possibilities of the area. In 1904, he founded The Winter Park Land Company and purchased from the Winter Park Company the original town site of Winter Park, consisting of 1,200 town lots, orange groves, and lots of "wild land." Morse had a dream — to build a "beautiful little city" with a major emphasis on culture.

At the age of 17 (in 1850), Morse had gone to work for E.&T. Fairbanks & Co. at St. Johnsbury Center, Vermont, as an apprentice for $50 a year. By 1870, he was a partner, and by 1880, he controlled Fairbanks Morse & Co., a fast-growing maker of industrial machines. In recollection, his peers attributed his success "to his concentration on building the character of the Company and its employees."

Morse knew that Winter Park's character would have to be directed and nurtured. He started by building the city's first modern offices at 122-30 Park Avenue South which housed the company offices, the Baby Grande Theater, and the Women's Christian Temperance Union Reading Room. He employed H.A. Ward and Herbert Barnum to run the company and sell the town lots. They were to sell with one eye toward his dictum that a good neighbor was more important than a high sales price.

In 1906, Morse gave a permanence to the beauty of Winter Park by donating Central Park, the property on the west side of Park Avenue from New England to Garfield, to the city. His deed contained the expressed condition that it always remain a park. He placed a reverter clause in the deed that provided the property would revert to his Winter Park

View of Park Avenue, looking south from Morse Boulevard, in 1936. Central Park is on the right and the Winter Park Land Company's office building is near left.

heirs if it were ever used for anything other than a park.

In 1914, to beautify North Park Avenue, Morse helped organize the Winter Park Country Club and leased the land along Webster and New York avenues to the Club for the token sum of $1 a year.

Always maintaining a low profile, with most of his gifts anonymous, Morse contributed very generously to the developments within the growing city, like the first town hall, Rollins College, the Winter Park Wom-

Mr. Morse's view of Park Avenue, looking south from Morse Boulevard, in 1904. (Depot on right).

en's Club and other civic projects. His continual emphasis on quality, culture, and character has been the guiding policy of The Winter Park Land Company to this day.

When Morse died in 1921, his guidance and benevolences to improve the quality of life in Winter Park had brought his dream close to reality. Since then, though many inevitable changes have occurred in the march of time, his granddaughter, Jeannette Genius McKean, has attempted to carry on the company's tradition of maintaining a lovely and unique community. Today, Winter Park is indeed the beautiful little city that Charles Hosmer Morse envisioned.

A testimonial to community cooperation

It became apparent in the early fifties that a hospital in the Winter Park area was sorely needed. Orlando was expanding, its two hospitals were desperately overcrowded, and they were miles away. In April 1951, a dedicated group of concerned citizens, determined to bring quality health care to their neighborhood, were granted a charter for a nonprofit corporation, the Winter Park Memorial Hospital Association.

The event made front-page headlines, and three weeks later the organization's first board of directors was elected. The volunteers faced the ominous task of raising $500,000 to break ground, all from private contributions. It was expected to take five years, but then a spark ignited the community — the city of Winter Park donated eighteen acres of land encompassing four fairways from the old Aloma Golf Course valued at $50,000. Donations poured in from private citizens and most every community group. The campaign, led by A.G. Bush, chairman of the building committee, went over the top in only two years.

The first spade of earth was turned on October 13, 1953, by Michael Zimmerman, then principal of Winter Park Elementary School. His $5 contribution was the first of nearly 3,000 received.

More than 2,500 citizens cheered sixteen months later as Mrs. Fred H. Albee, whose $150,000 contribution assured a successful fund drive, cut the ribbon at dedication ceremonies on January 16, 1955. An open house followed where guests admired a 50-bed hospital equipped with the latest medical equipment and patient rooms described by one columnist "where you feel like you're being cared for in a plush, big motel."

The doors officially opened February 8,

A community dream came true February 8, 1955 when Winter Park Memorial opened its doors as a 50-bed, not-for-profit, community hospital.

The East Wing, completed in 1978, brought the hospital's bed capacity to its current level of 301. It includes complete intensive care and surgery facilities, as well as a modern birthing center featuring six birthing rooms.

1955 with 42 employees led by Administrator Sanford Robinson and a team of physicians headed by Dr. Roland F. Hotard Sr., chief of staff. The first patient was Mrs. Edwin R. Smith, admitted by the late Dr. Russell J. Ramsey. At 2:05 a.m. the next day, the hospital's new delivery suite was christened with the birth of Brian Rocklon Scott, son of Mr. and Mrs. Gerald Scott. More than 2,000 patients were seen that first year, and by 1957 occupancy levels were consistently above 90 percent.

Expansion programs began in 1960 with the opening of the two-story, 100-bed Bush Wing which included 50 private rooms. A sophisticated X-ray suite, 24-hour emergency room services, expanded pediatric, obstetrical, and surgery sections would follow, and by 1965 the hospital boasted 261 beds as the North Wing opened (currently the West Wing). The 100,000th patient was admitted in 1971.

Expanded services to meet changing community health care needs had become a hallmark of the hospital. In 1973, for instance, the first Short Stay Surgery services in central Florida were initiated, eliminating a costly hospital stay for many patients. Responding to growing medical and community education needs, a 15,000-volume Medical Library and Education Building was dedicated in November 1976, including an auditorium where more than 10,000 area residents have attended hospital-sponsored health seminars. A full-body C.A.T. scanner installed in 1979 brought a constant flow of visitors from as far away as Egypt to observe one of the most advanced diagnostic radiology tools in the world.

The seventies brought skyrocketing growth to central Florida, and the board of trustees worked diligently to keep pace. One of the most comprehensive expansions came in 1978 as the three-story East Wing opened, bringing the hospital's bed capacity to its current level of 301. It houses complete intensive, coronary, and progressive care units as well as extensive surgery facilities. Then in early 1982, the area's first complete Birthing Center opened on the third floor, featuring six birthing rooms, a fully equipped nursery and hotel roomlike accommodations.

Today's work force exceeds 900, and the more than 400 members of the auxiliary contribute endless hours of volunteer service. The hospital's medical staff has grown to more than 400, representing nearly every major medical specialty.

As its 30th anniversary approaches, it is with extreme pride that Winter Park Memorial remains true to its roots as a private, not-for-profit, community hospital governed by a volunteer board of trustees chosen from an ever-growing Association membership. As described in an *Orlando Sentinel* editorial shortly before the hospital opened, "Winter Park Memorial Hospital . . . is a magnificent testimonial to the immense possibilities of community cooperation."

BIBLIOGRAPHY

The following bibliography includes only those books that are available in central Florida libraries. Much of the research for *Orlando: The City Beautiful* was conducted in primary sources — personal manuscript collections, diaries, public documents, and newspapers. Major research libraries consulted include:

Library of Congress, Washington, D.C.
National Archives, Washington, D.C.
P.K. Yonge Library of Florida History, University of Florida, Gainesville, Florida.
Southern Historical Collection, University of North Carolina, Chapel Hill, North Carolina.
Flowers Collection, Duke University, Durham, North Carolina.
Florida State Archives, Tallahassee, Florida.
Orange County Historical Museum, Orlando, Florida.

Valuable secondary material on Orlando and central Florida may be found in the *Florida Historical Quarterly* and the *Florida Anthropologist.*

Newspapers consulted were:
Apopka Chief (1923-1981)
Florida Agriculturist (1874-1892)
Orlando Daily Record (1892)
Orlando Orange County Reporter (1886)
Orlando Sentinel (title varies) (1911-1984)
Orlando South Florida Citizen (1896)
Orlando South Florida Sentinel (1896)
Tallahassee Floridian (1877-1893)

SELECTED BOOKS

Abbott, Karl P. *Open for the Season.* Garden City, N.J.: Doubleday & Co., 1950.

Akerman, Joe A., Jr., *Florida Cowman.* Kissimmee, Fla.: Florida Cattlemen's Assoc., 1976.

Bacon, Eve. *Oakland, The Early Years.* Chuluota, Fla.: The Mickler House Pub., 1974.
——— *Orlando: A Centennial History.* Chuluota, Fla.: The Mickler House Pub., 1975.

Barbour, George M. *Florida for Tourists.* Gainesville. Fla.: University of Florida Press, 1964.

Barrientos, Bartolome. *Pedro Menendez de Aviles.* (1567). Translated by Anthony Kerrigan. Gainesville, Fla.: University of Florida Press, 1956.

Blackman, William Fremont. *History of Orange County Florida: Narrative and Biographical.* Chuluota, Fla.: Mickler House Pub., 1973.

Blake, Nelson M. *Land Into Water — Water Into Land.* Tallahassee, Fla.: University Presses of Florida, 1980.

Brinton, Daniel B. *A Guide Book to Florida.* Philadelphia, Pa.: Inquirer Printing House, 1869.

Buker, George E. *Swamp Sailors.* Gainesville, Fla.: University Presses of Florida, 1975.

Bullen, Adelaide K. *Florida Indians of Past and Present.* New York, N.Y. and London: Kendall Books, 1974.

Carter, Clarence Edwin, compiler. *The Territorial Papers of the United States.* Vols. XXII-XXVI. Washington, D.C.: Government Printing Office, 1960.

Cohen, M. M. *Notices of Florida and the Campaigns.* Facsimile reproduction of the 1836 edition. Gainesville, Fla.: University of Florida Press, 1964.

Corse, Carita Doggett. *Florida, A Guide to the Southernmost State.* Compiled and written by the Federal Writers' Project of the Work Projects Administration for the State of Florida. New York, N.Y.: Oxford University Press, 1939.

Covington, James W., *The Billy Bowlegs War, 1855-1858.* Chuluota, Fla.: Mickler House Pub., 1982.

Dann, Carl. *Vicissitudes and Casathrophics.* Orlando, Fla.: Florida Press, Inc., 1929.

Davis, William Watson. *Civil War and Reconstruction in Florida.* Gainesville, Fla.: University of Florida Press, 1964.

Doherty, Herbert J. *Richard Keith Call, Southern Unionist.* Gainesville, Fla.: University of Florida Press, 1961.

Fisher, Jane. *Fabulous Hoosier.* Chicago: Harry Coleman and Co., 1953.

Forbes, James Grant. *Sketches, Historical and Topographical of the Floridas.* Facsimile reproduction of the 1821 edition. Gainesville, Fla.: University of Florida Press, 1967.

Fries, Kena. *Orlando in the Long, Long Ago . . . and Now.* Orlando, Fla.: Florida Press, 1938.

Gannon, Michael V. *The Cross in the Sand.* Gainesville, Fla.: University of Florida Press, 1967.

Gidding, Joshua R. *The Exiles of Florida.* Gainesville, Fla.: University of Florida Press, 1964.

Gore, Eldon H. *From Florida Sand to "The City Beautiful," A Historical Record of Orlando, Florida.* Orlando, Fla.: J. M. Cox, 1957.

Gore, Mahlon. *Florida Home, Far and Field: A Guide to Homeseekers, Towns and Investors.* Orlando, Fla.: Board of County Commissioners, 1897.

Griffin, John W. *The Florida Indian and His Neighbors.* Winter Park, Fla.: Rollins College, 1949.

Hanna, Alfred Jackson. *Fort Maitland: Its Origins and History.* Maitland, Fla.: The Fort Maitland Committee, 1936.

Harper, Roland M. *Geography of Central Florida.* 13th Annual Report of the State Geological Survey, 1921.

Hawkes, J. M. *The Florida Gazetteer.* New Orleans, La., 1871.

Hetherington, Alma. *The River of the Long Water.* Chuluota, Fla.: Mickler House Pub., 1980.

Hopkins, James T. *Fifty Years of Citrus: The Florida Citrus Exchange, 1909-1959.* Gainesville, Fla.: University of Florida Press, 1959.

Howard, C. E. *Early Settlers of Orange County, Florida: Reminiscent, Historic, Biographic.* Orlando, Fla., 1915.

Kendrick, Baynard Hardwick. *Orlando: A Century Plus.* Orlando, Fla.: Sentinel Star Co., 1976.

Langford, Carl T. *Hizzoner the Mayor.* Orlando, Fla.: Chateau Pub. Co., 1976.

Lanier, Sidney. *Florida: Its Scenery, Climate and History.* Facsimile reproduction of the 1875 edition. Gainesville, Fla.: University of Florida Press, 1973.

aumer, Frank. *Massacre.* Gainesville, Fla.: University of Florida Press, 1968.

azarus, William C. *Wings in the Sun: The Annals of Aviation in Florida.* Orlando, Fla.: Cobb's, 1950.

owery, Woodbury. *The Spanish Settlements Within the Present Limits of the United States.* 2 Vols. New York: Putnam, 1901.

yon, Eugene. *The Enterprise of Florida.* Gainesville, Fla.: University Presses of Florida, 1975.

MacDowell, Claire Leavitt. *Chronological History of Winter Park, Florida.* Winter Park, Fla.: *Winter Park Herald, 1950.*

Mahon, John D. *History of the Second Seminole War.* Gainesville, Fla.: University of Florida Press, 1967.

―――― *History of the Second Seminole War, 1835-1842.* Gainesville, Fla.: University of Florida Press, 1967.

Manucy, Albert. *Florida's Menendez.* St. Augustine, Fla.: St. Augustine Historical Society, 1965.

Martin, Sidney Walter. *Florida During the Territorial Days.* Athens, Ga.: University of Georgia Press, 1944.

Milanich, Jerald T. and Charles H. Fairbanks. *Florida Archaeology.* New York, N.Y. Academic Press, 1980.

Motte, Jacob Rhett. *Journey into Wilderness.* Ed. James F. Sunderman. Gainesville, Fla.: University of Florida Press, 1963.

Mowat, Charles L. *East Florida as a British Province, 1763-1784.* A facsimile reproduction of 1943 edition. Gainesville, Fla.: University of Florida Press, 1964.

Orange County Chamber of Commerce. *Industrial Survey of Orange County.* Orlando, Fla., 1940.

Orange County Immigration Society. *A General Description of Orange County, Florida: Its Facilities and Transportation,* 1881.

Pettingill, George R. *Story of Florida Railroads, 1835-1903.* Boston, Mass. 1952.

owers, Ormund. *One Man, One Mule, One Shovel,* Winter Park, Fla.: Anna Publishing, 1983.

yburn, Nita J. *A History of the Development of a Single System of Education in Florida, 1822-1903.* Tallahassee, Fla.: Florida State University, 1954.

obertson, Fred L. comp. *Soldiers of Florida in the Seminole Indian, Civil and Spanish American Wars.* Tallahassee, Fla.: Board of State Institutions, 1903.

omans, Bernard. *A Concise Natural History of East and West Florida.* A facsimile reproduction of 1775 edition. Gainesville, Fla.: University of Florida Press, 1962.

hofner, Jerrell H. *History of Apopka and Northwest Orange County, Florida.* Tallahassee, Fla.: Sentry Press, 1982.

―――― *Nor Is It Over Yet: Florida During the Era of Reconstruction, 1863-1877.* Gainesville, Fla.: University of Florida Press, 1974.

olis de Meras, Gonzalo. *Pedro Menendez de Aviles.* Facsimile reproduction of the 1567 manuscript. Translated by Jeanette Thurber Connor. Gainesville, Fla.: University of Florida Press, 1964.

Sprague, John T. *The Florida War.* A facsimile reproduction of the 1848 edition. Gainesville, Fla.: University of Florida Press, 1964.

Swanson, Henry F. *Countdown for Agriculture.* Orlando, Fla.: Designers Press, 1975.

Swanton, John R. *Early History of the Creek Indians and Their Neighbors.* Bureau of American Ethnology. No. 73. Washington, D.C., 1922.

Swanton, John R. *The Indians of the Southeastern United States.* New York, N.Y.: Washington Government Printing Office, 1946.

Tebeau, Charleton W. *A History of Florida.* Coral Gables, Fla.: University Miami Press, 1971.

Vignoles, Charles. *Observations Upon the Floridas.* Facsimile reproduction of the 1823 edition. Gainesville, Fla.: University Presses of Florida, 1977.

Webb, Wanton S. *Florida: Historical, Industrial and Biographical.* Jacksonville, Fla., 1885.

Williams, John Lee. *The Territory of Florida.* Facsimile reproduction of the 1837 edition. Gainesville, Fla.: University of Florida Press, 1964.

An Orlando service station, circa 1918.

INDEX

Numerals in italics indicate an illustration of the subject.

CREDITS

AUTHOR'S ACKNOWLEDGMENTS

I would like to express my appreciation to some of the people who have furnished assistance and encouragement in researching and writing this book. I am first of all indebted to Dr. William Warren Rogers of the Florida State University and Dr. Samuel Proctor of the University of Florida for many years of guidance and encouragement. I wish to thank Jean Yothers of the Orange County Historical Museum for two kinds of assistance, the absence of either of which would have diminished the book's worth. First, she possesses an incomparable knowledge of the history of Orlando which she generously shared with me. And, she permitted me the freedom to explore and use the magnificent photograph collection in the museum which has provided the majority of the pictures used in the book. I am most pleased with the prints which John Markham made from those pictures, and I am indebted to Philip Eschbach who, not only made many of the pictures in the first place, but who also interrupted his busy schedule to make additional photographs which were needed on short notice.

Donald A. Cheney, to whom this book is dedicated, also deserves special mention. Having lived in Orlando from 1889-1983, a period which almost spans the modern history of the city, and possessing a superb sense of history and an excellent memory, he was not only an excellent historical source himself, but it is largely to his credit that there is an Orange County Historical Museum. Henry Land and Raymer Maguire Jr., both of whom have extensive knowledge of the Orlando area, were also helpful. Dr. Paul W. Wehr, my colleague at the University of Central Florida, shared with me some of the rare material he has accumulated in his work on the area and its early inhabitants.

For their assistance on this project and many similar ones in the past, I wish to express my thanks to Elizabeth Alexander and Steve Kerber of the P.K. Yonge Library of Florida History at the University of Florida. Joan Morris of the Florida State Archives photographic division was helpful and understanding — as always.

The enthusiasm and energy with which Bud Brewer has supported the project has been a great encouragement to me. Betty Hicks, Frank Mendola, and Rebecca Umphrey of the Orange County Historical Museum staff are due my thanks, not only for their essential assistance, but also for their tolerance of my frequent visits to their facility during the past year. I must make special mention of their colleague, George Dilas, who took a deep interest in the book and assisted me in countless ways, but whose sudden death will prevent him from seeing it in print.

Both my wife Shirley and my secretary Christine Arcand deserve my thanks for editorial and clerical assistance, but just as important, for their scrupulous husbanding of my time during the project.

— Jerrell H. Shofner

Most historical photographs, maps, and art appearing in this book were furnished by the Orange County Historical Museum. Current color photography, with the exception of the photo appearing on page 129, was furnished by David C. Cotton (*The Orlando Sentinel*). Also, the two black-and-white prints appearing on page 57 and 143, respectively, were supplied by David C. Cotton. Other sources are noted here in alphabetical order and by page number (location on the page noted). Those photographs appearing in the chapter *Partners In Progress*, page 172 through 247, were provided by the represented firms.

Florida State Archives: 28, 38 bottom, 48/49, 52/53, 73, 74 top, 106/107, 122/123, 126/127, 128/129, 168/169, 256.

New York Historical Society: 27 (Lithograph by George Catlin).

Jean Yothers: 102 bottom.

P.K. Younge Library of Florida History: 17-19, 20 top and bottom, 21 top and bottom, 22/23, 24, 26 top and bottom, 29.

One of the English families who settled around Orlando in the 1880s.

Keeping score at the 1951 National Orange Picking Contest.

Concept and design by
Continental Heritage Press, Inc., Tulsa.
Printed and bound by Walsworth Publishing
Company.
Type is Garamond. Text sheets are Warrenflo.
Endleaves are Multicolor Antique.
Cover is Kingston Linen.